Ageing, Long-term Care Insurance and Healthcare Finance in Asia

This book uses a revised version of Kingdon's multiple-streams framework to examine health financing reforms in China, Hong Kong, Taiwan, and the Republic of Korea (ROK) as well as long-term care insurance (LTCI) reforms in Japan and Singapore. It shows that the explanatory power of the multiple-streams framework can be strengthened through enriching the concepts of policy entrepreneurs, ideas, and windows of opportunity in the original framework as well as bringing the theoretical lens of historical institutionalism into the framework.

Sabrina Ching Yuen Luk is Assistant Professor in Public Policy and Global Affairs, Nanyang Technological University, Singapore.

Routledge Studies in the Modern World Economy

For more information about this series, please visit: www.routledge.com/
Routledge-Studies-in-the-Modern-World-Economy/book-series/SE0432

Ageing, Long-term Care Insurance and Healthcare Finance in Asia

Sabrina Ching Yuen Luk

LONDON AND NEW YORK

First published 2020 by Routledge

2 Park Square, Milton Park, Abingdon, Oxon OX14 4RN
605 Third Avenue, New York, NY 10017

Routledge is an imprint of the Taylor & Francis Group, an informa business

First issued in paperback 2022

Publisher's Note

The publisher has gone to great lengths to ensure the quality of this reprint but
points out that some imperfections in the original copies may be apparent.

British Library Cataloguing-in-Publication Data
A catalogue record for this book is available from the British Library

Library of Congress Cataloging-in-Publication Data
Names: Luk, Sabrina Ching Yuen, author.
Title: Ageing, long-term care insurance and healthcare finance in Asia/
    Sabrina Ching Yuen Luk.
Other titles: Routledge studies in the modern world economy.
Description: Abingdon, Oxon ; New York, NY: Routledge, 2020. |
    Series: Routledge studies in the modern world economy | Includes
    bibliographical references and index.
Identifiers: LCCN 2019046802 (print) | LCCN 2019046803 (ebook)
Subjects: MESH: Aging | Health Care Reform | Insurance, Long-
    Term Care | Healthcare Financing | Aged | Asia
Classification: LCC RA395.A52 (print) | LCC RA395.A52 (ebook) |
    NLM WA 540 JA1 | DDC 362.1/04250952—dc23
LC record available at https://lccn.loc.gov/2019046802
LC ebook record available at https://lccn.loc.gov/2019046803

ISBN: 978-1-138-06948-0 (hbk)
ISBN: 978-1-03-233725-8 (pbk)
DOI: 10.4324/9781315115689

Typeset in Galliard
by Apex CoVantage, LLC

Dedicated to my father (Roger Luk) and my mother (Sandy Chu) for their support and unconditional love. To the memory of my godfather (Wing Lin Leung).

Contents

Acknowledgements

This book is the result of two years' hard work. I would like to express my deepest gratitude to my parents and elder brother for being the anchors of my soul and the pillars of my strength. This book is a testimony to their unconditional love and support throughout my prolonged pursuit of knowledge. I would also like to express my gratitude to Yongling Lam and Samantha Phua at Routledge for their professional advice and assistance in the publication of this book.

This book is a salute to scholars, both past and present, who have enhanced our knowledge of healthcare, long-term care, and ageing through their works.

Abbreviations

ACFTU	All-China Federation of Trade Union
ADL	activities of daily living
AFCs	age-friendly communities
A&E	accident and emergency
AI	artificial intelligence
CbICS	Community-based Integrated Care System
CCEJ	Citizen's Coalition for Economic Justice
CCP	Chinese Communist Party
CCSV	Community Care Service Voucher
CEPD	Council for Economic Planning and Development
CHE	catastrophic health expenditure
CHI	community health insurance
CHIAs	corporate health insurance associations
CHWE	Council on Health and Welfare for the Elderly
CIIS	Critical Illness Insurance Scheme
CMS	Cooperative Medical System
CPF	Central Provident Fund
CSSA	Comprehensive Social Security Assistance
CT	computed tomography
DAB	Democratic Alliance for the Betterment of Hong Kong
DFCs	dementia-friendly communities
DoH	Department of Health
DJP	Democratic Justice Party
DLP	Democratic Liberal Party
DPJ	Democratic Party of Japan
DPP	Democratic Progressive Party
DSP	Democratic Socialist Party
EHI	Employees' Health Insurance
EHV	Elderly Health Care Voucher
ERC	ElderShield Review Committee
ExCo	Executive Council
FHI	Farmers Health Insurance
FKTU	Federation of Korean Trade Unions

GDP	Gross Domestic Product
GEI	Government Employees Insurance
GHS	Government-funded Healthcare Scheme
GNP	Grand National Party
GOP	general out-patient
GOPC PPP	General Outpatient Clinic Public-Private Partnership Programme
HA	Hospital Authority
HKGCC	Hong Kong General Chamber of Commerce
HKSAR	Hong Kong Special Administrative Region
HPA	Health Protection Accounts
HPS	Health Protection Scheme
HRQOL	health-related quality of life
HSP	Health Security Plan
HWC	Health and Welfare Committee
IDP	intergenerational day program
IMF	International Monetary Fund
IoTs	Internet of things
IPs	Integrated Shield Plans
KIHASA	Korean Institute of Health and Social Affairs
KMIC	Korean Medical Insurance Corporation
KMT	Kuomintang
LDP	Liberal Democratic Party
LegCo	Legislative Council
LI	Labour Insurance
LIS	Labour Insurance Scheme
LTC	long-term care
LTCI	long-term care insurance
MAA	mutual aid association
MAS	Monetary Authority of Singapore
MEDISAGE	Saving Accounts for Long-Term Care
MHSA	Ministry of Health and Social Affairs
MHW	Ministry of Health and Welfare
MISG	Medical Insurance Study Group
MOF	Ministry of Finance
MOH	Ministry of Health
MOL	Ministry of Labor
MPs	Members of Parliament
MPF	Mandatory Provident Fund
MRI	magnetic resonance imaging
MSA	medical savings accounts
NCD	non-communicable diseases
NCMII	National Committee for Medical Insurance Integration
NCNP	National Congress for New Politics
NCRR	National Citizens' Response to Reform

NDRP	New Democratic Republican Party
NHI	National Health Insurance
NHIA	National Health Insurance Administration
NHIC	National Health Insurance Corporation
NHIS	National Health Insurance Service
NRCMS	New Rural Cooperative Medical System
OECD	Organization for Economic Co-operation and Development
PAP	People's Action Party
PAP.SG	People's Action Party Seniors Group
PARC	Policy Affairs Research Council
PHI	private health insurance
PPD	Party for Peace and Democracy
PRC	People's Republic of China
PWD	people with dementia
RDP	Reunification and Democracy Party
RMB	Renminbi
ROK	Republic of Korea
SCER	State Commission for Economic Restructuring
SHI	social health insurance
SID	supplier-induced demand
SOE	state-owned enterprise
SOP	specialist out-patient
SPF	social pooling fund
SPR	Singapore Permanent Resident
TFR	total fertility rate
Tw-DRGs	Taiwanese version of Diagnosis-Related Groups
UEBMI	Urban Employee Basic Medical Insurance
UHIC	Universal Health Insurance Coverage
UK	United Kingdom
ULD	United Liberal Democratic Party
URBMI	Urban Resident Basic Medical Insurance
US	United States
VHIS	Voluntary Health Insurance Scheme
WCIAS	Women's Committee for the Improvement of the Aged Society
WP	Workers' Party

1 Population ageing and financing health and long-term care in Asia

Trends in population ageing

Population ageing, which refers to an increase in the proportion of older persons, has become one of the most significant trends of the 21st century (United Nations Population Fund 2012). It is the result of the continued decline in fertility rates and an increase in life expectancy (World Health Organization 2010a). There are myriad reasons for fertility decline, including delayed marriage, conflict between work and family responsibilities (Jones 2007), higher education of women, the increasing labor force participation of women, the decline of child mortality, the high cost of raising a child, family planning (e.g. the use of contraception, counseling by experts) (Roser 2014), and government policies (e.g. China's one-child policy). There are also various reasons for an increase in life expectancy, including improved sanitation, safe drinking water, increased education, rising living standards, better nutrition, improved lifestyles, and greater access to quality health services (United Nations Economic and Social Commission for Asia and the Pacific 2017a: 19). From 1950 to 2017, the global population aged 60 years or over increased from 205 million to 962 million, representing almost a 4.7-times increase (United Nations Population Fund 2012: 13; United Nations 2017a: 2). By 2030, the global population aged 60 years or over is projected to reach 1.4 billion, and by 2050, the global population of older persons is projected to more than double its 2017 size, reaching nearly 2.1 billion (United Nations 2015: 9). 'Globally, the number of older persons is growing faster than the number of people in all younger age groups' (United Nations 2017b: 7). 'In 2018, for the first time in human history, persons aged 65 years or over outnumbered children under five years of age worldwide' (United Nations 2019: 16). Projections indicate that these two age groups will continue to grow in opposite directions (He *et al.* 2016: 3). By 2050, the proportion of the population aged 65 or over (15.6 percent) will be more than double that of children under five (7.2 percent) (He *et al.* 2016: 3). Moreover, the number of persons aged 65 years or over globally is projected to reach 1.5 billion by 2050, surpassing the number of adolescents and youths aged 15 to 24 years (1.3 billion) (United Nations 2019: 16).

'World regions vary in their particular phase of the demographic transition and differ in their speed of aging' (He *et al.* 2016: 6). In the 1950s, Europe and

North America were the world's oldest regions, with 12.1 percent and 12.4 percent of their population aged 60 years or over, respectively (Arivalagan 2019: 1). Latin America and the Caribbean had only 5.6 percent of their population aged 60 years or over during that period (Huenchuan 2013: 29). Asia was a young region in the 1950s, with only 6.8 percent of its population aged 60 years or over (Arivalagan 2019: 1). In 1980, the world's top ten countries or areas with the largest share of persons aged 60 years or over were located in Europe (United Nations 2017b: 8). They were Sweden (22.0 percent), Norway (20.2 percent), Channel Islands (20.1 percent), United Kingdom (UK) (20.0 percent), Denmark (19.5 percent), Germany (19.3 percent), Austria (19.0 percent), Belgium (18.4 percent), Switzerland (18.2 percent), and Luxembourg (17.8 percent) (United Nations 2017b: 9). Since the 2000s, however, 'Asia has become one of the world's most rapidly ageing regions, outpacing the rate of ageing in Europe and Northern America' (Arivalagan 2019: 1). To put this into historical context, the United States (US), Sweden, and France took 69 years, 85 years, and 115 years, respectively, to move from an ageing to an aged society (Garcia and Wong 2018: 10; United Nations Economic and Social Commission for Asia and the Pacific 2017b). In Asia, however, Japan took only 26 years to make the transition (Garcia and Wong 2018: 10), while 'China is expected to make the transition in 25 years, Singapore and Thailand in 22 years, and Viet Nam in only 19 years' (United Nations Economic and Social Commission for Asia and the Pacific 2017b: 3).

At present, Asia leads world regions in the size of its older population (He *et al.* 2016: 6). In 2017, Asia had nearly 549 million population aged 60 years or over, which constituted 57 percent of the world's population aged 60 years or over (United Nations 2017b: 5). 'In general, the countries of East Asia are furthest along in the population-aging process, followed by Southeast Asia and then South Asia' (East-West Center 2002: 83). By 2050, Asia is expected to have nearly 1.3 billion people aged 60 years or over (United Nations 2017b: 5). That same year, East Asia will continue to have the oldest population in Asia (UNFPA Asia Pacific 2017: 10), while Japan will host the oldest population in the region (Menon and Melendez-Nakamura 2009: 3). According to the survey conducted by Pew Research Center in 2013 on public awareness of ageing in 21 countries, the view that ageing was a major problem for their country was the most prevalent in East Asia (Pew Research Center 2014). The level of concern with ageing was the highest in Japan (87 percent), followed by the Republic of Korea (ROK) (79 percent) and China (67 percent) (Pew Research Center 2014: 11). Meanwhile, more than half of the public in Germany (55 percent) and Spain (52 percent) said that ageing was a problem (Pew Research Center 2014: 5). The survey also found that the public in Japan had the lowest confidence in having the ability to maintain an adequate standard of living in their old age (Pew Research Center 2014: 6).

Indeed, population ageing 'poses a number of challenges for governments, society and older persons themselves' (United Nations Development Programme 2017: 14). These challenges include ensuring secure income in old age, maintaining good health of older adults and their access to healthcare, and ensuring a supportive environment necessary for ageing in place (United Nations Population Fund 2012: 29–30). Many older adults are financially insecure because of loss of work ability, a lack of employability, low savings, and the lack of financial support from family. This has raised concerns about the ability of governments to provide adequate social protection and social security (e.g. pensions) for the growing number of older adults (United Nations Population Fund 2012: 29).

Population ageing puts significant strain on the healthcare system. The incidence and severity of chronic diseases increase sharply with age. As a result of overall life expectancy growing faster than healthy life expectancy, many older adults live longer but spend more years in poor health (United Nations Economic and Social Commission for Asia and the Pacific 2017a: 37). Since per capita healthcare costs for older adults over 65 are three to five times greater than for those under 65 (Safiliou-Rothschild 2009: 57), they become a particular financial burden for older adults or households with them (United Nations Economic and Social Commission for Asia and the Pacific 2017a: 37). How to provide affordable healthcare for older adults while ensuring the financial sustainability of healthcare systems is an important task for governments. As the population ages, it is necessary to create age-friendly communities (AFCs) which offer barrier-free housing and facilities, affordable, frequent, and reliable public transport services, and a wide range of community activities to foster social participation of older adults, including those with disabilities (World Health Organization 2007: 44). It is only through the creation of AFCs that older adults can live a safe, independent, and dignified life in their communities for as long as possible.

Financing health and long-term care in Asia

'Increasing age is frequently associated with increased health-care utilization and costs' (World Health Organization 2019a). It is also associated with a higher risk for disability 'as a result of an accumulation of health risks across a lifespan of disease, injury, and chronic illness' (United Nations Department of Economic and Social Affairs n.d.). In the face of an ageing population, it is imperative for governments to establish effective mechanisms to ensure that older adults have access to health and long-term care (LTC) services without financial burden (World Health Organization 2019a). At present, however, '[e]nsuring universal coverage for health and long-term care for older people is still a distant ambition in many countries' (World Health Organization 2019a) because many governments have limited financial resources and other funding priorities. Besides, health and LTC financing reforms are politically contentious. 'Health financing reform often involves complex interactions among many stakeholders of varying positions, power, and influence, within the health sector and beyond' (World Health Organization 2018). As regards LTC financing reform, it requires 'navigating deep divides in society, from the social safety net to taxes to individual responsibility and private sector initiatives' (Farrell 2016). In many cases, health or LTC financing reform encounters strong political opposition from vested interests.

The reform usually has to go through many years of experimentation, debates, and negotiations before it is finally implemented. The process can be costly, time-consuming, and frustrating.

Health financing

The purpose of health financing is to provide sufficient funds for the operation of health systems (Schieber *et al.* 2006: 225), to set the right financial incentives for providers (World Health Organization 2000: 95), and to ensure that all individuals have access to needed healthcare services without the risk of severe financial hardship (often called financial catastrophe or impoverishment) (World Health Organization 2010b: 72). The three key functions of a health financing system are revenue collection, pooling of funds, and purchasing of services (World Health Organization 2010b: 72). Revenue collection refers to the sources of funds for healthcare (McIntyre and Kutzin 2012: 77). Funds can come from domestic sources (e.g. households, businesses) and external sources (e.g. donor governments or agencies) (Schieber *et al.* 2006; Health Policy Plus n.d.). Pooling of funds refers to the accumulation of prepaid healthcare funds so that members of the pool collectively share the financial risk of paying for healthcare (McIntyre and Kutzin 2012; Health Policy Plus n.d.). 'Risk pooling addresses the unpredictability of illness, particularly at the individual level' (McIntyre and Kutzin 2012: 77) and promotes equity, as those with greater ability to pay and those with lower health risks subsidize financially poor and high-risk individuals (Health Policy Plus n.d.). Purchasing of services refers to 'the process of transferring pooled funds to healthcare providers to ensure that appropriate and efficient services are available to the population' (McIntyre and Kutzin 2012: 77). Services can be purchased from public and private providers (Schieber *et al.* 2006). In theory, there are five types of health financing models around the world: tax-funded model, social health insurance (SHI) model, private health insurance (PHI) model, mandatory savings model, and out-of-pocket model. In reality, most countries or cities adopt a pluralistic approach to finance health care. In Asia, healthcare financing models are quite diverse in terms of their development (Kwon 2011: 651) due to differences in history, political, economic, and social conditions.

Tax-funded model

The tax-funded model funds healthcare through government tax revenues. Tax revenues can be collected by local, provincial, or national government authority on incomes, purchases, sales, property, corporation profits, land, and the like (Roemer 1976; Savedoff 2004). This model seeks to make health services available on a universal basis and pool both income and health risks (McKenna *et al.* 2017). It has the advantages of providing equitable access to healthcare, having simple and low-cost administration, and redistributing wealth from high-income groups to low-income groups (Food and Health Bureau 2008: 58–9). But the major disadvantage of this model is the risk of unstable funding or underfunding because of competing public expenditures (International Labour Organization 2015). As the payer of healthcare, governments are likely to prioritize cost efficiency and containment (Blank and Burau 2007: 76) and 'weigh tradeoffs between health and roads, education, defense and other public functions' (Savedoff 2004: 7). Countries or cities using this model or variations of it include the UK, Italy, Spain, the Nordic countries, New Zealand, Cuba, and Hong Kong (Reid 2009a, 2009b).

Social health insurance (SHI) model

The SHI model funds healthcare through mandatory contributory schemes. It requires wage-related contributions that are shared by employers and employees to not-for-profit sickness funds designated for paying healthcare providers (Busse *et al.* 2004: 45). The SHI model is built on the principle of social solidarity. It 'does not discriminate against those who are older or have pre-existing medical conditions' (McKenna *et al.* 2017). Every insured person is entitled to the same comprehensive benefits package (Saltman 2004: 7), 'irrespective of their socio-economic status, ability to pay, or geographical location' (Busse *et al.* 2017: 882). The SHI model has the advantages of generating stable revenues and being more efficient at pooling both income and health risks (International Labour Organization 2015; McKenna *et al.* 2017). But the disadvantages of this model are that payroll contribution can lead to cost escalation and reduce the competitiveness of employers and employees in a global market (International Labour Organization 2015; McKenna *et al.* 2017). Countries or cities using this model or variations of it include Germany, the Netherlands, Austria, Belgium, Japan, the ROK, China, and Taiwan.

Private health insurance (PHI) model

The PHI model funds healthcare through individually purchased health insurance schemes or employer-sponsored health insurance, which are often (but not always) voluntary (OECD Study on Private Health Insurance 2004). For individually purchased health insurance schemes, the level of premium charged to an individual depends on an assessment of his or her risk profile at the time of purchase. Factors considered include age, gender, lifestyle habits (e.g. tobacco use, alcohol consumption), medical history, and family history of disease. Individuals under the high-risk category are more likely to pay higher premiums. As regards employer-sponsored health insurance, the level of premium is based on 'group risk, typically estimated across employees of a single firm or occasionally a single industry' (McKenna *et al.* 2017). All members of the group pay the same premium amount for the same benefit package. The PHI model has the advantages of providing financial protection against unexpected illness or injury as well as providing more choices of hospitals, doctors, and services. But the disadvantages of the PHI model include expensive premiums for high-risk groups, such as those with pre-existing medical conditions, encouraging the tendency to over-supply and over-use healthcare due to moral hazards and incurring high administration costs for claims processing and reimbursement (Food and Health Bureau 2008: 82–3). The PHI model is the predominant health financing model in the US (Huber 1999).

The mandatory savings model

The mandatory savings model funds healthcare through medical savings accounts (MSAs). 'MSAs are individual savings accounts that are restricted to spending on health or medical care' (Hanvoravongchai 2002: 1). The model is built on the principles of self-reliance and self-accountability (Hsiao 1995: 261). Pooling 'occurs across an individual's lifetime – individuals save during economically active, healthy years and spend in elderly years when need for healthcare is increased' (Hsu 2010: 4). The mandatory savings model has the advantages of empowering an individual and disciplining him or her to plan ahead and be aware of his or her medical needs (Scheffler and Yu 1998: 274). It can 'prevent consumer moral hazards and create proper incentives for wise health care purchasing decisions' (Hanvoravongchai 2002: 3). Being both the consumer and purchaser of healthcare services, the MSA holder has an incentive to reduce usage as well as compare services to obtain lower prices (Scheffler and Yu 1998: 274). But the disadvantage of the mandatory savings model is that it limits risk pooling between the rich and the poor, and between the healthy and the sick (Hanvoravongchai 2002: 3). 'Those with chronic diseases or those persistently unemployed may not accumulate enough savings for necessary health care' (Hanvoravongchai 2002: 3). High deductibles also deter those with limited or no savings from seeking necessary medical care (Hanvoravongchai 2002: 3). The mandatory savings model is the predominant health financing model in Singapore.

The out-of-pocket model

The out-of-pocket model funds healthcare through 'direct payments made by individuals to health care providers at the time of service use' (World Health Organization 2019b). Direct payments are part of the health financing landscape in all countries relying on user fees and copayments to raise additional revenue to fund services, encourage more rational and responsible use of medical services, and contain health system costs (McKenna *et al.* 2017; World Health Organization 2019b). But the disadvantage of the out-of-pocket model is that it has no risk pooling (Food and Health Bureau 2008: 70). Direct payments would impose a disproportionate financial burden on vulnerable populations, including chronic patients, low-income patients, the elderly, and those receiving extensive and costly treatments (Food and Health Bureau 2008: 70). Vulnerable populations may not seek medical treatment or delay seeking medical treatment, which in turn leads to deterioration in health status (McKenna *et al.* 2017). They may fall into poverty due to illness.

Long-term care financing

Since the 1990s, policymakers in different countries have raised serious concerns over the financial sustainability of LTC systems due to rapidly ageing populations. LTC refers to 'the care for people needing support in many facets of living over a prolonged period of time' (Colombo *et al.* 2011: 39). The need for LTC 'is a consequence of sickness or frailty causing dependency on others' (Joshua 2017: 9). LTC can be provided in institutional, community, and home settings (Rivers *et al.* 2000: 472) and encompasses a wide array of services ranging from rehabilitation and nursing care to assistance with activities of daily living (ADL), such as getting in and out of bed, walking, bathing, dressing, cooking, and managing money (Colombo *et al.* 2011; Rivers *et al.* 2000). LTC can be funded by general taxation (e.g. Sweden, Denmark, Finland, and Norway), social insurance (e.g. the Netherlands, Germany, Japan, and the ROK) and means-tested 'safety net' mechanisms (e.g. the UK, Medicaid in the US) (Joshua 2017). But informal care by unpaid family members and friends is the main pillar of most LTC systems (Joshua 2017: 12).

In traditional Asian-Pacific societies, most LTC 'is unpaid and provided by family members, particularly women' (United Nations Economic and Social Commission for Asia and the Pacific 2018: 1). However, shrinking family sizes, youth migration, and increasing female labor force participation have made informal care provision more difficult (United Nations Economic and Social Commission for Asia and the Pacific 2018). Additionally, 'with an increasing gap between life expectancy and healthy life expectancy, the care needs of older persons have grown and become more complex' (United Nations Economic and Social Commission for Asia and the Pacific 2018: 1). Hence, several governments in Asia have introduced long-term care insurance (LTCI) to help people pay for LTC services received at home or in a nursing home in the event they become unable to care for themselves due to cognitive impairment, chronic illness, or disability.

Japan introduced LTCI for the elderly in 2000. The ROK introduced LTCI in 2008 to provide eligible seniors with benefit coverage for domiciliary services and institutional service (Chon 2014). Taiwan introduced LTC Plan 1.0 in 2008 and LTC Plan 2.0 in 2017 (Chiu *et al.* 2019). The former aimed to establish 'state-subsidized care for the elderly and disabled, covering home nursing, meals, and transportation, as well as rehabilitation and respite care services' (Fulco 2018). The latter aims to establish an integrated community-based LTC system that includes healthcare, disability prevention care, dementia care, and family caregiver support services (Chiu *et al.* 2019; Fulco 2018; Lu 2017).

China introduced a pilot program for LTC insurance in 15 cities in 2016 to provide care protection for the disabled elderly. Singapore introduced a severe disability insurance scheme called ElderShield in 2002, which provided basic financial protection for those who needed LTC, especially in old age (HealthHub 2019). It will introduce CareShield Life in 2020, which is an enhanced version of ElderShield to provide higher and lifetime payouts to severely disabled claimants (ElderShield Review Committee 2018).

The Hong Kong Special Administrative Region (HKSAR) has yet to have LTC insurance. But it launched the First Phase and Second Phase of the Pilot Scheme on Community Care Service Voucher (CCSV) for the Elderly in September 2013 and October 2016, respectively, which allowed eligible elderly persons to receive community care services that best suit their needs under the 'money following the user' funding approach (The Government Information Centre 2019). Eligible elderly persons can choose home-based service and/or center-based service and, if necessary, may use residential respite service and/or speech therapy service' (The Government Information Centre 2019). But a study conducted by a think tank called Our Foundation Hong Kong found that factors such as copayments and lack of flexibility in voucher service provision reduced the attractiveness of the Pilot Scheme (One Foundation Hong Kong 2016). Professor Yeoh Eng-kiong, who was Secretary for Health, Welfare and Food of the HKSAR Government (1999–2004) and led the study of Our Foundation Hong Kong, said that the government should consider introducing an insurance scheme to fund LTC services like the model adopted in Japan (Tsang 2016).

Analytical foundation: a refined version of multiple-streams framework

This study examines health financing reforms in China, Hong Kong, Taiwan, and the ROK and LTC financing reforms in Japan and Singapore. It uses a refined version of multiple-streams framework to explain the divergent health financing and LTC reforms in these six Asian countries.

Kingdon's multiple-streams framework

In the mid-1980s, John Kingdon, who, based upon 247 interviews with top decision makers, developed the multiple-streams framework to examine agenda setting and alternative specifications in the areas of healthcare policy and transportation policy in the federal government of the US. The multiple-streams framework contains three major policy streams and have the following characteristics:

1   The problem stream: This stream regards problem recognition. Within this stream, Kingdon distinguished between a condition and a problem. A condition is an undesirable phenomenon that people are willing to accept or tolerate. A problem, on the other hand, is an undesirable phenomenon that is perceived as appropriate for governmental action. A condition exists objectively; a problem does not (Yame 2002: 20). An objective condition becomes a problem when such condition is 'subjectively perceived to be undesirable and therefore defined as a problem' (Lauer 1976: 122). A problem is socially constructed and gains the attention of governmental decision makers because of systematic indicators, focusing on events such as crises or disasters or through formal or informal feedback from the operation of existing programs that attract government and public attention (Kingdon 1984).

Legitimacy is evidenced when the public sphere – for example, policymakers, the public, and the media – takes up the problem for discussion or action (Sims and Miskel 2003: 3).

2 The policy stream: This stream regards the generation of policy alternatives that are the potential solutions to such policy problems (Béland 2016: 230). Such policy alternatives compete to win acceptance by policy communities consisting of specialists both inside and outside of government in a given policy area. Policy alternatives are viable only if they are able to meet two criteria: technical feasibility and value acceptability. The former means that policy alternatives must be 'worked out and capable of being implemented' (Kingdon 1984: 151), while the latter means that policy alternatives must be 'acceptable in the light of the values held by members of the policy community' (Kingdon 1984: 151). Besides, viable policy alternatives are tailored to an anticipated budget constraint, win the acceptance of the general public or a more specialized public, and gain the approval of elected officials. 'The process of alternative specification narrows the large set of possible alternatives to that set from which choices actually are made' (Kingdon 1984: 205).

3 The political stream: This stream regards political opportunities. Explanation for low- or high-agenda prominence is associated with various political forces, including swings in national mood, election results, changes of administration, partisan or ideological distributions in Congress, and interest group advocacy campaigns. In this stream, consensus-building takes place through a bargaining process (Kingdon 1984: 171). Coalitions 'are being built through the granting of concessions in return for support of the coalition' (Kingdon 1984: 167).

According to Kingdon (1984), these three streams 'are largely independent of one another, and each develops according to its own dynamics and rules' (20). However, the three streams converge when windows of opportunity are open to allow policy entrepreneurs to push their pet proposals and thereby increase the likelihood of their proposals rising on the decision agenda. Windows are opened by events in either the problem or political streams, but they do not stay open long. If problem windows or political windows pass without action, they may not open again for a long time (Kingdon 1984: 178). Policy entrepreneurs are those who are willing to invest their time, energy, political capital, money, and other resources in pushing their pet proposals into prominence and play the roles in prompting important people to pay attention, coupling solutions to problems or coupling both problems and solutions to politics. They can be found both inside or outside of government, such as career bureaucrats, elected officials, lobbyists, academics, or journalists. Meanwhile, the role of ideas is important in agenda-setting and alternative specifications. Ideas play the role in 'the construction and especially, the classification of policy problems' (Béland 2016: 232). For example, numbers are 'powerful ideational constructions that can have a strong impact on both policy and politics' (Béland 2016: 233). Certain ideas are advocated and diffused by policy entrepreneurs through different means and channels in order to let both policy communities and larger publics get used to such ideas and build acceptance for the proposals (Kingdon 1984: 134–7). The receptivity to ideas of a given type is a critical factor that explains the prominence of an item on the agenda (Kingdon 1984: 76). Policy change takes place because certain ideas take hold and grow. In sum, the multiple-streams framework takes into account the dynamic nature of policy-making (Kingdon 2011). '[A]gendas are set by problems or politics, and alternatives are generated in the policy stream' (Kingdon 1984: 21). Timing, agency, and the role of ideas are emphasized in the multiple-streams framework (Béland 2016).

Kingdon's multiple-streams framework has been widely used by scholars to examine a particular policy in other countries, such as health policy in an African state (Ridde 2009), diabetes care in Ireland (Hugh *et al.* 2014), environmental public policies in Brazil (Alves 2014), and the implementation of targets on asylum, defense procurement, and climate change in Britain (Boswel and Rodrigues 2016). Besides, its applicability and relevance are explored in comparative policy research (Béland and Howlett 2016: 221). The multiple-streams framework and some of its concepts are used to examine the dynamics of policy reforms in the US, Britain, France, and Chile (Keeler 1993), telecommunications policy in Britain and France (Zahariadis 1992), public enterprise privatization in Britain and Germany (Zahariadis and Allen 1995), sugar policy reform in the European Union (Ackrill and Kay 2011), policy choice in the European Union (Zahariadis 2008), labor market policies in Germany and Sweden (Spohr 2016), educational reforms in Ghana (Boasiako and Asare 2015), and asylum policy in Swiss member states (Sager and Thomann 2017). Meanwhile, the framework has also been extended to examine other stages of the policy cycle, including the decision-making stage (Zahariadis 1992), implementation stage (Exworthy *et al.* 2002; Ridde 2009), and termination stage (Geva-May 2004). According to Béland and Howlett (2016: 223), Kingdon's multiple-streams framework has been used to examine over 300 cases. It 'has provided great insight into and understanding of the workings of policy making across different countries and policy fields' (Zahariadis 2007: 80) and has 'made important contributions to policy theory, and to the empirical literature' (Cairney and Jones 2016: 38).

Critiques of Kingdon's multiple-streams framework

Nevertheless, the multiple-streams framework is not without criticism. First, it is criticized for ignoring institutional constraints on agenda-setting (Mucciaroni 1992; Zohlnhöfer *et al.* 2016). The multiple-streams framework is grounded in the behavioral tradition of political science (Spohr 2016: 257). It conceives of politics as the 'political climate', referring to such things as swings in national mood and party turnover in Congress and emphasizes the fluid, changeable aspects of politics (Mucciaroni 1992: 465). It views the role of institutions almost exclusively in situational terms, which constitutes part of the changing 'political climate', and thereby neglecting those aspects of political life that either change very slowly, change infrequently, or do not change (Mucciaroni 1992: 465–6). Second, the framework is criticized for being ahistorical (Mucciaroni 1992; Weir 1992). It focuses on recent trends and immediate events in the problem or political stream, which serve as catalysts for pushing items onto the agenda (Mucciaroni 1992: 471). But problems evolve over time, and '[i]tems that reach the agenda in any given period have their roots in the conditions, events and choices of the past' (Mucciaroni 1992: 470). It is insufficient to simply say that the issue becomes salient when indicators signal trouble or when a crisis occurs and hence historically grounded explanations should be considered (Mucciaroni 1992: 471). Third, the framework is criticized for viewing the problem, policy, and political streams as independent streams that do not converge until windows of opportunity are open (Weir 1992; Zahariadis 2007). A historical perspective would show that the streams are linked in important ways over time (Weir 1992: 191). 'The conception of what problems are and how they should be defined very often depends on previous policies, which establish some groups as authoritative voices in a particular field' (Weir 1992: 191). It means that 'changes in one stream can trigger or reinforce changes in another, making coupling much less fortuitous and the process more purposive' (Zahariadis 2007: 81). Hence, it is more appropriate to view streams as interdependent (Zahariadis 2007: 81).

A refined version of multiple-streams framework

The stages model of policy-making, which is also known as the 'linear model' (Thomas and Grindle 1990), the 'sequential model', or the 'heuristic stages model' (Kulaç and Özgür 2017: 146) 'has been used extensively to understand the policy process and its key phases' (Dovlo *et al.* 2016: 216). The model 'theorises that policy processes are rational, balanced, objective and analytical' (Dovlo *et al.* 2016: 216). There are numerous variants of the models, with the number of stages varying from four to nine (Anderson 2015; Brewer and deLeon 1983; Foyle 1999; Hogwood and Gunn 1984; Ripley 1985). 'In recent work, a five-stage model of the policy process has been most commonly used' (Howlett and Giest 2015: 17), which consists of the stages of agenda-setting, policy formulation, decision-making, policy implementation, and policy evaluation (Howlett and Giest 2015: 17).

The stages model has two main advantages. The first advantage is that it 'facilitates the understanding of public policy-making by breaking the complexity of the process into a limited number of stages' (Howlett and Ramesh 1995: 12). Another advantage is that the stage model 'is not culture bound' (Anderson 2015: 6) and 'can readily be used to examine policymaking in foreign political systems' (Anderson 2015: 6) or 'make a comparison between different countries in case of each stage' (Kulaç and Özgür 2017: 149). But the main disadvantage of the stage model is that it fails to reflect the real policy-making processes, and it is treated as a textbook approach (Nakamura 1987). In reality, 'policy-making processes are seldom linear and stage-like' (Auer 2007: 542) because they are messy and highly political (Dovlo *et al.* 2016: 216). The stages 'are often compressed or skipped, or followed in an order unlike that specified by the logic of applied problem-solving' (Howlett and Ramesh 1995: 12).

The multiple-streams framework was originally developed to examine public policy agenda-setting in presidential democracy in the US. In 1991, Sabatier (1991: 151) suggested that the multiple-streams framework should be expanded to include the entire policy process. Since then, scholars have examined the subsequent stages of the policy process with some modifications of the framework. This study aims to examine the processes of health financing and LTCI reforms in the agenda-setting, formulation, decision-making, and implementation stages. While previous studies suggest that every stage comprises three streams, this study suggests another interpretation of three streams in different stages of policy-making. In the agenda-setting stage, problem recognition is the most important. The focus should be on the problem stream. In the formulation stage, analysis and identification of preferred alternatives is the most important. The focus should be on the policy stream. In the decision-making and implementation stages, there are negotiations involving multiple stakeholders and the predominance of certain ideas. The focus should be on the political stream. This study emphasizes that the problems, policy, and political streams are linked in important ways over time due to historical forces. To increase the explanatory power of the multiple-streams framework and its applicability to other political systems or other countries, the author decontextualizes the framework by enriching some important concepts in the original framework as well as bringing the theoretical lens of historical institutionalism into the framework. This study aims to examine how the combined forces of policy entrepreneurs, ideas, windows of opportunities, history, and institutions in different streams shape the processes of health financing and LTCI reforms.

Policy entrepreneurs

In the original framework, 'there is both a functional and physical separation of policy entrepreneurs and decision-makers' (Ackrill and Kay 2011: 74). The framework refers to policy entrepreneurs as 'people willing to invest their resources in return for future policies they favor' (Kingdon 1984: 214). They can be found both inside or outside of government, such as career bureaucrats, elected officials, lobbyists, academics, or journalists. They 'are not decision-makers in [the] public sector and their role is limited to influencing governmental agenda setting' (Bakir and Jarvis 2017: 467) by introducing, translating, and implementing innovative ideas into public sector practice (Roberts and King 1991: 152). But critics argued that such distinction is too stark because policy entrepreneurs 'may not simply sell ideas to decision-makers, but be involved directly in decision-making' (Ackrill and Kay 2011: 74). It means that policy entrepreneurs can be both promoters of policy ideas and elite decision makers (Bakir and Jarvis 2017: 466). This may be particularly true in less democratic political regimes when political leaders or key figures within the government exercise immense power over policy-making. They have authority, capital, and other resources to advocate their proposals through different channels. There is a possibility that they are both policy entrepreneurs and decision-makers at the same time. Hence, the concept of policy entrepreneurs should also be extended to cover decision-makers.

Meanwhile, policy entrepreneurs can also function as institutional entrepreneurs when they have the ability to mobilize ideas and utilize discourse in various stages of public policy-making toward policy and institutional changes (Bakir 2009: 573–4). They use framing to justify new practices as appropriate, valid, and indispensable (Garud *et al.* 2007: 962). This, in turn, can mobilize coalitions of diverse groups and 'generate the collective action necessary to secure support for and acceptance of institutional change' (Garud *et al.* 2007: 962). Institutional entrepreneurs 'break with existing rules and practices associated with the dominant institutional logic(s) and institutionalize the alternative rules, practices or logics they are championing' (Garud *et al.* 2007: 962). They 'exercise judgement regarding the extent that deviations may be tolerated in the present and may also be worthwhile to create new futures' (Garud and Karnøe 2001: 6). They are fully aware that deviations may threaten existing orders and create inefficiencies in the present (Garud and Karnøe 2001: 6) 'but also aware that such steps are required to create new futures' (Garud and Karnøe 2001: 6). In sum, institutional entrepreneurs are 'agents of change who initiate divergent actions that shake up institutionalised practices and who actively participate in mobilising resources to implement this change' (Breton *et al.* 2014: 80).

Ideas

In the original framework, the concept of ideas is not clear. According to Kingdon (1984), 'ideas can come from anywhere' (75). They confront one another and combine with one another in various ways (Kingdon 1984: 123). Ideas that survive and prosper meet some criteria (Kingdon 1984: 123). Although the term 'ideas' was featured in the book abundantly (Béland 2016: 231), its meaning is very vague. There is a need for greater clarity of the concept of ideas. This study borrows the study of Campbell (1998), which identified four types of ideas, namely, programmatic ideas, paradigms, frames, and public sentiments. Programmatic ideas and paradigms are cognitive in nature, while frames and public sentiments are normative in nature (Campbell 1998: 385). Programmatic ideas are policy prescriptions. They are technical and professional ideas that help policy makers devise concrete solutions to their policy problems (Campbell 1998: 386). 'They are often presented in policy briefs, position papers, advisory memos to policy makers and congressional testimony' (Campbell 1998: 386). Paradigms are 'cognitive background assumptions that constrain action by limiting the range of alternatives that [are] likely to [be] perceive[d] as useful and worth considering' (Campbell 1998: 385). Frames are normative concepts that policy makers use to legitimize policy solutions in order to muster public support (Campbell 1998: 394). Public sentiments are broad-based attitudes or assumptions held by large segments of the general public about what is desirable or not (Campbell

1998: 392). They 'constrain the normative range of legitimate solutions available to policy makers' (Campbell 1998: 385). Bringing these four types of ideas into the multiple-streams framework can provide a clear picture about the role of ideas in different stages of policy-making.

While ideas alone cannot sufficiently explain policy change, paying close attention to ideas is necessary to account for the direction and meaning of policy change because ideas help explain the behavior, policy decisions, and strategic choices of actors (Béland and Waddan 2012: 8). Policy change is usually associated with new ideas rising to political prominence (Luk 2014a, 2017). 'The newness of the idea is determined by its context, by the relevant unit of adoption' (Roberts and King 1991: 150). Although an idea may have been developed earlier elsewhere, the idea is 'new' if people involved in developing and implementing it consider it to be new (Roberts and King 1991: 150). New ideas can rise to political prominence due to delegitimization of old ideas (Luk 2014a: 15, 2017: 8), which is 'rooted in dissatisfaction with or a recognition of the inadequacy of existing belief structures' (Berman 2001: 234). Besides, policy makers trade old ideas for new ones if they think that new ideas seem to be better 'road maps' than old ones to guide them through difficult or rapidly changing situations (Berman 2001: 235).

Windows of opportunities

In the original framework, windows of opportunity narrowly refer to events in the problem stream such as crises or disasters or changes in the political stream such as a shift in national mood, change of administration, a change in personnel, or a shift in the partisan or ideological distribution of seats in Congress (Kingdon 1984: 176–8). However, the explanatory power of the multiple-streams framework can only be strengthened if the concept of windows of opportunity can also include other types of environmental pressures. This study enhances the concept of windows of opportunity by bringing in the concept of environmental triggers developed by Cortell and Peterson (1999). Environmental triggers refer to domestic or international events, whether a crisis or non-crisis, alone or in combination, that open windows of opportunity for policy makers to make institutional change possible (Cortell and Peterson 1999: 183–5). Such events discredit existing institutions and policies and hence produce pressure for change or reform (Cortell and Peterson 1999: 184). International environmental triggers include (1) war, (2) geopolitical conflict, (3) a changing balance of power, (4) macro-economic change, dislocation, and shock, (5) international norms, organizations and treaties, and (6) technological change (Cortell and Peterson 1999: 185). Domestic environmental triggers include (1) revolution, (2) civil war, (3) coup d'état, (4) election/change of government, (5) economic growth rate, (6) demographic change, and (7) social movement or conflict (Cortell and Peterson 1999: 185). According to Cortell and Peterson (1999: 186), environmental triggers may generate costs measured in terms of political, social, or economic dislocations that lead to demands for changes in policy practices. They may also shift national mood and increase policy makers' autonomy from short-term political constraints to innovative (Cortell and Peterson 1999: 187). Nevertheless, whether policy makers would act on a window of opportunity depends on their perceptions of the desirability, feasibility, and scope of change (Cortell and Peterson 1999: 188) and whether the prevailing institutional arrangements 'create opportunities for, or place limits on, an official's ability to translate her desire for structural change into policy' (Cortell and Peterson 1999: 190).

Historical institutionalism

In the original framework, there is an insufficient attention to the role of institution in the policy and political streams. While the role of institutions may be less decisive at the agenda-setting stage (Zohlnhöfer *et al.* 2016: 248), the role of institutions matters most at the decision-making stage because 'formal institutions are those that are assigned decision-making or veto powers' (Zohlnhöfer *et al.* 2016: 244). Institutions 'define which actors participate in which constellation in the adoption of policies and which policy options are institutionally permissible' (Zohlnhöfer *et al.* 2016: 247). The role of institutions is particularly important in the political stream because it determines whether policy entrepreneur(s) can gain the majority support needed to get their pet project adopted (Zohlnhöfer *et al.* 2016: 249).

In response to the criticisms that the multiple streams framework is ahistorical and neglects the impact of institutions on policy-making, this study combines the framework with the theoretical lens of historical institutionalism to examine the distinct role of institutions in affecting policy entrepreneurs' goal-setting, policy preferences, and strategies; defining the channels in which ideas can be absorbed and translated into policy; and responding to the effects of environmental pressures or shifting contextual conditions. Historical institutionalism emerged in the early 1990s as a distinct tradition of institutional analysis to examine the roles of institutions and history in structuring and shaping political behaviors and outcomes over time (Fioretos *et al.* 2016; Steinmo 2008: 118). In general, historical institutionalists define institutions as "macrostructures and institutional assemblages like the welfare state or national economic systems" (Fioretos *et al.* 2016: 6), formal organizations, the rules or conventions promulgated by formal organizations, standard operating procedures, routines (Hall and Taylor 1996: 938), informal rules and norms (Steinmo 2008: 124). Institutions define 'appropriate behavior for specific groups of actors in specific situation[s]' (March and Olsen 1998: 948).

Institutions play three important roles. First, institutions play a determinant role in distributing power among actors in a given polity (Luk 2014a: 8). Historical institutionalism emphasizes asymmetrical power relations (Luk 2014a: 8). It 'sees different institutional structures as setting different political rules of the game' (Shih *et al.* 2012: 307) that privilege some actors and groups in society while putting others at a disadvantage (Thelen and Steinmo 1992: 2). Institutional position, responsibilities, and relationships with others affect how actors interpret and pursue their self-interests, define their goals, choose their policy preferences, and determine their strategies (Luk 2014a: 8). Due to uneven distribution of power, some actors 'are central to the development of policy whereas others are ineffectual, forced to accept gains and losses determined by others' (Pierson 1994: 40).

Second, historical institutionalism sees political institutions as structuring the flow of ideas and shaping the absorption and diffusion of ideas (Hall 1992; King 1992; Thelen and Steinmo 1992; Weir 1992). The structure of political institutions, the formal rules and procedures governing policy-making define the channels and mechanisms by which ideas penetrate the policy-making process and are promoted, adopted, and implemented as policy (King 1992; Thelen and Steinmo 1992: 24; Campbell 2002: 30). For example, decentralization and institutional fragmentation of the American political system empowers business actors to oppose progressive economic and social ideas (Béland 2009: 708).

Third, institutions respond to changes in the external environment by changing their meaning and functioning (Thelen and Steinmo 1992). Open-systems theory, which assumes considerable interdependence between institutions and their environments, sees changes in the latter triggering adaptive responses within the institutions (Milakovich and Gordon 2013: 164). Institutions constantly need to balance pressures, responses and demands, and resources to ensure their stability in the long run, which permits continued functioning in the manner expected by leaders, workers, and people outside the institutions (Milakovich and Gordon 2013: 165). Crises or shifts in external conditions do not necessarily lead to dramatic institutional change, such as institutional breakdown (Thelen and Steinmo 1992). Instead, gradual or incremental institutional change can take place. The concept of 'institutional dynamism' indicates that changes in the broader political or socioeconomic context enable previously latent institutions to suddenly become salient or existing institutions being put in the service of different ends when old or new actors are empowered to pursue new goals or adopt new strategies (Thelen and Steinmo 1992: 16–18).

Path dependence is another important concept in historical institutionalism. Path dependence refers to 'specifically those historical sequences in which contingent events set into motion institutional patterns or event chains that have deterministic properties' (Mahoney 2000: 507). 'With path dependence, each step in a particular direction makes it more likely that a unit will continue to follow that same direction' (Mahoney *et al.* 2016: 82). It means that there is 'an inertial tendency towards continuing along the same path rather than changing direction regardless of the advantages of the alternatives' (Luk 2014a: 9). The inertial tendency can be explained by one or a combination of several types of self-reinforcing mechanisms, including investment effects, learning effects, coordination effects, and adaptive expectation effects (Pierson 1994, 2000). Investment effects mean that high set-up or fixed cost provides individuals with a strong incentive to stick with a single option in order to exploit the option to the full extent, and further investment will be made to support this option. Learning effects is learning by using leads to accumulate knowledge, skills, and experience. Efficiency gained from iterations and cost reduction because of a more skillful performance (faster, more reliable, and with fewer errors) creates a strong incentive for individuals to stick with the chosen option (Sydow *et al.* 2009: 700). Coordination effects 'build on the benefits of rule-guided behavior' (Sydow *et al.* 2009: 699). More actors adopting a specific institution such as the right-hand traffic rule can significantly reduce coordination costs because their behaviors can be anticipated and reactions can be considered in advance (Sydow *et al.* 2009: 699). Adaptive expectation effects 'relate to the interactive building of preferences' (Sydow *et al.* 2009: 700). Individuals are willing to adopt a particular practice because they expect others to do the same and wish to end up on the winning side (Sydow *et al.* 2009: 700). The subsequent self-fulfilling prophecies make a particular practice more attractive (Sydow *et al.* 2009: 700). These self-reinforcing mechanisms create positive feedback loops that 'essentially remove certain alternatives from the menu of political possibilities' (Pierson 2004: 12) and hence 'forsaken alternatives become increasingly unreachable with the passage of time' (Pierson 2004: 13). This indicates that timing and sequencing of particular events matter because subsequent self-reinforcing processes generate irreversibility, affecting the consequences of later developments (Pierson and Skocpol 2002: 701).

When the concept of path dependence is applied to understand a policy path, one needs to know that 'a policy passed at time T_1 may significantly change the range of possible options at time T_2' (Hacker 2002: 53). While it is important to know *which* decisions are taken, it is also important to know *when* those particular decisions are taken because the same decisions will not necessarily have the same effect at different stages of the path (Oliver and Mossialos 2005: 11). There are five conditions pushing policy development down a particular path. These include circumstances when (1) a policy generates the creation of large-scale institutions with substantial set-up costs; (2) a policy benefits sizable organized interest groups; (3) a policy embodies long-lived commitments; (4) institutions are of necessity densely interwoven with the broader features of an economy or society; or (5) features of the environment within which a policy is implemented make it harder to respond to unanticipated policy outcomes (Hacker 2002: 55). These conditions make policy reversal difficult to obtain.

Chapter outline

This study will use the revised version of the multiple-streams framework to examine health financing reforms in China, Hong Kong, Taiwan, and the ROK as well as LTCI reforms in Japan and Singapore. Chapter 2 gives a detailed account of the urban health insurance reform in China and examines challenges to the current multi-layered social health insurance system. Chapter 3 examines the mandatory health insurance reform fiasco in Hong Kong in 1999, the implementation of the voluntary health insurance scheme in 2019, and challenges to the current public healthcare system. Chapter 4 gives a detailed account of the process of LTCI reform in Japan and challenges to the current LTC system. Chapter 5 examines the compulsory LTCI reform in Singapore, which leads to the implementation of CareShield Life in 2020. Chapter 6 gives a detailed account of the process of the National Health Insurance (NHI) reform in Taiwan and challenges to the current NHI system. Chapter 7 examines the process of Integration Reform in the ROK and challenges to the current single-payer system. Chapter 8 examines ways to achieve healthy ageing in Asia.

2 China

The urban health insurance reform

Introduction

China is the world's most populous country with approximately 1.4 billion people. It has become an ageing society since 1999 and had 9.5 percent of the population aged 65 and over in 2015 (Center for Strategic and International Studies 2016). It has established a multi-layered health insurance system covering 95 percent of its population (China Daily 2018). This chapter gives a detailed account of the process of urban health insurance reform, examines why a mandatory social health insurance system was implemented in 1998, and identifies challenges to the current multi-layered health insurance system.

The problem of rising healthcare costs had crippled the free healthcare system since the early 1980s and subsequently led to its collapse in the early 1990s. The process of reforming the health financing system was protracted. After carrying out local experimentation for more than ten years, the central government finally decided to introduce a social health insurance system funded by contributions from both employers and employees. The social health insurance system was technically feasible because local experimentation showed that it could effectively curb the rapid growth of medical expenses. It also promoted the new ideas of individual responsibility and social solidarity that were endorsed by political leaders. Changes in political leadership and China's transformation into a market-based economy created a window of opportunity for reforming the health financing system. A centralized political system put political leaders in an advantageous position to implement health financing reform without any political opposition. The State Council, representatives from different ministries, and Vice-Premier Zhu Rongji were policy entrepreneurs in the reform process. Representatives from different ministries negotiated, bargained, and compromised their stances before they reached a consensus on the design of the health financing model. The social health insurance system was the outcome of consensus-building among policy entrepreneurs.

After years of substantial efforts, the government has established a multi-layered health insurance system covering urban employees, urban residents, and the rural population. However, the current multi-layered health insurance system is plagued by the problems of huge insurance fund deficits, insufficient financial protection for the insured, and insufficient medical protection for the elderly. How to provide affordable and sustainable healthcare for its population will remain an important task for the central government.

Pre-reform era

On 1 October 1949, the Chinese Communist Party (CCP) founded the People's Republic of China (PRC) under the leadership of Mao Zedong. During Mao's era, the government provided free healthcare services for urban employees through two schemes: the Labour Insurance Scheme (LIS) (*laodong baoxian*) and the Government-funded Healthcare Scheme (GHS) (*gongfei yiliao*). In rural areas, people obtained healthcare services through a low-cost prepayment system called the Cooperative Medical System (CMS) (Liu 2013: 30–1). The development of the urban-rural dual healthcare financing system was strongly impacted by changes in Sino-Soviet relations, economic factors, and the ideology of communism (Luk 2017: 27–8). China's decision to side with the Soviet Union as its major ally in 1950 led to China adopting the Leninist political system characterized by the top-down state-centric structure of decision-making and authority relations (Greenhalgh and Winckler 2005) as well as the Soviet-style centrally planned economy emphasizing heavy industrial development over agriculture (Tang and Parish 2000: 19). Policy-making was 'largely the domain of the central party-state, with local governments seen as implementing bodies' (Duckett 2011: 14). Following the Soviet Union, China adopted a *danwei*-based welfare system in urban areas. In urban China, all publicly owned organizations where people worked – including governmental organizations, enterprises, scientific, educational, and healthcare organizations – were generally classified as *danwei*, which literally meant work units (Gu 2001a: 92). *Danwei* offered its formal employees permanent employment (Gu 2001a: 92) and provided employees with 'comprehensive, generous, non-contributory welfare benefits from housing, education, [and] social security to health care' (Luk 2014a: 39).

The *danwei*-based welfare system 'underpinned a tacit agreement between the state and the working class, which is called the "Soviet social contract" by Western scholars' (Gu 2001a: 92). Under such a contract, 'the communist state provided economic and social security in return for the workers' political compliance' (Gu 2001a: 92). The provision of free medical care to urban employees ensured a healthy workforce to support social and economic development (Luk 2017: 33). 'Drawn from the Soviet Union experience, as well as from the fundamental ideology of communism' (Yang 2010: 296), the state monopolized and nationalized health resources to increase equality and accessibility to healthcare (Yang 2010: 296). Hospitals were nationalized and were classified as non-profit work units, while all hospital employees became salaried state employees (Gu 2001b: 201). Led by elite medical professionals, the Ministry of Health (MOH) and its subordinate bureaus ran or had oversight over most hospitals, determined the annual budgets of hospitals, and appointed hospital employees (Duckett 2011: 22–3; Yu and Ren 1997: 436). The price of health service was controlled by the government at a level below the cost (Liu and Hsiao 1995: 1097). In the late 1950s, the deterioration of the Sino-Soviet relationship led to a radical shift in the focus of healthcare development from urban areas to rural areas (Luk 2017: 34). In the late 1960s, Mao wrested health policy from the MOH and strongly promoted the CMS and barefoot doctors in rural areas (Duckett 2011: 23).

Labour Insurance Scheme (LIS)

The LIS was formally established after *the Labour Insurance Regulations of the People's Republic of China* came into effect on 1 March 1951 (Government Administration Council 1951). It initially covered workers and staff in state-owned, private, joint public-private, or cooperative factories and mines employing 100 or more workers as well as those working in railway enterprises, shipping enterprises, post and telecommunications enterprises, and the subsidiary units of these enterprises (Government Administration Council 1951). In 1953, the LIS was extended to cover workers and staff in capital construction units of factories, mines, transportation enterprises, and state-owned construction companies (Luk 2017: 37). In 1955, there was nationalization of industry and private enterprises. Private enterprises were virtually extinguished, and private ownership was rooted out (Zhang 2008: 326). Public ownership became the sole ownership in the nation, including state and collective ownership (Zhang 2008: 326). The LIS was extended to cover workers in the state-owned forestry industry, aquaculture industry, petroleum industry, aviation industry, finance industry, and the foreign trade sector (Li 2009: 34) as well as workers in collective-owned enterprises (which were owned by local or district governments) (Hu *et al.* 1999: 309). The LIS also covered workers' direct dependents and retired workers (Li 2009: 34). By 1956, the LIS had covered 23 million workers (Li 2009: 34–5). In 1989, the LIS covered about 127 million people (excluding direct dependents), accounting for 10.6 percent of China's population (Liu and Hsiao 1995: 1095).

Although it was called an insurance scheme, the LIS was not a health insurance scheme in the real sense because there was no premium contribution and the scheme was not managed by any insurance institutions (Luk 2014a, 2017). The funding source of the LIS came from the labour insurance fund, which was contributed to by employers, according to *The Labour Insurance Regulations. The Labour Insurance Regulations* stipulated that employers were required to contribute 3 percent of their total payroll to the labour insurance fund every month (Government Administration Council 1951). In 1957, employers were required to contribute 4.5 to 5.5 percent of their total payroll to the labour insurance fund every month (Li 2009: 35), depending on the types of industries or enterprises. The labour insurance fund shall not be deducted from the wages of workers and staff. While 70 percent of the labour insurance fund was deposited into the account of the respective primary trade union committees of the enterprises concerned (Government Administration Council 1953), the rest of it was deposited into the account of the All-China Federation of Trade Union (ACFTU) so that 'a certain degree of redistribution could be effected between enterprises of varying financial commitments (Lee 2000: 140). The ACFTU, which was 'the state-led body that governed all trade unions in China' (Gu 2001b: 199) and 'the highest leading organ for directing the labour insurance work throughout the country' (Government Administration Council 1953: 28), entrusted the People's Bank of China to take custody of the labour insurance fund (Government Administration Council 1953).

The labour insurance fund was used for the payment of relief benefits, invalid pensions or allowances, maternity benefits, death benefits, old-age pensions, and for funding the LIS. The LIS covered the fees for consultation, treatment, ordinary medicines, and hospitalization of workers and staff who sought medical treatment at the enterprise-run hospital or clinic, or in a specially designated hospital (Government Administration Council 1953: 13). Workers and staff had to pay the fees for expensive medicines, meals at the hospital, and travel expenses on their own (Government Administration Council 1953: 13). Most large enterprises with more than 1,000 employees organized their own hospitals (inside hospitals), while most medium-sized enterprises with 200 to 1,000 employees had their own clinics to provide outpatient services for their employees (Liu and Hsiao 1995: 1095–6). Small enterprises relied on contracted hospitals to provide all health services for their employees (Liu and Hsiao 1995: 1096). Contracted hospitals would clear the bill with the enterprises upon completion of treatment (Yu and Ren 1997: 437). The LIS also covered treatment fees and half the cost of ordinary medicines of direct dependents of workers and staff (Government Administration Council 1953: 15). Direct dependents of workers and staff had to pay inpatient fees, meals at the hospital, fees for expensive medicines, travel expenses, and all other expenses on their own (Government Administration Council 1953: 15).

In 1966, *the Circular on Several Questions Concerning the Improvement of the Labour Health Insurance System* was jointly issued by the Ministry of Labour (MOL) and the ACFTU to increase the amount of medical expenses borne by workers. According to *the Circular*, workers and staff had to pay the fees for registration, home visits, nutrients, and tonics on their own, while employers paid the fees for expensive medicines (Ministry of Labour and the All-China Federation of Trade Union 1966). Direct dependents of workers and staff had to pay the fees for registration, examination, laboratory tests, and half the cost of surgery and medicines (Ministry of Labour and the All-China Federation of Trade Union 1966). In January 1967, immediately after the beginning of the Cultural Revolution (1966–1976), the ACFTU was formally dissolved and virtually all enterprise unions ceased to function (Naughton 1997: 177). The enterprise management itself had to take over the administration of the benefits and social security system (Naughton 1997: 177). In February 1969, the Ministry of Finance (MOF) issued *the Opinions on the Reform of Several Systems in the Financial Work of State-owned Enterprises*, which in effect suspended the drawing of the labour insurance fund in state-owned enterprises (SOEs) and converted the amount of money originally contributed to the labour insurance fund to enterprises' non-operating expenditures (Wang 2017: 5). From then on, enterprises became responsible for financing and administering the labour insurance (Lee 2000: 140). In November 1969, enterprises were required to draw 11 percent of their payroll to establish the employee welfare fund, with 5.5 percent of it used to pay the medical expenses of workers and staff (Li 2009: 35). In other words, the LIS became a work-unit-based welfare scheme (Gu 2001b: 200).

Government-funded Healthcare Scheme (GHS)

The GHS initially began in 1951 as a pilot scheme in some communist revolutionary base areas and ethnic-minority areas (Government Administration Council 1952). In July 1952, the GHS was formally established after the Government Administration Council had issued *the Directive Regarding the Implementation of the Government-funded Healthcare and Prevention Scheme for Personnel of the People's Governments, Parties, Organizations and Institutions at Various Levels in the Nation*. According to the *Directive*, the GHS would be rolled out in phases. It initially covered government employees, workers, and staff employed in trade unions, youth leagues and women's leagues, personnel in cultural, educational, health, and economic-construction institutions, and disabled military personnel (Government Administration Council 1952). It was then extended to cover cadres, university and college students in January 1953 and retired employees of the state and government institutions in June 1956 (Liu 2013).

Those covered by the GHS were given a GHS card, and they carried the card to seek medical treatment at the designated clinic or hospital (Ministry of Health 1952). The GHS was funded by the Treasury according to per capita health spending for employees set by the central government (Li 2009: 37). Per capita health spending for employees rose from Renminbi (RMB) 18 in 1953 to RMB 25 in 1962 and RMB 30 in 1978 (Li 2009: 37). The GHS covered both outpatient and inpatient expenses for consultation, treatment, surgery, medicines, and hospitalization (Government Administration Council 1952). Patients only paid for meals at the hospital and travel expenses on their own (Government Administration Council 1952). If they had financial difficulties, they could receive subsidies from the institution they worked for, and such subsidies would be treated as administrative expenses of the institution (Government Administration Council 1952). The GHS was managed by the GHS Management Committees established at various levels of government (Ministry of Health 1952). In 1989, the GHS covered 26.5 million people, accounting for 2.4 percent of the population (Liu and Hsiao 1995: 1095).

Cooperative Medical System (CMS)

Prior to 1955, healthcare payment in rural areas was dominated by the fee-for-service model (Luk 2017: 40). The vast majority of the rural population avoided seeking medical care when they were ill, due to lack of money. The rudiment of the CMS could be traced back to 1950 when peasants in the northeast provinces, based on the spirit of mutual aid, established cooperative medical stations in villages by collecting financial contributions and food (e.g. grain, eggs, and potatoes) from individuals (Cao 2006; Li 2009; Liu and Cao 1992). In 1955, the agricultural cooperative movement accelerated the development of cooperative medical stations in rural areas (Liu and Cao 1992; Wang 2009). In Mishan Township, Gaoping County, Shanxi, the funding of the cooperative medical station came from three sources: an annual healthcare fee of RMB 0.5 contributed by individual peasants, 15 to 20 percent of the public welfare funds contributed by the agricultural cooperative, and drug charges contributed by doctors (Cao 2006; Wang 2009). Peasants who had paid the annual healthcare fee were entitled to receive preventive healthcare services (Wang 2009: 375). They were exempt from paying fees for registration, injections, surgery, and home visits except for drug charges (Cao 2006: 136; Wang 2009: 375).

The MOH, which praised Mishan village for establishing a reliable socialist organizational basis for the provision of preventive healthcare, disseminated the Mishan experience with the approval of the State Council (Wang 2009: 375). Subsequently, cooperative medical stations were established in villages in Shanxi, Henan, Hebei, Hunan, Guizhou, Shandong, and Shanghai (Sun 2009). By 1957, more than 10,000 cooperative medical stations had been established in China (Wang 2009: 375). The phrase 'cooperative medical system' soon appeared in a newspaper under the MOH in September 1958 and then in a central government document in November 1959 (Wang 2009: 376–7). The confirmation and promotion of the CMS by the MOH and Mao Zedong made the CMS grow rapidly, and its coverage rate increased rapidly (Liu and Cao 1992: 504). The CMS had covered about 80 percent of the rural population by the end of the 1960s and 90 percent of the rural population in 1979 (Liu and Cao 1992: 504).

There was not a single model of the CMS in the nation (Wang 2009). The CMS varied across regions in terms of operation, contribution, and medical coverage (Luk 2017: 41). The CMS could be run by a brigade, a commune, or by both (Wang 2009: 381). The funding of the CMS came from three sources: the annual income of an individual peasant, the brigade or commune welfare fund, and government subsidies (Li 2009; Liu 2013). But the economic condition of rural localities affected the amount of funding contributed to the CMS, which in turn affected the level of medical coverage enjoyed by peasants. The percentage of the annual income contributed by an individual peasant could vary from 0.5 to 2 percent (about RMB 4 to 8) (Li 2009: 56). The portion of brigade or commune welfare fund contributed to the CMS could vary from 30 percent to 90 percent (Wang 2009: 381). In general, the level of medical coverage could be divided into three types: (1) free treatment and free drugs; (2) free treatment but drugs were paid by peasants out of pocket; and (3) exempting part of the drug costs, but examination and inpatient fees were paid by peasants (Shi 2003: 47). The cost of cooperative medical service was kept at an affordable level by relying on low-cost barefoot doctors to raise herbs and make Chinese medicine on their own (Wang 2009: 380–1). The CMS was managed by the CMS Management Committee (Liu and Cao 1992: 501).

The process of the urban health insurance reform

The problem stream

The provision of free healthcare services through the LIS and GHS greatly improved the health conditions of urban workers. The mortality rate decreased from about 12.3 percent in 1955 to 9.5 percent in 1965, and about 6.8 percent in 1985 (Zheng 2009: 258). Meanwhile, life expectancy drastically increased from 57 years in 1957 to 68 years in 1982 (Zheng 2009: 258). But the provision of free healthcare services encouraged over-consumption of medical services and a serious waste of medical resources due to a lack of cost consciousness among the LIS and GHS beneficiaries (Li 2009). During Mao's era, over-consumption and waste did not lead to any serious financial problems in the operation of the free healthcare system because of low drug prices (Gu 2001b: 201). Nevertheless, over-consumption of medical services became one of the key drivers of the rapid growth of healthcare expenditures in the 1980s. Other drivers included 'the marketization and commercialization of hospitals' (Gu 2001b: 204), a drastic increase in the number of LIS and GHS beneficiaries (Luk 2017: 45), and ageing of the covered population (Liu and Hsiao 1995: 1095).

The rapid growth of healthcare expenditures became a serious problem when China, under the leadership of Deng Xiaoping, transformed itself from a centrally planned economy into a market economy in 1978. Decentralizing the fiscal system from the 1980s 'gave local governments greater autonomy and responsibility to determine their own spending' (Duckett 2011: 44), including their spending on health. This drove local governments to spend in areas that would increase their tax revenues, such as industrial development (Duckett 2011: 44). Local governments' incentives to spend on growing the economy greatly increased in the 1980s and 1990s when their performance was 'mainly measured in economic terms, such as the growth of GDP, industrial outputs, fiscal revenues, and foreign direct investment' (Jing *et al.* 2015: 55). Since the government performance evaluation system gave all kinds of awards, bonuses, commissions, and subsidies to high-performing local governments (Jing *et al.* 2015: 55), it 'encouraged local government leaders to invest in promoting growth rather than in health and social provision' (Duckett 2011: 45). Consequently, local governments reduced their budgetary commitment to health (Duckett 2011: 41). 'Government subsidies decreased and accounted for only about 10 percent of average public hospital revenues' (Luk 2015: 49). This led to 'substantial changes in hospital management and operational approaches for generating revenues' (Liu *et al.* 2004: 42). To compensate for the lack of government subsidies, the MOH, which 'regained control of health policy-making again' (Duckett 2011: 42), 'began reforms of health system fee and pricing structures that allowed hospital scope for increasing revenues from non-budgetary sources' (Duckett 2011: 48), and these were approved by the State Council (Duckett 2011: 51). Public hospitals were given substantial financial autonomy to charge for their services and to sell drugs at a profit (World Bank 2010: vii). They were also permitted to charge higher fees to patients covered by LIS or GHS than they did to self-pay patients (Duckett 2011: 86). They began to run like for-profit organizations (Luk 2015: 49).

'[P]rice liberalization applied to many new drugs and items of medical equipment, some of which were imported from abroad' (Gu 2001b: 205). The use of higher-than-average charges on drug prescriptions and new, expensive, high technology care became a common practice among public hospitals to make up budget shortfalls (Hu *et al.* 1999: 310). 'On average, the drug expenditure accounted for about 67 percent of total expenditure per visit' (Yu and Ren 1997: 446), which was well above global average. CT scanners and MRIs were used by hospitals to earn more profits (Yu and Ren 1997: 446). A bonus system was also introduced to increase the performance of hospital doctors (Luk 2017: 44). Under this system, the amount of bonus the doctor received depended on the quantity of services provided (e.g. medical procedures, tests, and examinations) or the revenue generated by the doctors through service provision and drug prescription over a revenue target (Liu and Mills 2005). In order to receive more bonuses, doctors engaged in supplier-induced demand (SID), leading patients to take unnecessary medications or have unnecessary tests, procedures, treatments, and surgical operations. SID, 'couple[d] with asymmetric information between patients and doctors' (Liu *et al.* 2004: 42), led to a rapid increase in healthcare expenditures.

Meanwhile, a drastic increase in the number of LIS and GHS beneficiaries from 15 million in 1952 to about 154 million in 1989 also drove up healthcare expenditures (Liu and Hsiao 1995: 1096). This was the result of an increase in the number of retirees (Hu *et al.* 1999: 310). Ageing of the covered population was another reason for the rise in healthcare expenditures because older people usually had heavier disease burden and greater medical needs than younger people (Luk 2017: 25–6). As a result, there was a drastic increase in both the overall LIS and GHS expenditures and the average per capita medical expenses of LIS and GHS participants. One study showed that in the 1980s, GHS medical expenses increased annually by about 21 percent and the LIS by 17 percent, which were greatly higher than the 13 percent growth rate in fiscal revenue of the same period (Peng and Chen 2011a: 410). Another study showed that the overall LIS expenditure rose from RMB 2.73 billion in 1978 to 6.47 billion in 1985, while the overall GHS expenditure rose from RMB 570 million in 1979 to about RMB 1.54 billion in 1985 (Zheng 2009: 260). The average per capita medical expenses of LIS participants rose from RMB 36.1 in 1978 to RMB 44.3 in 1980 and RMB 65.1 in 1985 (Zheng 2009: 260). From 1990 to 1992, the average per capita medical expenses of LIS participants increased by 32 percent, rising from RMB 187.6 to RMB 248 (Zheng 2009: 260). From 1953 to 1979, the average per capita medical expenses of GHS participants increased by 52 percent, rising from RMB 26.25 to RMB 39.9 (Zheng 2009: 260). From 1985 to 1992, the average per capita medical expenses of GHS participants increased threefold, rising from about RMB 72.6 to RMB 220 (Zheng 2009: 260).

The rapid growth of healthcare expenditures imposed an extremely heavy financial burden on enterprises and the government. Under the economic reform, both SOEs and collective-owned enterprises faced market competition (Hu *et al.* 1999: 310) and became solely responsible for their own profits and losses (Hsü 2000: 850). Profits retained 'could be used for bonuses, employee welfare benefits, and further industrial innovations' (Hsü 2000: 850). However, many enterprises 'earned no profit and approximately one third had net losses' (Hu *et al.* 1999: 310). They were financially incapable of paying the medical expenses of their employees (Luk 2014a, 2017). Some of them cut costs by laying off workers. This led to laid-off workers losing their LIS entitlement. By 1990, most enterprises found that the LIS cost equaled 8 to 9 percent of their payroll (Hu *et al.* 1999: 310). Paying such cost hindered their financial viability and weakened their competitiveness in the marker economy (Luk 2014a: 65). For less profitable enterprises or enterprises that had many retired workers, they were unable to preserve sufficient labour insurance funds to pay for the medical expenses of their employees (Hu *et al.* 1999). They cut back on provisions, although this contravened national LIS policy (Duckett 2011: 86). As a result, many employees became 'underinsured' or 'uninsured' (Luk 2017: 45). 'Uninsured' employees also included those working in newly emergent private enterprises such as foreign-funded enterprises and shareholding enterprises (Peng and Chen 2011a: 410), because no standard medical benefit requirement existed for these enterprises (Gu 2001b: 208; Hu *et al.* 1999: 310). According to the MOH, out-of-pocket payment for urban healthcare accounted for 37.3 percent of total health expenditures in 1990, which was 14 percent higher than the figure in 1980 (Aitchison 1997: 46).

Meanwhile, a continuous drain on the state budget due to the rapid growth of healthcare expenditures also made it difficult for the government to sustain the GHS (Luk and Preston 2016: 111). In fact, the central government from the mid-1980s onwards launched a series of health financing reforms to contain medical costs (Gu 2001b; Li 2009; Luk 2017), but the result was unsatisfactory. In the early 1990s, there was the collapse of the LIS and GHS due to insufficient financial support from the enterprises and the government (Luk 2017: 45). Many workers who were originally covered by the LIS or GHS ended up personally paying for their medical expenses out of pocket. The proportion of the urban population who sought self-treatment when being ill increased from 77 percent to 88 percent from 1993 to 1998 (Gao *et al.* 2001: 306). Financial difficulty was cited as a major obstacle to seeking treatment from a doctor (Gao *et al.* 2001: 307). The collapse of the LIS and GHS compelled the government to introduce a new health financing model in the late 1990s.

The policy stream

The central government spent more than ten years carrying out different pilot experiments before it finally decided to introduce a new contribution-based medical insurance model nationwide in 1998. For the period of 1984–89, the central and local governments explored different ways to reduce medical expenditures while ensuring that patients received appropriate care. In April 1984, the MOH and the MOF jointly issued *Notification of Further Strengthening the Management of the Government-funded Healthcare Scheme*, which stated that pursuing the GHS reform was imperative and encouraged local governments to experiment with different solutions on the premise of ensuring equality and efficiency so that drug waste and the risk for misuse and abuse of the GHS could be reduced (Ministry of Health and Ministry of Finance 1984). Decentralization was adopted as the GHS reform strategy because the economic reform 'promoted decentralized decision making at the local level' (Wang 2002: 168). 'Local governments were responsible for solving their own problems in their own ways' (Yu and Ren 1997: 439–440).

In 1987, the MOH and the MOF jointly convened the first National Experience Sharing Meeting to exchange views on reforming and managing the GHS in all localities (Peng and Chen 2011a: 412). In February 1988, the State Commission for Economic Restructuring (SCER), which was an agency responsible for the overall design of the national economic system with the State Council Premier serving as its director (Peng and Chen 2011a: 133–4), submitted Premier Li Peng the *Report on the Issue of Reforming Social Protection and the Medical System* (Peng and Chen 2011a: 413). It pointed out that the health financing reform, which involved multiple government agencies, required the establishment of a special taskforce to conduct research on the reform plan (Peng and Chen 2011a: 413).

In March 1988, the Research Group on Health Insurance System Reform, consisting of representatives from eight ministries and committees, was formed with the approval of the State Council to propose a reform plan for the LIS and GHS. In July 1988, the Research Group drafted *the Tentative Design of the Reform of Medical Insurance Scheme for Employees*, which proposed the gradual establishment of a highly socialized and diversified medical insurance scheme for employees with medical expenses shared by the country, employers, and employees (Peng and Chen 2011a: 413). Subsequently, the State Council chose four medium-sized cities, including Dandong, Siping, Huangshi, and Zhuzhou, as the pilot cities to carry out health financing reform experiments in March 1989 (Gu 2001b; Zheng 2009: 263). The main reform experiments included: (1) copayment schemes requiring workers to pay part of their medical expenses; (2) a social pooling scheme to cover the medical expenses of retired workers; and (3) a social pooling scheme to cover workers' catastrophic health expenditures (Li 2009: 42). While copayments aimed to cut healthcare spending and reduce unnecessary medical treatment, risk pooling aimed to share uneven enterprise health spending burdens (Duckett 2011: 82–3).

Meanwhile, some local governments also undertook reform measures to contain medical costs. For example, financial contracting with enterprises was introduced in which the government appropriated certain amounts of healthcare funds for enterprises to pay the medical expenses of their employees (Gu 2001b: 209). Enterprises had to cover any healthcare spending beyond the contracted amount on their own (Gu 2001b: 209). Some local governments introduced 'pre-payment to hospitals according to the number of beneficiaries in their areas, and specifying a fixed fee for services' (Dong 2001: 7). It aimed at transferring financial risk to hospitals and increasing their incentives to achieve effective cost control. Nevertheless, health financing reform in the exploration stage were piecemeal and incremental (Luk 2017: 47–8). It was limited to certain funding adjustments to increase the cost consciousness of patients and minimize healthcare providers' moral hazard behaviors without having any institutional change in the free healthcare system. It failed to address the fundamental weaknesses that existed in financing, payment, and management within the LIS and GHS (Dong 2001: 8). Hence, the reform failed to reverse the national tendency of soaring health expenditures (Gu 2001b: 209). The continued fiscal crisis compelled the central government to commence a new round of pilot reform on the health financing system (Gu 2001b: 209).

Nevertheless, the pilot reform on the health financing system was interrupted by the 1989 Tiananmen Square protest. There was the retreat from reform in the years 1989–1991. In early 1992, Deng's historic tour of southern China marked a return to reform and opening up. In May 1992, the Small Group on Healthcare System Reform was established under the leadership of the State Council to conduct a comprehensive study on reforming the LIS and GHS (The General Office of the State Council 1992). It consisted of representatives from the SCER, the MOH, the MOL, the MOF, the Bureau of Personnel, the Pharmaceutical Bureau, the Price Bureau, and ACFTU (The General Office of the State Council 1992). 'The diversity of the participants represented an admission by the central government of the political complexity of health care reform' (Aitchison 1997: 87). The State Council instructed representatives from the SCER to take charge of overall routine work, representatives from the MOH to examine plans for the GHS, and representatives from the MOL to examine plans for the LIS (The General Office of the State Council 1992). The Small Group was required to write a briefing report on the current situation, problems, procedures, and experience of reforming the health financing system for internal reference (The General Office of the State Council 1992). It was also required to convene seminars, draw up the draft of the reform plan, and revise it after discussion with local governments and authorities in charge. It had to address any problems through consultation and deliberation among group members and report the revision result to the State Council (The General Office of the State Council 1992).

Indeed, at the central government levels, all of the interested ministries and bureaus were battling to control the reforming health financing system (Aitchison 1997: 6). This was because ministries and bureaus operated largely independently on a daily basis, and they took divergent positions on health financing reform (Luk 2014a: 61–2). For example, the SCER, which was established in the early 1980s to study and guide the overall economic reform, 'emphasized efficiency and favoured less government involvement in health care financing' (Luk 2014a: 61). The MOF, which was responsible for the funds for the GHS and tax administration, wanted to limit healthcare costs and created a health financing system that was less of a burden to the central government finances (Aitchison 1997: 85–6). The MOH, which was responsible for managing hospitals, 'wanted to ensure that the interests of hospitals and physicians would not be affected by health insurance reform' (Luk 2017: 52). The MOL, which was responsible for allocating labor and overseeing the LIS and the welfare of the urban labor force, was interested in retaining and even expanding its supervisory control through new laws and regulations (Aitchison 1997: 29–30; Duckett 2011: 92). The Price Bureau was anxious to maintain its roles in assigning the costs of medicines and medical services under the health financing reform (Aitchison 1997: 86). The Pharmaceutical Bureau, which was responsible for administration of pharmaceutical factories and the production of drugs, was anxious to prevent price restrictions on medicines (Aitchison 1997: 86). When representatives from different ministries and bureaus came together to form the Small Group, they bargained with each other, hoping to create a health financing system that could suit their own interests best. But the bargaining process was time-consuming, and members within the Small Group struggled to resolve differences and find common ground. By the end of 1992, the Small Group produced a compromise health insurance plan funded by the state, employers, and employees (Duckett 2011: 84), 'where the burden of health care remained substantially with the state and capitation was used to control health care costs' (Aitchison 1997: 87). However, the plan was not favored by Vice-Premier Zhu Rongji, who was 'determined at all costs to relieve the central government of the burden of health care costs' (Aitchison 1997: 87). Inspired by the Singaporean health financing model, Zhu decided that the burden of cost should fall more on employers and employees, and the individual account should be adopted to limit healthcare consumption (Aitchison 1997: 88). While all representatives of the Small Group disliked Zhu's plan, they sought to delay national implementation by carrying out local experimentation over the next few years (Aitchison 1997: 89; Duckett 2011: 84).

In November 1993, the Third Plenary Session of the 14th Central Committee of the Communist Party of China clearly stated that medical insurance for urban employees should be borne jointly by employers and employees, and a medical insurance model combining individual medical savings accounts (MSA) and the social pooling fund (SPF) should be established (Li 2009: 48). In January 1994, Premier Li Peng held the Work Meeting of the Premier to focus on the reform of the health insurance system and study the relationship among the government, enterprises, employees, and hospitals (Zhou and Zhang 2017: 130). In April 1994, the SCER, together with the MOL, the MOF and the MOH, issued *Opinions on Test Sites for Reforming the Healthcare System for Staff and Workers* (hereafter the 1994 Opinions). According to the 1994 Opinions, basic medical protection should be provided for all urban employees. The level and mode of the basic medical protection should match the country's level of productivity and the capacities of the various parties concerned (The State Commission for Economic Restructuring *et al.* 1994). The state and enterprises should not bear all of the medical expenses (The State Commission for Economic Restructuring *et al.* 1994). Hence, a health insurance model that combined individual MSA and the SPF should be established, and the funding would come from premium contributions made by both employers and employees (The State Commission for Economic Restructuring *et al.* 1994). In November 1994, the State Council approved the selection of Zhenjiang in Jiangsu Province and Jiujiang in Jiangxi Province (the two *jiangs*) as two pilot cities to implement the new medical insurance model (The State Council 1994) because these two medium-sized cities had better economic conditions and had made certain achievements in managing and reforming the GHS (Peng and Chen 2011b: 144–5). Following the guidance of the State Council, the two *jiangs* in December 1994 implemented the pilot reforms on the basis of their respective realities.

In January 1996, leaders from 11 ministries attended a meeting which summarized the reform experience in the two *jiangs* (Peng and Chen 2011b: 147). The reform experience showed that the establishment of a medical insurance model combining individual MSA and SPF was proven to be correct (Peng and Chen 2011b: 148). The use of individual MSA as a demand-side cost control mechanism could achieve an economic efficiency in healthcare utilization because the insured would be more cost conscious when healthcare payments were linked to their own 'assets', which were the funds in their individual MSA (Liu *et al*. 2004: 47). Meanwhile, the use of SPF could maximize the risk pooling capacity when the insurance pool was socialized over the entire local community (Liu *et al*. 2004: 47), 'providing insurance for all cross-sector employed individuals regardless of their health status and individual characteristics' (Liu *et al*. 2004: 47). By combining individual MSA and SPF, the two-*jiangs* model could effectively curb the rapid growth of medical expenses, and basic healthcare of employees was guaranteed in a better way (Peng and Chen 2011b: 148).

In April 1996, the General Office of the State Council held a four-day work conference to discuss questions concerning the expansion of the trials of medical insurance reform to the entire nation (Peng and Chen 2011b: 299). Based on the successful pilot reform experience in the two *jiangs*, the State Council in May 1996 decided to expand the reform to '57 cities in 27 provinces, autonomous regions and provincially ranked municipalities across the country' (Gu 2001b: 209). It made clear stipulations regarding 'the objectives, the basic principles, and the main contents, policy and organizational leadership of the expansion of trials' (Peng and Chen 2011b: 299). While local governments in the expanded reform primarily followed the insurance model in the two *jiangs* (Liu *et al*. 2004: 44), they 'were given considerable room to feature their plans with characteristics that may better meet their local needs and socioeconomic conditions' (Liu *et al*. 2004: 44–5). For example, they could use different instruments such as copayment, capping, and provider payment schedules to contain costs (Liu *et al*. 2004: 47). The Leading Small Group of the State Council on the Pilot Spots of Health Insurance System Reform for Urban Employees was established to supervise and guide local governments to carry out the pilot reforms, monitor the progress of the reforms, and evaluate their outcomes (Luk 2014a: 61).

The political stream

In January 1997, the Central Committee of the Communist Party of China and the State Council jointly issued the *Decision Concerning Health Reform and Development*, which called for the use of the contribution-based medical insurance model to provide basic medical protection for all urban employees (The Central Committee of the Communist Party of China and the State Council 1997). In the first half of 1998, the Leading Small Group of the State Council on Reforming the Medical Insurance System for Enterprise Staff and Workers drafted, on the basis of summing up useful experience from pilot reforms, a report on *the Decision of the State Council Concerning the Establishment of the Urban Employee Basic Medical Insurance System* (Peng and Chen 2011b: 303). In late November 1998, 'the State Council held a national work conference on the medical insurance system in Beijing' (Peng and Chen 2011b: 303). In the conference, 'experience of all pilots nationwide was summarized and the work on reforming the medical insurance system was formally arranged' (Zhou and Zhang 2017: 140).

Vice Premier of the State Council Li Lianqing stressed at the conference that a new basic medical insurance system for urban employees must be established in the nation (Peng and Chen 2011b: 303).

In mid-December 1998, the State Council promulgated a landmark decree known as *the Decision of the State Council Concerning the Establishment of the Urban Employee Basic Medical Insurance* (hereafter the 1998 Decree) (The State Council 1998). According to the 1998 Decree, a compulsory scheme known as the Urban Employee Basic Medical Insurance (UEBMI) would be implemented nationwide. Based on the principle of broad coverage (Peng and Chen 2011b: 304), the State Council required all urban work units in both the public and private sectors and their employees to participate in the UEBMI. Urban work units included the SOEs, collective enterprises, foreign-invested enterprises, privately owned enterprises, government organizations, public institutions, social organizations, and private non-enterprise units (The State Council 1998). Work units and their employees were required to make a compulsory contribution to the UEBMI. Retired employees could also join the UEBMI without paying any insurance premium. The contribution rate for work units, at the minimum, had to be at the level of 6 percent of an employee's total wage bill (The State Council 1998). The contribution rate for employees, at the minimum, had to be at the level of 2 percent of an employee's total wage bill (The State Council 1998).

The Basic Medical Insurance fund (hereafter the BMI fund) was formed by an individual MSA and an SPF. Premiums contributed by the employees would fully go into the MSA. As regards premiums contributed by work units, 30 percent of it would go into the MSA, while the rest of it would go into the SPF (The State Council 1998). The MSA mainly covered insured employees' general outpatient and emergency medical expenses, and prescribed drug charges (Luk 2017: 49). The SPF mainly covered inpatient charges (including inpatient observation in emergency rooms) (Luk 2017: 49). The BMI fund would be managed and supervised by the Ministry of Labor, Social Security, and the MOF (The State Council 1998). Local governments were required to formulate the UEBMI implementation plans based on the general framework laid down in the 1998 Decree. But they were given discretion to determine and adjust contribution rates, payment thresholds, ceilings, and reimbursement ratios of the BMI in accordance with socioeconomic conditions (Luk 2017: 49). In sum, the implementation of the contribution-based UEBMI to provide medical coverage for all urban employees could minimize the risk of adverse selection by patients and favorable selection by providers while maximizing risk pooling capacity (Liu *et al.* 2004: 46).

Changes in political and economic contexts

The successful implementation of the UEBMI was due to several reasons: changes in political and economic contexts, a highly centralized polity and top-down decision-making model, decentralization and 'trial and error' strategies, and ideology. First, changes in the economic context due to changes in the top party-state leadership and ruling ideologies opened a window of opportunity for reforming the health financing system from the mid-1980s onwards. When Deng Xiaoping came to power in 1978, he decided to restore the economy that was seriously damaged by the Cultural Revolution (1966–76). He sought to make the nation strong and prosperous and thought that 'only major reform would permit the CCP to remain in power' (Lieberthal 2004: 127). He emphasized the need to continue strong one-party rule and linked CCP legitimacy closely to his ability to deliver the economic goods (Saich 2004: 57). He denounced Mao's egalitarianism as 'a dangerous notion that retarded economic growth' (Saich 2004: 60). He endorsed the ideology of economic pragmatism, 'the efficiency first' principle, and the idea of market forces, which became key components of the new governing philosophy (Guo 2010: 21–4). His endorsement of economic pragmatism could be reflected in his dicta such as 'To get rich is glorious' and 'Let some people get rich first'. His focus on economic growth led to a lowering of health as a priority and a declining government budgetary commitment to health (Duckett 2011: 41–2). Implementing the commercializing reforms in health by the MOH worsened the problem of moral hazards inherent in the LIS and GHS systems (Gu 2001b: 202). Rapid increase in health expenditures turned into a fiscal crisis for both the enterprises and the state (Gu 2001b). This prompted the government to transform the LIS and GHS systems into a new health insurance system that could fit well with the market economy (Gu 2001b).

A centralized political system

Second, a centralized political system without any separation of executive, legislative, and judicial powers enabled the government to reform the health financing system without any political impediments (Luk 2014a). 'China is a unitary state with political power concentrated at the central government level' (Wang 2002: 163). The central government enjoyed a monopoly on setting reform objectives and formulating reform policies. It adopted a top-down approach to inform decision-making. In the 1980s and 1990s, policy-making remained dominated by senior leaders within the party-state and central government ministries (Duckett 2011: 15). A centralized, bureaucratically dominated polity and closed policy-making process prevented non-state interest groups from playing a role (Duckett

2011). Public opinions exerted little influence on policy-making. The general public was weak 'because they had no opportunity to vote leaders out of office' (Duckett 2011: 19). They could hardly participate in policy-making through lobbying or other civil society activities (Duckett 2011: 16), and they were barred from voicing their opposition to policies they disliked. The CCP dominated the state apparatus through 'its control of the media through which it shaped the ideological climate in which the entire populace lived' (Lieberthal and Oksenberg 1988: 5).

Negotiations, bargaining and consensus-building

During the health reform process, the State Council, several ministries, and Vice-Premier Zhu Rongji played an important role in shaping the design and content of the health insurance model. Due to authoritarian politics, however, employees and recipients of healthcare had limited influence on health financing reform (Duckett 2011). The State Council worked closely with ministries during the process of urban health financing reform. It was the highest organization of state administration exerting leadership over various ministries, commissions, committees, and bureaus (Saich 2004: 133). Many ministries and bureaus had vested interests in the health financing reform. But no single ministry had authority over the others (Lieberthal 1992). During the reform process, each ministry tried to 'maintain the privileges of its constituents at the same time as increasing its own portion of the health care policy-making pie' (Aitchison 1997: 93). The MOF, which funded hospitals and the GHS, was fiscally conservative (Duckett 2011). It 'sought to restrain health-care costs and wanted a system that would not place heavy demands on central government finance' (Duckett 2011: 88). It therefore preferred a decentralized social insurance model rather than a tax-funded model because the former could shift fiscal responsibilities to local governments and thereby reduce the state's fiscal commitment (Duckett 2011: 88). The MOH, which wanted to ensure revenues for public hospitals, 'preferred demand-side constraints on health spending, for example patient copayments' (Duckett 2011: 77) and 'resisted attempts to impose supply-side controls on hospitals' (Duckett 2011: 18). The MOL, which 'had as its traditional purview in health care the administration of health care provision to all of China's state workers' (Aitchison 1997: 85), fought to retain control of LIS's successor program and the urban social security portfolio, of which the UEBMI was a part (Duckett 2011: 77). 'Fragmentation of authority encouraged a search for consensus among various organs' (Lieberthal 1992: 9) in order to reform the health financing system. 'This consensus, in turn, required extensive and often elaborate deals to be struck through various types of bargaining stratagems' (Lieberthal 1992: 9).

The structures that linked the top and the bottom of the system required negotiations, bargaining, exchange, and consensus-building (Lieberthal 1992: 12). Recognizing that health financing reforms involved a trade-off between the competing interests of various ministries, the State Council formed ad hoc small groups (*xiaozu*), leading small groups (*lingdao xiaozu*), or research groups to let representatives of various ministries come together to examine different reform plans, exchange ideas, and reach consensus on the contents of health insurance reforms. Since leading small groups or small groups only consisted of ministerial representatives and were 'largely hidden from public view' (Lieberthal 2004: 217), they faced little political opposition in the policy-making process. However, the compromise health insurance plan proposed by the Small Group 'could not wholly prevail against the decision of one key political actor' (Aitchison 1997: 87). The intervention of Vice-Premier Zhu Rongji led to the plan being adjusted to reduce the state's fiscal commitment while increasing those of employers and employees (Duckett 2011: 84). The result was a new health insurance model based on contributions from both employers and employees. Other important roles played by the State Council included choosing pilot cities for health financing reforms and organizing work conferences to allow leaders from different ministries and representatives from local governments to discuss health insurance reforms.

Decentralization-based and 'trial and error' strategies

Third, the adoption of decentralization-based and 'trial and error' strategies facilitated local experiments that eventually grew into a nationwide health insurance reform. During Deng's era, the central government replaced compulsory planning with guidance planning and shifted the emphasis from direct to indirect control (Leung 1998: 624). The central government, which assumed the role of macro control at the top, only delineated broad guiding principles for reform (Leung 1998: 624). Under administrative decentralization, local governments were encouraged to experiment with different solutions to contain medical costs according to local circumstances and capacity (Leung 1998). The adoption of 'trial and error' strategies helped minimize resistance and facilitate readjustments through feedback from local governments (Leung 1998: 624). After several years of experimentation and evaluation, the central government promoted the successful experiences or models through legislations (Leung 1998: 624). Local governments were empowered to enact local statutes in light of local circumstances when implementing health insurance reforms (Wong *et al.* 2006: 25–6). They enjoyed a wide discretion in determining 'the contribution rate, funding structure, payment structure, medical coverage and reimbursement ratio of health insurance schemes' (Luk 2017: 53).

Ideational forces

Fourth, ideology plays an important role in shaping the design of the health insurance model. During Deng's era, the old ideas of free healthcare and egalitarianism were no longer embraced by political leaders and key bureaucratic actors because they 'were regarded as one of the root causes of rising health care expenditure and impediments to promote economic reform further' (Luk

2014a: 67). Instead, the new ideas of individual responsibility and social solidarity gained political prominence as reflected in the institutional design of the new health insurance model. The new health insurance model combined the individual MSA and the SPF. The government sought to achieve individual responsibility through premium contribution from an individual and the individual MSA. When individuals were asked to pay premiums, they would take more responsibility for healthcare decisions and became more cost-conscious. The individual MSA resembled the Medisave account in Singapore because Vice-Premier Zhu Rongji drew on Singapore's experience in financing healthcare. The government also sought to achieve social solidarity and promote the idea of mutual aid through the SPF because the SPF could redistribute funds from the healthy to the sick and ensure financial protection against catastrophic health expenditures. The SPF resembled sickness funds of a statutory health insurance system in Germany, indicating that the government borrowed experience from Germany when designing the new health insurance model.

Challenges to the current multi-layered social health insurance system

After implementing the UEBMI, the Chinese government had gradually implemented the New Rural Cooperative Medical System (NRCMS) in 2003, the Urban Resident Basic Medical Insurance (URBMI) in 2007 and the Critical Illness Insurance Scheme (CIIS) in 2012. Both the NRCMS and the URBMI are voluntary schemes funded by individual contributions and annual subsidies from the central and local governments. The NRCMS mainly covers inpatient expenses for rural residents. The URBMI covers inpatient and outpatient expenses for catastrophic illnesses for non-working urban residents, including young children, primary and secondary school students, the severely disabled, and the elderly (Luk 2017: 63). The CIIS provides NRCMS and URBMI participants with financial protection against critical illnesses, on top of their basic medical insurance reimbursement (Luk 2017: 64). In January 2016, the government decided to adopt a gradual approach to integrate NRCMS and URBMI so that a unified health insurance system would be set up for urban and rural residents (The State Council 2016). The unified health insurance system is expected to 'break the urban-rural dichotomy, strengthen the efficiency of risk pooling, provide better financial protection, and achieve equal medical treatments' (Luk 2018: 32). In 2018, China's basic medical insurance covered 1.35 billion people, accounting for 95 percent of the total population (China Daily 2018). It shows that the Chinese government has made unremitting efforts to provide basic medical protection for different segments of the population. It has almost achieved universal health insurance coverage through the establishment of a multi-layered health insurance system.

Nevertheless, the multi-layered health insurance system is plagued by several problems, including medical insurance fund deficit, high out-of-pocket expenses, and insufficient medical protection for the elderly. First, the medical insurance fund deficit has been reported in many places where insured people cannot get reimbursed for their medical expenses. For example, in 2013, a total of 225 districts in China experienced a deficit in the UEBMI funds, and a total of 108 districts experienced a deficit in the URBMI funds (Beijing Business Today 2014). By 2024, there will be an accumulated deficit of RMB 735.3 billion in the UEBMI funds, according to the estimate of *Green Book of Health Reform and Development 2014* (Li 2015). Experts said that improvements in health insurance coverage, an ageing population, and the unreasonable growth of health expenditures are the main causes of the medical insurance fund deficit (Li 2015). The unreasonable growth of health expenditures is caused by SID, high drug prices, and health insurance fraud committed by healthcare providers and physicians (Luk 2017). SID is still a common practice among doctors to increase their incomes. High drug prices are due to markups from wholesale to retail price. Public hospitals still heavily rely on drug sales to gain substantial revenues. Common fraudulent practices such as falsifying medical records and fake hospitalization (*gua chuang zhu yaun*) result in quick depletion of health insurance funds (Luk 2017: 80).

Second, the problem of high out-of-pocket expenses remains unsolved. In order to earn higher kickbacks from pharmaceutical companies, doctors usually prescribe expensive, imported drugs that are excluded from *the National Basic Medical Insurance Drug Formulary List* for reimbursement (Luk 2014a: 72). Insured persons have to pay for these drugs on their own. High out-of-pocket expenses is also caused by having unnecessary surgeries and prolonged hospital stays. At present, both NRCMS and URBMI participants face higher out-of-pocket expenses than UEBMI participants because their health insurance schemes mainly cover inpatient expenses. But the problem of falling into poverty or falling back into poverty due to illnesses is serious among NRCMS participants who lack the financial means to pay for medical bills (Luk 2017: 73).

Third, the fragmented design of the current social health insurance system fails to provide sufficient medical protection for the elderly (Luk 2018: 32). China has yet to establish a health insurance scheme tailored for the elderly. The level of health insurance coverage enjoyed by older people depends on which health insurance scheme they participate in. The UEBMI provides a more comprehensive medical coverage for retired or older people than the NRCMS and the URBMI. Disparities in insurance coverage leads to health inequalities among the elderly. Although the majority of older people are covered by basic medical insurance, they still have to bear high out-of-pocket medical expenses. In 2017, out-of-pocket medical expenses for older people accounted for 50 percent of total medical expenses in the nation (China Ageing Finance Forum 2018). Those who cannot afford their medical bills may delay seeking medical care or give up their medical treatment, leading to health deterioration.

Ensuring the financial sustainability of the health insurance system will continue to be an important task for both the central and local governments. The introduction of a zero-markup policy for essential drugs in 2009 failed to reduce the average expenses and out-of-pocket expenses of patients because public hospitals increased other fees (e.g. treatment fees, surgical fees) and provided unnecessary services to compensate for the loss of drug revenues (He and Zhou 2017; Ye *et al.* 2015). How to ensure affordable healthcare for insured and uninsured persons remains a challenge. At present, many patients 'bypass the primary health-care system (i.e. the gatekeepers) to go to hospitals for more specialised consultations and higher insurance reimbursements' (Li *et al.* 2017: 2591). To control the growth of health spending, however, the government has to strengthen the primary care system through greater investment in primary care infrastructure, improving the education level and qualification of primary care doctors, and further promoting the family practice contract services. The government also has to strengthen its anti-fraud capacity to combat health insurance fraud that is usually committed on a large scale and on a collective basis. It can promulgate state law against health insurance fraud, set up an insurance fraud bureau to investigate health insurance fraud, establish a public fraud reporting system, and use data mining technology to detect health insurance fraud (Luk 2017: 90–6). Shrinking working-age population and early retirement will reduce the revenue of the UEBMI fund in the long run. To increase the revenue of the UEBMI fund, the government is conducting a feasibility study on the policy for retired employees to pay health insurance premiums (Guo 2016). Premium contributions from retired employees may help increase the financial stability of the UEBMI fund.

Conclusion

By 2040, China will become a super-aged society with 22 percent of its people aged 65 and over (Eberstadt 2018). The demand for healthcare will continue to increase. In order to provide affordable and sustainable healthcare for its population, the government needs to strengthen its efforts to address high drug prices, combat health insurance fraud, reduce urban-rural disparities in healthcare, and ensure more equitable access to healthcare for its population.

3 Hong Kong

The mandatory health insurance reform fiasco

Introduction

Hong Kong tops global life expectancy rankings (Hollingsworth 2017). In 2018, average life expectancy was 82.2 years for males and 87.6 years for females (Centre for Health Protection 2019a). But the growing burden of chronic diseases has posed a major fiscal sustainability challenge to the free healthcare system. This chapter examines why the mandatory health insurance reform failed in 1999, while the voluntary health insurance scheme was implemented in 2019. It also identifies challenges to the current free healthcare system.

The mandatory health insurance reform was the most controversial health financing reform in Hong Kong. A 15-member team of economists, public health specialists, physicians, and epidemiologists from Harvard University were policy entrepreneurs in this reform. However, the mandatory health insurance scheme proposed by the Harvard Team faced severe opposition from legislators, political parties, medical practitioners, employers, the general public, and even pro-Beijing interest groups. Opponents argued that the mandatory nature of the scheme violated freedom of choice, while the idea of individual responsibility was contrary to the widespread belief that free healthcare was a fundamental right and legal entitlement for all (Luk 2014a). The poor economic circumstance did not open a window of opportunity to implement the mandatory health insurance reform. The proposal for the mandatory health insurance scheme gave opponents a very bad impression that the government was very inconsiderate and wanted to shirk its responsibility in financing healthcare at a time of economic difficulty. The Chief Executive's lack of political legitimacy and the disjointed political system also made it very difficult for the government to secure majority support for this unpopular reform.

In recent years, the government has been promoting community-based primary care services to solve the problems of overcrowding and acute manpower shortage in public hospitals. In 2019, a voluntary government-regulated private health insurance scheme was implemented as a supplementary financing option. It is expected that the new scheme can encourage the insured to obtain private healthcare services and alleviate the pressure on the public healthcare system.

Pre-reform era

On 1 July 1997, Hong Kong became the Hong Kong Special Administrative Region (HKSAR) after its handover from British to Chinese rule. The HKSAR had a dual-track healthcare system encompassing the public and private sectors. The public sector was the predominant provider of secondary and tertiary healthcare services, while the private sector was the major provider of primary healthcare services (Food and Health Bureau 2008: 121). The HKSAR inherited a British-style public healthcare system funded by general taxation. Hong Kong residents only paid nominal fees when they obtained medical services from public hospitals or clinics. Charges for general out-patient (GOP) service were HK$37, which included medication and covered roughly 19 percent of the actual average cost per consultation for GOP service (Liu and Lee 1997: 12). Charges for specialist outpatient (SOP) service were HK$44, which included medication and covered roughly 10 percent of the actual average cost per consultation for SOP service (Liu and Lee 1997: 12). Charges for inpatient care at public hospitals were HK$68 per day (Liu and Lee 1997: 12), which covered meals, medicine, X-rays, and different tests (Cheung and Gu 2002: 36). The cost recovery rate for inpatient services was about 4 percent (Liu and Yue 1998: 34). Public hospitals provided 90 percent of inpatient care services and were managed by the Hospital Authority (HA), which was an independent statutory body established in 1990 (Liu and Lee 1997: 4).

Similar to the colonial government, the HKSAR government upheld the principle that 'no one should be denied adequate healthcare due to lack of means'. The public healthcare system provided the Hong Kong population with universal access to healthcare (Food and Health Bureau 2008: 127) and served as an essential safety net for the population (Food and Health Bureau 2008: 37). Recipients of Comprehensive Social Security Assistance (CSSA) were exempted from payment of fees for public healthcare services upon production of a valid medical fee waiver issued especially to them (The Government Information Centre 2008). 'In 1996/97, there were an estimated number of 97,000 CSSA in-patient and 538,000 out-patient episodes' (Liu and Yue 1998: 53). Non-CSSA recipients, including chronically ill patients, low-income patients, and elderly patients (Food and Health Bureau 2008: 127) could apply for a fee waiver at the Medical Social Service Unit of public hospitals and clinics or the Integrated Family Service Centres of the Social Welfare Department (The Government Information Centre 2008 March 12). A one-off waiver would be issued to non-CSSA recipients for hospitalization or unscheduled attendance at GOP clinics, while a period waiver would be issued to non-CSSA recipients for frequent follow-up medical treatment within a period of time (The Government Information Centre 2008). Medical items for which fees may be waived covered injections and dressings, Accident and Emergency (A&E) service, GOP service (non-episodic cases), SOP service, day hospital service, and community care (The Government Information Centre 2008).

The private sector provided 70 percent of outpatient service and 10 percent of inpatient service in Hong Kong (Liu and Lee 1997: 22). It provided a choice for those who were able and willing to pay for private healthcare services (The Government Information Centre 2015). Fees charged by private doctors for out-patient services usually varied from HK$100 to HK$250, or more for a specialist consultation (Food and Health Bureau 2008: 128). Charges in private hospitals varied from HK$350 a day for a bed in a general ward to HK$900 or more for a bed in a higher-class ward (Food and Health Bureau 2008: 129). Patients had to pay for all services, and some of the services such as diagnostic tests and surgical operations were charged separately and on an itemized basis (Food and Health Bureau 2008: 129). They could pay the fees out of pocket or by using private medical insurance (Liu and Lee 1997: 13).

The process of the 1999 health financing reform

The problem stream

Since the mid-1980s, the problem of rising healthcare expenditures had become more and more serious. In the years between 1986/87 and 1996/97, public healthcare expenditures increased nearly six times from HK$4,303 million to HK$25,051 million (Liu and Yue 1998: 12). In relative terms, public health-care expenditures as a proportion to Gross Domestic Product (GDP) increased from 1.3 percent in 1986/87 to 2 percent in 1996/97 (Liu and Yue 1998: 12). There were two main reasons for rising healthcare expenditures: (1) the ageing population, and (2) the success of the HA. Since the 1980s, the popula-tions had been showing a continuing ageing trend (Census and Statistics Depart-ment 2012: 9). The percentage of population aged 65 and above increased from 6.6 percent in 1981 to 8.7 percent in 1991 and 10.2 percent in 1996 (Census and Statistics Department 2012: 4). The elderly dependency ratio, which was the number of persons aged 65 and over per 1,000 persons aged between 15 and 64, increased from 97 in 1981 to 125 in 1991 and 143 in 1996 (Census and Statistics Department 2012: 4). Population ageing increased healthcare needs because old age 'is often accompanied by deteriorating health and chronic illnesses' (Hong Kong Government 1993: 15). Compared to younger persons, elderly persons consumed more healthcare resources and put a greater strain on the healthcare system. In 1991, elderly persons aged 60 or above (13 percent of the popula-tion) accounted for 32 percent of outpatient at government outpatient clinics, while elderly persons aged 65 or above (8.8 percent of the population) took up 37 percent of the bed days in public hospitals (Hong Kong Government 1993: 15). The survey conducted by the Census and Statistics Department showed that elderly persons aged 65 and above had the highest rate of hospitalization in 1995, while they ranked second in the rate of doctor consultation in 1996 (Liu and Yue 1998: 60–1). It was estimated that healthcare expenditures would increase as the population continued to age. In 1992, the cost of providing primary healthcare to those aged 60 and above at government outpatient clinics was HK$141 mil-lion, whereas the cost of providing inpatient treatment to those aged 65 and above was HK$2,721 million (Hong Kong Government 1993: 15). Given the projected increase in the size of these age groups, the cost of providing primary healthcare to those aged 60 and above would be HK$178 million, whereas the cost of providing inpatient treatment to those aged 65 and above would be HK$3,838 million in 2001 (Hong Kong Government 1993: 15). These represented a cost increase of 26 percent and 41 percent, respectively. How to meet the healthcare needs of the increasing number of older persons while ensuring the financial sustainability of the free healthcare system became an important task of the HKSAR government after the handover in 1997.

The success of the HA was another reason for rising healthcare expenditures in Hong Kong. Since the mid-1960s, the colonial government had focused on the expansion of hospital beds to meet the demands of the growing population (Hong Kong Government 1964, 1974). Such historical development resulted in a healthcare system that placed more emphasis on curative care (Liu and Yue 1998: 14) and the government's heavy involvement in the financing of expensive hospital care (Wong 1996: 450). The government heavily subsidized the HA. Since its establishment in 1991, the HA had been allocated between 73 percent and 84 percent of public healthcare expenditures for hospital services (Liu and Yue 1998: 37). In 1996/97, HK$21 billion was allocated to HA for hospital services, representing about 84 percent of the public healthcare expenditures (Liu and Yue 1998: 37) and accounted for 96 percent of HA's total income (Liu and Yue 1998: 49). The HA was the victim of its own success (Yuen 1997: 396; The Legislative Council 1999). Its commitment to the ongoing upgrading of wards and quality improvement in health services as well as its no-turn-away policy led to a drastic increase in patient load in public hospitals (Yuen 1997: 393–6; Luk 2014a: 113). In 1996/97, there were a total of 948,265 patient discharges, 6,121,160 specialist outpatient attendances, and 2,080,006 A&E attendances (Hospital Authority 1997: 108), representing an increase of 35 percent, 48 percent, and 48.3 percent from 1992/93 respectively. Only the number of general outpatient attendances decreased from 801,108 in 1992/93 to 754,572 in 1996/97 (Hospital Authority 1997: 108).

Due to experiencing sharp declines in occupancy, private hospitals 'voiced concern at their diminishing market share' (Gauld 1997: 33) and formed the Private Hospital Association to call on the government to limit access to public services to the most needy through means-testing (Wong 1996; Yuen 1997). Heads of private hospitals also lobbied the government to 'bring patients back to their wards and to draw a line between free welfare and charged services provided in public hospitals' (Wong 1996: 452). Meanwhile, the colonial government feared that continuous increase in public healthcare expenditures due to subsidizing the HA would cause serious fiscal problems for the government unless other sources of funding could be found (Yuen 1997: 398). It faced formidable challenges to contain healthcare spending while maintaining universal access to healthcare services (Gauld 1997: 34). After all, the burden of healthcare expenditures would ultimately fall on the public since they had to pay tax to finance the public healthcare system (Liu and Yue 1998: 11). How to finance healthcare in a better way was a major concern of the colonial government.

In fact, the colonial government in the early 1990s tried to address the problem of rising health expenditures by examining alternative ways to finance healthcare and proposing some reform options in a consultation document issued in 1993. But its reform was shelved due to strong opposition from legislators and the general public. The colonial government appointed a Medical Insurance Study Group (MISG) in 1991 and a committee in 1992 to respectively study the health insurance scheme which could suit the Hong Kong context and develop a long-term fee and waiver strategy (Gauld and Gould 2002: 120). In 1993, the findings and views of the MISG and the committee were incorporated into the government's first consultation document *Towards Better Health* (Gauld and Gould 2002; Cheung and Gu 2002), which was commonly known as *The Rainbow Report* because of the rainbow logo on the document cover. *The Rainbow Report* proposed five reform options:

1   the percentage subsidy approach, which raised fees based on a percentage of the actual operating costs;
2   the target group approach, which introduced more expensive semi-private beds and itemized charges at public hospitals based on the principle of cost recovery, while groups with less ability to pay were granted waivers;
3   the coordinated voluntary insurance approach, which encouraged the take-up of private health insurance schemes approved by a designated statutory body;
4   the compulsory comprehensive insurance approach, which required all households in Hong Kong to join a health insurance scheme centrally administered by the government that covered primary and hospital care in both public and private sectors; and
5   the prioritization of the treatment approach, which focused on treating patients with higher-priority conditions.

(Hong Kong Government 1993: 27–38)

However, 'none of the options or a combination of them had the general support of the community' (Legislative Council Secretariat 2005: 1). Given that funding was a more sensitive issue (Gauld 1997: 35) and confronting the legislators and the public during the political transition period was a bad idea (Luk 2014a: 119), the colonial government 'decided at the end of the consultation period that the status quo should be maintained' (Legislative Council Secretariat 2005: 1). Hence, rising healthcare expenditures became an issue that was left for the HKSAR government to deal with.

The policy stream

In October 1997, Chief Executive Tung Chee-hwa announced in his inaugural policy address that the government would carry out a comprehensive review of the existing healthcare system in 1998 to draw up suitable long-term policies (Hong Kong Special Administrative Region Government 1997). In November 1997, the Health and Welfare Bureau commissioned a 15-member team of economists, public health specialists, physicians, and epidemiologists from Harvard University to provide a comprehensive assessment of the existing healthcare financing and delivery system and propose strategic options to improve the system (The Harvard Team 1999). Led by Professors William Hsiao and Winnie Yip, the Harvard Team received advice and guidance from the government-appointed Steering Committee consisting of government officials, professors, medical and business leaders (The Harvard Team 1999: 2). The Harvard Team and the Steering Committee met every six to eight weeks to discuss 'issues confronting the current system, the objectives of the health care system, and viable reform options' (The Harvard Team 1999: 2). The Harvard Team also received guidance and assistance from the Working Group whose members came from the Treasury, the Financial Services Bureau, the Health and Welfare Bureau, the Department of Health (DoH), and the HA (The Harvard Team 1999: ii). During its study, the Harvard Team obtained data by making use of local and overseas information already available, conducting surveys of residents, doctors, and patients, and consulting more than 200 people, including scholars, members from different political parties, representatives from healthcare professional groups and associations, insurance companies, major employers, and patients' rights group (The Harvard Team 1999). In February 1999, the Harvard Team submitted the final report to the Health and Welfare Bureau. In April 1999, the 472-page Harvard consultancy report entitled *Improving Hong Kong's Health Care System: Why and For Whom?* (hereafter the *Harvard Report*) was released for public consultation for three months.

The *Harvard Report* identified four major weaknesses in the existing healthcare system, including highly variable quality of care, the highly compartmentalized health care system, dominance by hospital-based services, and the questionable long-term financial sustainability (The Harvard Team 1999: 4–9). The Harvard Team pointed out that these weaknesses were the result of the policy of benign neglect adopted by the government, which only stepped in when a problem became serious and whose solutions failed to deal with interrelated concerns (The Harvard Team 1999: 8). This left Hong Kong without a coherent overall policy for organizing or financing healthcare (The Harvard Team 1999: 8). Regarding financial sustainability of the existing system, the Harvard Team forecasted that public health expenditures as a share of total public expenditures would increase from 14 percent in 1996/97 to about 22 percent by the year 2016 under status quo (The Harvard Team 1999: 74). However, the low tax and balanced budget requirements imposed by Hong Kong's Basic Law meant that it was impossible to get extra financial resources through additional taxation (Cheung and Gu 2002: 43). In order to improve financial sustainability of the existing system, the Harvard Team identified five reform options based on the following guiding principle:

Every resident should have access to reasonable quality and affordable health care. The government assures this access through a system of shared responsibility between the government and residents where those who can afford to pay for health care should pay.

(The Harvard Team 1999: 9)

The guiding principle endorsed by the Harvard Team was different from the existing principle in several ways. First, unlike the existing principle that ensured the provision of adequate healthcare, the guiding principle focused on the provision of affordable healthcare with reasonable quality. Second, the guiding principle introduced the idea of shared responsibility. It meant that 'the government did not expect to shoulder the complete costs itself' (Gauld and Gould 2002: 128). Third, the guiding principle pointed out that residents who were more financially capable should pay for healthcare, which was different from the existing principle that healthcare would be provided for people regardless of their economic status. Based on the guiding principle, the Harvard Team identified the five reform options:

Option A: maintaining the status quo;
Option B: capping the government budget for healthcare;
Option C: raising user fees at public hospitals and clinics;
Option D: implementing a Health Security Plan (HSP) and Saving Accounts for Long-Term Care (MEDISAGE), a two-tier mandatory health insurance scheme which required both employers and employees to jointly contribute about 1.5 to 2 percent of employees' wages to the HSP to pay inpatient and outpatient medical expenses, and 1 percent of employees' wages to MEDISAGE to purchase long-term care insurance at the age of 65. The concept of 'money follows the patient' was introduced by establishing the Health Security Fund, Inc. to pay a standard payment rate to the public or private healthcare provider chosen by a patient (The Harvard Team 1999: 13); and
Option E: competitive integrated system which adopted the HSP and MEDISAGE option and reorganized the HA into 12 to 18 regional Health Integrated Systems to provide preventive, primary, outpatient, and hospital care (The Harvard Team 1999: 92–112).

In the *Harvard Report*, the Harvard Team evaluated the five reform options against five specific objectives of reform: (1) maintaining and improving equity; (2) improving quality and efficiency; (3) improving financial sustainability; (4) meeting the future needs of the population; and (5) managing overall health expenditure inflation (The Harvard Team 1999: 91–2). To the Harvard Team, Option A should not be accepted because maintaining the status quo was neither organizationally nor financially sustainable in light of projected demographic or epidemiological changes (The Harvard Team 1999: 92). Option B should not be accepted because capping the government budget would inevitably lead to lower quality care and less access to public health services (The Harvard Team 1999: 11). Option C should not be accepted because raising user fees failed to improve efficiency and quality of care and led to the poor and sick facing a financial barrier to access healthcare (The Harvard Team 1999: 96–7). Based on the evaluation result, the Harvard Team concluded that only Option D and Option E should be accepted because they could meet all of the reform objectives. It recommended that Hong Kong adopt Option D in the interim, which would build the foundation for the adoption of Option E in the long run (The Harvard Team 1999: 17). The Harvard Team said that it heavily relied on international experience when developing reform options (The Harvard Team 1999: 10). It drew upon the experience of Singapore and Japan to develop Option D and the experience of the United Kingdom, the United States, Germany, and Australia to develop Option E (The Harvard Team 1999: 88–9). It was obvious that the *Harvard Report*, through recommending Option D and Option E, aimed to 'alter the current funding concept to bring about a structural and a system change' (The Legislative Council 1999).

The political stream

Major political parties, legislators, representatives of business communities, medical doctors, scholars, and the public reacted negatively to the *Harvard Report*. The 1999 health financing reform ended in failure because of three main reasons: (1) a disjointed political system, (2) the difficult economic circumstances, and (3) the institutionalization of old ideas.

A disjointed political system

First, a disjointed political system made it impossible for the HKSAR government to gather wide political support for health financing reform. There was the lack of cohesion within the Executive Council (ExCo), a poor relationship between the ExCo and senior civil servants, and a tense relationship between the ExCo and the Legislative Council (LegCo). Being the first Chief Executive of the HKSAR, shipping tycoon Tung Chee-hwa lacked political legitimacy. He 'was seen as essentially selected by Beijing' (Cheung 2005: 141) and endorsed by the undemocratically constituted Selection Committee consisting of 400 pro-China and business elites (Cheung 2005; Luk 2014a). The ExCo, which was an organization assisting the Chief Executive in policy-making, consisted of members coming from a wide variety of backgrounds (Ma 2007: 62). These members included top government officials, previously pro-British figures, pro-China figures, members from pro-government parties and representatives from big businesses (Cheung 2005: 139; Ma 2007: 62). 'Such a mix was not conducive to forging a cabinet-style leadership sharing common interests and a collective agenda' (Cheung 2005: 139).

The ExCo presided over by the Chief Executive had a poor relationship with senior civil servants because of mutual distrust between the two sides as well as the rivalry between the two sides for policy-making powers under two competing 'executive-led' paradigms – one centered on the supremacy of the Chief Executive and the other centered on the traditional notion of bureaucratic polity

(Cheung 1997, 2004, 2007). Being a businessman and an outsider to the bureau-cratic polity, Tung did not share the same visions, ethos, and norms with the British-groomed senior civil servants (Ma 2007: 64–5). He thought that the civil service was unable to serve him well (Cheung 2005: 142). Meanwhile, senior civil servants' suspicion of communism and vigilance over possible intervention by Beijing made them mistrustful of Tung Chee-hwa, who declared loyalty to Beijing (Fong 2015). From Tung's perspective, the 'executive-led' principle was tantamount to a more presidential kind of executive government whereby the Chief Executive 'should take the lead in agenda-setting and expect full sup-port and cooperation from his civil-servant ministers' (Cheung 2004: 5). From senior civil servants' perspective, however, the 'executive-led' principle meant adherence to the colonial-era tradition of government by civil servants, with the Chief Executive, like the previous governors, giving formal approval to top civil servants' policy recommendations at the ExCo (Cheung 2004: 5). 'Despite the change of sovereignty and government, top civil servants [were] still keen to keep their policy-making powers largely intact' (Cheung 1997: 735). They perceived themselves as playing a leadership role in policy-making (Lee 1999: 947–8). But Tung's paternalistic political personality and his aspiration to be a strong leader made him treat senior civil servants as his subordinates (Lee 1999; Lau 2002a). Hence, his relationship with senior civil servants was very poor and 'there was a general lack of respect and support by top bureaucrats for his vision and reform agenda' (Cheung 2005: 142).

In fact, Tung's decision to commission scholars from Harvard University to review the existing healthcare system and recommend reform options for improv-ing healthcare finance was due to his belief that overseas scholars were more com-petent and more experienced, and the fame and reputation of Harvard University could easily win public acceptance (Luk 2014a: 124). Senior civil servants who were in the Steering Committee and the Working Group only provided assistance and guidance for the Harvard Team. In reality, the Harvard Team did not work with the Steering Committee well because these two parties lacked communica-tion and interaction. Being the member of the Steering Committee and legislator representing the medical profession in the LegCo, Dr. Che-hung Leong com-plained in the LegCo meeting held in May 1999 that the Steering Committee did not have the opportunity to discuss the issue of healthcare financing with the Harvard Team and monitor the work of the Harvard Team. According to Dr. Leong,

> this Committee was never given the chance to steer the consultation, its comments and criticisms were seldom taken on board nor were they ever explained nor even acknowledged by the consultant. Incidentally, the Steer-ing Committee never received, let alone endorsed, the Report before it went to the print.
>
> (The Legislative Council 1999)

There was no further information about why there was the lack of communica-tion and interaction among the Harvard Team and the Steering Committee. But it reflected that the government-appointed Steering Committee failed to carry out its roles during the process of health financing reform. Meanwhile, some members of the Steering Committee were not happy about the composition of the Steering Committee or had reservation about the findings of the Harvard Team. As Dr. Leong said in the LegCo meeting, the lack of grassroots input such as patients' rights groups was another fallacy of the Steering Committee (Hong Kong Standard 1998; The Legislative Council 1999). Since patients were the users of the health system, their input could have helped overseas experts understand what local patients really wanted and increased the acceptance of the *Harvard Report*. Professor Peter Yuen, who was a member of the Steering Committee, had reservations about the HSP because of 'the huge administrative cost that it would incur and the likelihood that it would change providers' behaviour and create additional expenses' (Legislative Council Secretariat 1999b). Besides, he thought that the Harvard Team had overestimated the growth in healthcare expenditures because the Team made the projection based on some questionable assumptions (Legislative Council Secretariat 1999b). He suggested that the government consider exploring 'alternative ways to enlarge its income for financing health services such as by raising user fees or increasing taxation especially in profits tax' (Legislative Council Secretariat 1999b). If there was sufficient communication between the Steering Committee and the Harvard Team, the latter could have proposed reform options that were more acceptable to communities.

The tense relationship between the ExCo and the LegCo also limited the capacity of the HKSAR government to secure majority support from legislators for its health financing reform (Luk 2014a: 122). Under the Basic Law, there was a clear separation of power between the ExCo and the LegCo, and there was no overlap of membership as in colonial days (Cheung 2007: 20). With the delinking of the ExCo and LegCo, 'there was no guarantee that the legislature would necessarily support government, not to mention give it a majority' (Cheung 2007: 25). The ExCo had a low political reputation because most of the ExCo members appointed by Tung had strong connections with big business and were pro-China (Lau 2002a: 13), and 'their own business and professional interests [were] a constant source of conflict-of-interest allegations' (Lau 2002a: 13). Most of the ExCo members were detached from the local population and did not have any political networks to mobilize popular support for Tung's policies (Lau 2002a: 13). On the contrary, the LegCo was the most representative political institution constituted by election (Ma 2002: 365). It 'regarded its role as mainly a watchdog over the government' (Cheung 2000: 2) and was a key arena for policy debates (Cheung 2004: 9). This caused the ExCo to accuse the LegCo of being over-critical of the government (Ma 2002: 349), and some ExCo members to question if the LegCo 'had in effect become an "opposition" body' (Cheung 2000: 2). While legislators did not have constitutional powers to overturn a government policy decision (Cheung 2004: 9), they could veto government bills, funding requests, or even the budget (Cheung 2000: 2). Hence, the government could not ignore views from legislators at the policy panels (Cheung 2004: 9) and had to 'seek policy legitimation through answering to the LegCo'

(Ma 2002: 367). In the LegCo, there were 18 panels that roughly corresponded to the policy bureaus of the HKSAR government (Ma 2002: 359). These panels allowed legislators to pass motions, express their views on certain issues, demand government officials in charge of the respective policies to provide information or take certain actions, or push for policy changes (Ma 2002: 359). The Panel on Health Services monitored and examined government healthcare policies and provided a forum for legislators to exchange and disseminate views on healthcare policies (The Legislative Council Commission 2019). It was where the meeting and debate on the 1999 health financing reform took place.

The introduction of the indirect election of legislators based on functional constituencies in 1985 and the direct election of legislators in 1991 'saw the emergence of political parties and elected legislators as new political actors' (Cheung 2007: 22). The Democratic Party, Democratic Alliance for the Betterment of Hong Kong (DAB), and the Liberal Party were three dominant political parties exhibiting divergent views on the politics of Hong Kong (Lam 2003: 225). In theory, the HKSAR government could get support from the DAB and the Liberal Party for the *Harvard Report* because the former was the pro-Beijing and pro-government party, while the latter was the pro-business party. In reality, however, health financing reform involved lots of vested interests (Luk 2014a: 124) so that even the DAB and the Liberal Party could not easily support the government for fear of jeopardizing their future electoral fortunes. In fact, legislators from both the DAB and the Liberal Party shared a similar position with that of the Democratic Party that the mandatory health insurance scheme would bring economic hardship to the local people in times of economic downturn. Hence, the 1999 health financing reform was shelved due to lack of LegCo support.

The difficult economic circumstances

Timing mattered. The difficult economic circumstances failed to open any window of opportunity for the government to secure majority support for the two-tier mandatory health insurance scheme (Luk 2014a: 127). From late 1997 until the end of 1999, Hong Kong was buffeted by the Asian financial crisis (Information Services Department 2002: 19). Such a crisis was 'unprecedented in its severity, duration and the scope of its impact' (Lau 2002b: viii). The GDP growth rate decreased from 5.1 percent in 1997 to -5.5 percent in 1998 (Xiao 2007: 192). The stock market plummeted, and the asset price bubble burst (International Monetary Fund 2001: 202–3). 'By mid-1998, property prices were down about 40 percent from their peak a year earlier' (International Monetary Fund 2001: 203). Many people, including middle-class citizens, 'encountered negative equity, bankruptcy and debt problems' (Lo 2015: 110). A wave of business collapses and closures inevitably led to layoffs (Lee *et al.* 2004: 132). The unemployment rate rose from 2.2 percent in 1997 to a record high of 6.3 percent in 1999 (Census and Statistics Department 2000: ix). Those who remained in their jobs faced salary freezes or reductions (Yau *et al.* 2007: 218). Both the LegCo members and the general public thought that the two-tier mandatory health insurance scheme proposed by the *Harvard Report* was inappropriate and untimely (Luk 2014a: 127). The proposal for the mandatory health insurance scheme gave the LegCo members, different political parties, and the general public a very bad impression that 'the government had an urgent desire to shirk its responsibility in financing health care at a time of economic difficulty' (Luk 2014a: 128). As legislator Dr. Che-hung Leong said in the LegCo meeting,

> The introduction of contributory saving and insurance, with possible progressive increase in contribution percentage, could pave the way for the Government to slowly relinquish its responsibility on health care and progressively increase the burden on the public to pay on their own.
>
> (The Legislative Council 1999)

In fact, legislators from different political parties worried that introducing the mandatory health insurance scheme during the economic downturn would only increase the financial burden of both employers and employees, especially when employers and employees were already required to make contributions to the Mandatory Provident Fund (MPF) scheme starting in December 2000. The MPF scheme was a compulsory personal savings scheme for retirement protection (Mandatory Provident Fund Schemes Authority 2010). The initial Mandatory Provident Fund Schemes Ordinance was passed in 1995 to provide a broad framework for the establishment of the MPF System and was substantially amended in 1998 for the effective operation and enforcement of the MPF System (Mandatory Provident Fund Schemes Authority 2010: 2). Employers and employees who were covered by the MPF System were each required to regularly contribute 5 percent of the employee's relevant income to an MPF scheme, subject to the minimum and maximum relevant income levels (Mandatory Provident Fund Schemes Authority 2019). Their financial burden would increase further if they also had to make contributions to the mandatory health insurance schemes. This explained why the mandatory health insurance scheme was very unpopular among legislators, political parties, and the business sector.

Legislator Sum Yeung, who was a member of the Democratic Party and member of the LegCo Panel on Health Services, said that it might not be the right time to introduce the mandatory health insurance scheme, as the working population would have to contribute 5 percent of their wages to the MPF scheme in 2000 (Legislative Council Secretariat 1999a). Legislator Cyd Ho, who was a member of another pro-democracy party called the Frontier, argued that introducing the mandatory health insurance scheme was tantamount to broadening the tax base (Legislative Council Secretariat 1999a). She worried that the mandatory contribution would impose a heavier financial burden on the lower- and middle-income groups and thought that the government should continue to finance healthcare services through taxation (Hong Kong Standard 1999b). Similarly, the pro-Beijing and pro-government DAB argued that the proposed mandatory health insurance scheme was 'hardly different from a new tax' (Hong Kong Standard 1999f). Legislator So-yuk Choi, who was a DAB member, doubted whether the government could convince employers and employees to participate in the mandatory health insurance scheme in times of economic downturn and high unemployment (The Legislative Council 1999). Legislator Yuen-han Chan, who was also a DAB member, said that 'she preferred the current health care system to remain unchanged' (Legislative Council Secretariat 1999c). Meanwhile, legislator Howard Young, who was a member from the pro-business Liberal Party, said that it was not at all a wise move by the government to introduce the mandatory health insurance scheme when employees were 'struggling hard for their survival in the midst of pay reductions and layoffs' (The Legislative Council 1999). The mandatory health insurance scheme on top of the MPF scheme would also increase the operating costs of business, which inevitably weakened the competitiveness of companies and discouraged foreign investment (The Legislative Council 1999).

The pro-Beijing forces in Hong Kong, including the Hong Kong General Chamber of Commerce (HKGCC) and the Hong Kong Federation of Trade Union, also failed to support the proposed mandatory health insurance scheme. The HKGCC, which represented and safeguarded the interests of business communities, was strongly opposed to the mandatory health insurance scheme because employers would face an increased financial burden resulting from contributing to the mandatory health insurance scheme during the time of economic downturn (Hong Kong Standard 1999a). It argued that the mandatory health insurance scheme on top of the MPF scheme would further reduce their profit margins (Hong Kong Standard 1999a). The proposed mandatory health insurance scheme would require another contribution from employers, which seemed to be unnecessary because the HKGCC said that many employers had already offered various levels of medical allowances to employees and such allowances were good enough (Hong Kong Standard 1999a). Meanwhile, the Hong Kong Federation of Trade Union, which was a pro-Beijing labor union-cum-party (Wong 2015: 100), worried that employees would face an increased financial burden resulting from contributing to the mandatory health insurance scheme, especially when the economic condition may not improve in the near future (Hong Kong Standard 1999a).

The institutionalization of old ideas

The ideas of free healthcare and fairness also affected public acceptance of the mandatory health insurance scheme. The government failed to cultivate stakeholder interest and support for the mandatory health insurance scheme because such a scheme 'could hardly fit into the context of Hong Kong where the idea of free health care was deeply embedded in the public health care system' (Luk 2014b: 21). The mandatory health insurance scheme required citizens to take on the financial responsibility of their medical expenses, which was contrary to the widespread popular belief that healthcare was a fundamental right and legal entitlement for all (Luk 2014a: 126). Since 1960, the government had been upholding the principle that 'no one should be denied adequate health care through lack of means'. This drove the government to provide heavily subsidized medical services irrespective of patients' socioeconomic status. In 1990, the enactment of the Hospital Authority Ordinance, which stated that the HA should uphold the principle that 'no one should be denied adequate medical treatment through lack of means', strengthened the role of public hospitals as a strong safety net and institutionalized the ideas of free healthcare, universal access to healthcare, and equality in healthcare (Luk 2014a: 126). The public healthcare system generated positive-feedback effects so that a strong and wide base of support was created for free healthcare (Luk 2014b: 22). This in turn led to strong public resistance to the mandatory health insurance scheme proposed by the Harvard Team. The public was against the mandatory nature of the scheme because 'it deprived them of their freedom to choose' (Luk 2014a: 126). Many citizens regarded the mandatory contribution as a tax in disguise, increasing the financial burden of the middle class (Health and Welfare Bureau 2000: 86). Meanwhile, some political parties criticized that the idea of mandatory contribution aggravated social disparity because personalizing the issue of healthcare in the name of individual responsibility would increase the financial burden of the low-income groups and the poor (Luk 2014a, 2014b).

The Hong Kong Medical Association, which represented the majority of the registered medical practitioners, argued that the two-tier mandatory health insurance had 'the disadvantage of focusing the drawing of the additional resources only on those who work and their employers' (The Hong Kong Medical Association 1999: 7). Besides, it argued that the *Harvard Report* limited itself to discussing the two-tier mandatory health insurance scheme that was obviously favored by the Harvard Team (The Hong Kong Medical Association 1999: 11), thereby greatly 'prejudicing a fair understanding and consideration by any reader of the report and ultimately a fair judgement amongst the various options' (The Hong Kong Medical Association 1999: 11). In fact, a survey conducted by the Hong Kong Policy Research Institute found that the proposed mandatory health insurance scheme had the least amount of public support compared to other health financing options. The survey found that while about 60 percent of 881 respondents acknowledged the need for health reform, most of them (40 percent) preferred the status quo, which was followed by a rise in tax (23.3 percent), raising fees (19.4 percent), and the mandatory health insurance scheme (12 percent) (Hong Kong Standard 1999d). Another survey conducted by the Democratic Party in April 1999 showed that about 80 percent of 516 respondents was opposed to contributing to the HSP, and 20 percent of them said that the mandatory health insurance scheme was unfair (Hong Kong Standard 1999e). Besides, about 51 percent of respondents said that cost control in hospitals and increasing resources to prevent diseases were better alternatives than implementing the mandatory health insurance scheme (Hong Kong Standard 1999e). These surveys showed that many respondents were strong defenders of free healthcare and favored less-radical approaches such as cost control when implementing health financing reform.

Since the release of the *Harvard Report*, the government had 'remained largely neutral and left it to the consultants to sell their own recommendations' (Gauld and Gould 2002: 130). Secretary for Health and Welfare Katherine Fok said that 'the government did not have a stance regarding the healthcare financing proposals contained in the Harvard Report' (Hong Kong Standard 1999c) but would like to steer the public debate on to wider and deeper issues such as the role of primary healthcare and how the healthcare system should be reformed to benefit future generations (Hong Kong Standard 1999g). But having no stance on the Harvard Team's recommendations 'gave the impression that the government did not agree with, or have confidence in, the findings (Gauld and Gould 2002: 130). In fact, DAB chairman Jasper Tsang argued that it was the unpopularity of the *Harvard Report* that made the HKSAR government quickly distance itself from the Harvard Team's proposed reform options (Hong Kong Standard 1999f). He said that the *Harvard Report* was unpopular because the clearest message the public received from the debate was that they had to pay more for healthcare if the Harvard proposal was adopted (Hong Kong Standard 1999f).

After the public consultation period had come to an end, 'the government appeared unwilling to take the initiative and move forward on any of the Harvard Team's reform options' (Gauld and Gould 2002: 138). In mid-October 1999, the Secretary for Health and Welfare announced that the government would study and analyze 2,100 submissions received during the public consultation period and would issue another health consultation document in 2000 to seek public support for its proposed way forward (Legislative Council Secretariat 2000). Legislator Dr. Che-hung Leong 'interpreted the government's action as yet another indication of its lack of political wisdom and courage to proceed with controversial policies' (Gauld and Gould 2002: 138). The government was 'unprepared to push ahead with measures which failed the crucial test of common acceptability' (Gauld and Gould 2002: 139) for the fear of facing high political costs (Luk 2014b).

Implementing the Voluntary Health Insurance Scheme in 2019

In December 2000, the HKSAR government released a public consultation document entitled *Lifelong Investment in Health*, which proposed to introduce medical savings through a scheme of Health Protection Accounts (HPA) (Health and Welfare Bureau 2000: 57). The HPA was designed to 'assist individuals to continue to pay for heavily subsidised medical services after retirement' (Health and Welfare Bureau 2000: 58). However, due to a poor economy and mixed response from the community, the government in 2004 said that further studies would be needed to carefully examine the role of the HPA and develop new financing options that would be sustainable in the long-term (Health, Welfare and Food Bureau 2004: 21).

During 2008 to 2010, the government carried out two stages of public consultation on healthcare reform. In March 2008, the government released the first-stage consultation document entitled, *Your Health Your Life*. It aimed at consulting the public on the pros and cons of reforming the free healthcare system through introducing six possible supplementary financing options, including social health insurance, out-of-pocket payments (i.e. increase user fees), mandatory medical savings accounts, mandatory private health insurance, voluntary private health insurance, and personal healthcare reserve (i.e. mandatory savings and insurance) (Food and Health Bureau 2008). Since the outcome of the first-stage consultation 'revealed strong public resistance to any supplementary healthcare financing options of a mandatory nature' (Legislative Council Secretariat 2016: 1), the government in October 2010 proposed a voluntary and government-regulated private health insurance scheme called the Health Protection Scheme (HPS) in the second-stage public consultation. The objective of the HPS was to provide an alternative to individuals who were able and willing to use and pay for private healthcare services through enhancing the accessibility, quality, and transparency of health insurance in the market (Food and Health Bureau 2014: 8). A number of key features were proposed for the HPS, including no turn-away of subscribers and guaranteed renewal for life; covering pre-existing conditions subject to a waiting period; making higher risk groups insurable with High-Risk Pool reinsurance; and standardizing health insurance policy terms and definitions (Food and Health Bureau 2010: viii). The outcome of the second-stage consultation showed that the public supported the introduction of the HPS to provide value for money choices to the community and enhance transparency, efficiency, and competition of the private healthcare sector (Food and Health Bureau 2011: vi).

To take forward the HPS, the government established a Working Group and a Consultative Group on the HPS to make recommendations on matters concerning the implementation of the HPS (Food and Health Bureau 2014: 8). In December 2014, the government renamed the HPS to Voluntary Health Insurance Scheme (VHIS) and put forth the detailed proposals for implementing VHIS for public consultation (Food and Health Bureau 2014: 5–6; Legislative Council Secretariat 2016: 3). Under the public consultation, the government proposed that insurers selling and/or effecting individual hospital insurance must comply with the Minimum Requirements prescribed by the government (Food and Health Bureau 2014: 9). The 12 Minimum Requirements aimed to improve accessibility and continuity of individual hospital insurance as well as enhance the quality, transparency, and certainty of insurance protection (Food and Health Bureau 2014: 9). The outcome of the public consultation released in January 2017 showed that there was 'broad support for the concept and policy objectives of the VHIS in general' (Food and Health Bureau 2017a: 4). Many respondents agreed that 'the proposed Minimum Requirements approach would enhance the accessibility, quality and transparency of individual Hospital Insurance' (Food and Health Bureau 2017a: 4) and the introduction of the VHIS 'would help alleviate the pressure on the public healthcare system' (Food and Health Bureau 2017a: 4). Based on the advice of the ExCo, the government decided to implement the VHIS through a non-legislative framework, which helped reduce the unintended impact of a new regulatory framework on the insurance sector and benefit the public with enhanced protection as soon as possible (Food and Health Bureau 2017b: 6). In March 2018, the Food and Health Bureau published

Code of Practice for Insurance Companies under the Ambit of the VHIS, which set out the required conduct and practices with which VHIS providers must comply (Food and Health Bureau 2019a). The VHIS Office was established under the Food and Health Bureau to implement the VHIS. On 1 April 2019, the VHIS was fully implemented for individuals to purchase Certified Plans as offered by the participating insurance companies (The Government of the Hong Kong Special Administrative Region 2019). A tax deduction under salaries tax and personal assessment will be given to 'taxpayers who pay qualifying premiums under a Certified Plan of VHIS for themselves or their specified relatives' (GovHK 2019).

Challenges to the free healthcare system: the current situation

Public hospitals have been overcrowded and overloaded for a long time due to increasing demand for service and a chronic shortage of manpower (Zhang 2018). The high demand for A&E departments is attributable to their convenience and accessibility and limited out-of-hours services provided by private outpatient clinics (The Research Office of the Legislative Council Secretariat 2019: 2). The situation of non-urgent patients using emergency services is serious.

For example, there were 2,079,000 people visiting A&E departments from June 2017 to June 2018 (Lou 2018). Of them, 61 percent were non-urgent cases (Lou 2018). The long waiting time for A&E services and the decline in service performance level for urgent and semi-urgent cases have been of concern (The Research Office of the Legislative Council Secretariat 2019: 20). In 2017, an increase in emergency fees from HK$100 to HK$180 per attendance was ineffective in cutting queues and waiting times for urgent cases (Lou 2018). In the same year, more elderly persons used emergency services because the medical fee waiver for public healthcare services was extended to cover Old Age Living Allowance recipients aged 75 and above (Lou 2018). The overcrowding issue in A&E departments worsens during the winter flu season. Non-urgent patients have to wait up to eight hours at all A&E departments (Tsang 2017; Kao and Tsang 2019).

Over the past ten years, there has been a drastic increase in the demand for specialist outpatient service. The number of specialist outpatient (clinical) attendances rose from 5,915,390 in 2008/09 to 7,716,670 in 2017/18, representing a 30 percent increase (Hospital Authority 2010, 2018). While the median waiting time of urgent cases for a first appointment at SOP clinics is less than one week, that of non-urgent cases for a first appointment at SOP clinics is excessively long. The longest (90th percentile) waiting time of non-urgent cases ranged from 12 to 181 weeks from April 2018 to March 2019 (Hospital Authority 2019a). Additionally, the demand for inpatient services has grown rapidly. The number of inpatient discharges and deaths rose from 1,268,808 in 2008/09 to 1,819,622 in 2017/18, representing a 43 percent increase (Hospital Authority 2010, 2018). Public hospitals treat 90 percent of inpatients while employing just 40 percent of doctors (Zhang 2018). Packed wards and the shortage of manpower have put doctors and nurses under tremendous pressure. During the winter flu season, over-capacity occurs in many public hospitals (Cheng 2019a; Kao and Tsang 2019). For example, the average inpatient bed occupancy rate in public hospitals reached 109 percent in January 2019 (Hospital Authority 2019b). As a result, temporary beds are laid along corridors or in between fixed ones in public hospitals (Kao and Tsang 2019). Doctors and nurses are overloaded while receiving inadequate overtime pay. In January 2019, over 100 nurses protested against staffing shortages at public hospitals (Cheung 2019) while over 200 public hospital doctors 'attended a rally to express their discontent over heavy workload and inadequate overtime pay' (Cheng 2019b).

Demand for public healthcare service will continue to increase due to an ageing population and the growing burden of chronic diseases. The life expectancy at birth has been rising steadily over the past three decades. From 1986 to 2018, the life expectancy at birth of males increased from 74.1 years to 82.2 years while that of females increased from 79.4 years to 87.6 years (Census and Statistics Department 2017a, 2019: 4). According to *Hong Kong Population Projections 2017–2066*, the number of elderly persons aged 65 and over is projected to more than double by 2036 (Census and Statistics Department 2017b: 5). It is projected to reach 2.37 million (31.1 percent of the total population) in 2036 and 2.59 million (36.6 percent) in 2066 (Census and Statistics Department 2017b: 5–6). With longevity, the healthcare needs of older persons, especially hospitalization needs, increases. Data revealed by the *Report of the Strategic Review on Healthcare Manpower Planning and Professional Development* shows that the hospitalization needs of people aged 65 or above is about nine times more than younger people, while that of people aged 85 and above is almost 20 times more than those aged under 65 (Food and Health Bureau 2017c: 45). An elderly patient 'on average stays 9.7 days per admission to hospital, as compared to 5.3 days of a non-elderly patient' (Food and Health Bureau 2017c: 45). This unavoidably puts huge strains on the public healthcare system.

Similarly, the growing burden of chronic diseases puts a significant strain on the public healthcare system. The data revealed by the Census and Statistics Department showed that the rate of Hong Kong residents suffering from chronic health conditions increased with the age of residents (Census and Statistics Department 2017c: 16). The rate significantly increased from 12.5 percent for those aged 35–44 to 26 percent for those aged 45–54 (Census and Statistics Department 2017c: 16). The rate further increased to 44.5 percent for those aged 55–64 and then 74.3 percent for those aged 65 and above (Census and Statistics Department 2017c: 27). The rate of Hong Kong residents suffering from hypertension was the highest (13.7 percent), followed by high cholesterol (7.2 percent), and diabetes mellitus (5.8 percent) (Census and Statistics Department 2017c: 16). From 2001 to 2018, cancer, pneumonia, cardiovascular diseases, and cerebrovascular diseases were the leading causes of death in Hong Kong (Centre for Health Protection 2019b).

In order to reduce significant health, social, and economic impacts of non-communicable diseases (NCD) on its population, the HKSAR government in

2018 released the document called *Towards 2025: Strategy and Action Plan to Prevent and Control Non-communicable Diseases in Hong Kong* (hereafter the SAP) (Department of Health 2019). 'The SAP aims to reduce [the] NCD burden including disability and premature death in Hong Kong by 2025' (The Hong Kong Special Administrative Region of the People's Republic of China 2018: viii). It defines nine local targets to be achieved by 2025, sets new strategic directions in line with World Health Organization's recommendations, identifies a spectrum of intersectoral actions to be carried out to achieve the nine local targets, and develops key indicators to track national progress and achievements in NCD prevention and control (The Hong Kong Special Administrative Region of the People's Republic of China 2018). The government envisages that the implementation of the SAP helps the Hong Kong population enjoy higher standards of health and better quality of life at every age, thereby increasing productivity and achieving sustainable development in Hong Kong (The Government of the Hong Kong Special Administrative Region 2018).

Acute manpower shortage remains a major challenge for public hospitals. Many doctors and nurses leave public hospitals for private hospitals because of poor working conditions, heavy workloads, excessive paperwork, long work hours, and poor overtime pay. 'The annual turnover rate for doctors in public hospitals has hovered between 4 and 5 percent over the past few years' (Cheung and Tsang 2019). But it rose to a record high of 5.7 percent in 2017/18 (Tsang 2018), which was identical to the rate for nurses (Ng 2018). According to the projection in the *Report of the Strategic Review on Healthcare Manpower Planning and Professional Development*, there will be shortfalls of 1,007 doctors, 1,669 nurses, and 933 physiotherapists by 2030 (Food and Health Bureau 2017c). To solve the problem of acute manpower shortage, the HA 'has formulated a series of short, medium and long term measures to retain staff and strengthen its manpower' (Food and Health Bureau and Hospital Authority 2019: 4). In the short run, the HA will continue to recruit qualified local graduates, have active and flexible recruitment of part-time staff, rehire retired healthcare professionals, and increase the rates of Fixed Rate Honorarium as well as the Special Honorarium Scheme allowance for Doctors (Food and Health Bureau and Hospital Authority 2019: 4–6). Other measures include recruitment of non-locally trained doctors with limited registration, enhancement of promotion prospects, better training opportunities for medical staff, flexible work arrangement, and the development of a long-term manpower plan (Food and Health Bureau and Hospital Authority 2019: 7–9).

To solve the overcrowding problem in public hospitals, the government has been promoting community-based primary care services over the past few years. A web-based electronic database called the Primary Care Directory (www.pcdirectory.gov.hk) is introduced to facilitate the public to search for registered doctors, dentists, and Chinese medicine practitioners that suit their needs (Department of Health 2012). 'Access to the mobile website of the Primary Care Directory with QR code is available at the waiting area of some A&E departments' (The Government of the Hong Kong Special Administrative Region 2017). But whether the Primary Care Directory is effective in diverting patients from public hospitals to community-based clinics is uncertain because the government does not provide further information on this matter. Another way to promote community care is the introduction of the General Outpatient Clinic Public-Private Partnership (GOPC PPP) Programme in 2014. Under the GOPC PPP Programme, clinically stable patients of HA GOP clinics with hypertension and/or diabetes mellitus are invited to receive treatment from private doctors at their clinics. Each of them can receive 10 subsidized visits per year and only pay the HA GOPC fee of HK$50 directly to private doctors after each consultation (Legislative Council Secretariat 2018: 2). The Programme was initially rolled out in three districts and subsequently extended to cover 13 more districts. 'As at early March 2015, over 3,600 invited patients and 84 private doctors had already enrolled in the Programme' (Legislative Council Secretariat 2018: 3).

The Elderly Health Care Voucher (EHV) Scheme, launched on a pilot basis in January 2009 and regularized in January 2014, aims to reduce the reliance of elderly persons on public healthcare services and enhance primary care for them (Food and Health Bureau 2019b: 1; Legislative Council Secretariat 2019: 1). It implements the 'money follows the patient' concept through providing healthcare vouchers to elderly persons for the purchase of private primary healthcare services in their local communities (Legislative Council Secretariat 2019). At present, every person aged 65 or above and holding a valid Hong Kong Identity Card is eligible to receive the annual voucher amount to HK$2,000 (Hong Kong Special Administrative Region Government 2018). Vouchers can be used for curative, rehabilitative, and preventive services (e.g. health assessment, dental checkup). But they 'cannot be used for inpatient services, pre-paid healthcare services and day surgery procedures, such as cataract surgery or endoscopy services' (Hong Kong Special Administrative Region Government 2018). 'The voucher amount used each time shall not exceed the fee for healthcare service delivered on that occasion' (Hong Kong Special Administrative Region Government 2018). Over 8,300 healthcare providers had enrolled in the EHV Scheme as of the end of March 2019 (Health Care Voucher Unit 2019: 7). As a relief measure, an additional one-off HK$1,000 worth of vouchers was provided to each eligible elder on 26 June 2019 (Hong Kong Special Administrative Region Government 2019). The financial cap on the cumulative amount of healthcare vouchers was also adjusted upward from HK$5,000 to HK$8,000 on the same day as a regular measure to allow users greater flexibility (Legislative Council Secretariat 2019).

The EHV Scheme is meant to provide additional healthcare choices for elderly persons so that they have better access to care that best suits their needs (Food and Health Bureau 2019b: 1). It is also meant to provide a partial subsidy with a view to promoting shared responsibility for healthcare among elderly persons and to ensure their appropriate use of healthcare services (Legislative Council Secretariat 2019: 4). It has become a popular scheme among elderly persons over time. In 2009, 29 percent of eligible elderly persons were using vouchers (Food and Health Bureau 2019b: 3). In 2018, there were about 1.2 million elderly persons using vouchers, which accounted for 94 percent of the eligible population

(Food and Health Bureau 2019b: 1). From 2009 to 2018, the total voucher amount claimed increased from HK$40 million to HK$2.8 billion (Food and Health Bureau 2019b: 3). A survey conducted in 2016 showed that the EHV Scheme was well received by the majority of elderly respondents. It found that 95 percent of elderly respondents considered the EHV Scheme convenient to use, while 72 percent of elderly respondents considered the coverage of healthcare services by the EHV Scheme sufficient (Food and Health Bureau 2019b: 3–4). It also found that the EHV Scheme 'encouraged dual use of public and private healthcare services' (Food and Health Bureau 2019b: 4), although 'the use of vouchers might not have any immediate impact on public healthcare service utilisation' (Food and Health Bureau 2019b: 4). In 2019, the DoH developed some enhancement measures for the EHV Scheme, with an emphasis on promoting primary and preventive care (Food and Health Bureau 2019b: 8). These measures included allowing the use of vouchers at District Health Centres and educating elderly persons on the wise and proper use of vouchers through health talks conducted by 18 Visiting Health Teams of the DoH and easy-to-understand illustrations (Food and Health Bureau 2019b: 9).

Conclusion

To conclude, the mandatory health insurance scheme proposed by overseas' experts was too radical to be accepted by multiple stakeholders. It could hardly fit into the context of Hong Kong, where the idea of free healthcare was deeply embedded in the healthcare system. Poor timing and a disjointed political system greatly impeded the implementation of the mandatory health insurance reform. The successful implementation of a voluntary health insurance scheme in 2019 shows that a milder reform option is more politically feasible and publicly acceptable. Ensuring the fiscal sustainability of the free healthcare system will remain a challenge for the government. More emphasis on preventive and community care and extending the EHV Scheme can be helpful in reducing the immense pressure on the free healthcare system.

4 Japan
The long-term care insurance reform

Introduction

This chapter gives a detailed account of the process of long-term care insurance (LTCI) reform in Japan. In the 1980s, a rapidly ageing population and rising healthcare costs exacerbated by the problem of 'medicalization of elderly care' drove the government to develop the LTC system and find an appropriate way to finance LTC. Welfare bureaucrats, the Study Group of the Total Plan for the Elderly established by the Ministry of Health and Welfare (MHW), the Prime Minister's Advisory Council on Social Security, and the MHW-appointed Study Group on Elderly Care and Self-support System were policy entrepreneurs in this reform. They proposed to fund LTC by social insurance, which aimed to promote the idea of universal coverage for all elderly Japanese. The prior initiation of LTCI in Germany in the 1990s gave Japan a good argument to adopt a social insurance model (Campbell *et al.* 2009). However, the process of passing the LTCI bill was not smooth due to the inability of the MHW to reconcile conflicting and competing interests among multiple stakeholders. In order to pass the LTCI bill, the MHW and the ruling party had to incorporate the principle proposed by the opposition party into the LTCI bill and make compromises that weakened the effectiveness of the LTCI system in solving the problem of 'medicalization of elderly care'. After the passing of the LTCI bill, the ruling party, out of electoral concerns, revised the LTCI system, which resulted in obstructing accomplishment of the objective of socializing care for the elderly. At present, Japan is a super-aged society. The government needs to make continued and unremitting efforts to ensure fiscal sustainability of the LTCI system, secure adequate professional care workers for the elderly, and provide necessary support for family caregivers.

Pre-reform era

Before the implementation of LTCI in 2000, Japan had three types of health insurance schemes: Employees' Health Insurance (EHI), National Health Insurance (NHI), and health insurance for the elderly (Fukawa 2002: 4). In 1961, Japan achieved universal health insurance coverage (UHIC) in 1961 through two separately developed social health insurance systems: EHI and NHI.

Employees' Health Insurance (EHI)

Modelled after German sickness funds, EHI was first introduced to employees in mining and factory companies with 15 or more employees by the Health Insurance Law of 1922, the implementation of which was delayed until 1927 due to serious socioeconomic disruptions that followed the Great Kanto Earthquake of 1923 (Fujii and Reich 1988; Fukawa 2002; Powell and Anesaki 1990: 88). It protected employees against work-related and non-work-related disease, injury, and death, and provided them with subsidies for childbirth costs (Sugita 2012: 40). It covered up to 180 days of treatment for a single work-related disease or injury and a maximum of 180 days per year for a combination of non-work-related diseases and injuries (Sugita 2012: 40). It required employers and employees to contribute equally while the state paid 10 percent of the cost (Kasza 2002: 419). But participation in EHI was not mandatory for companies (Sugita 2012: 40). The total numbers enrolled 'were estimated at fewer than 2 million; the total population at the time was close to 56 million' (Powell and Anesaki 1990: 88).

EHI was originally implemented by the Japanese government to prevent workers from being attracted to socialism (Sakamoto *et al.* 2018: 7), secure a healthy labor force, achieve industrial harmony, foster the development of core industries, and co-opt major corporations under the umbrella of corporate health insurance associations (CHIAs) to achieve supervisory control (Sugita 2012). EHI was then extended to cover 'all employees in workplaces with more than five full-time equivalent workers in 1934, and to office workers and dependants [sic] in 1939' (Ikegami *et al.* 2011: 1108). This was part of a government effort to recruit healthy soldiers as the war with China intensified in the 1930s (Ikegami *et al.* 2011: 1108; Sakamoto *et al.* 2018: 8). In 1943, EHI covered 70 percent of the population (Ikegami *et al.* 2011: 1108). EHI was divided into different plans according to the occupation of subscribers (Fujii and Reich 1988). In the 1980s, it contained eight plans: government-managed health insurance, society-managed health insurance, seamen's insurance, day laborers' health insurance, national public service mutual aid association (MAA) insurance, local public service MAA, public corporation employees MAA insurance, and private school teachers and employees MAA insurance (Fujii and Reich 1988: 12). After revision, EHI contained three main plans in 1997: society-managed health insurance, government-managed health insurance, and MAA insurance (Fukawa 2002: 5).

National Health Insurance (NHI)

NHI was established after the enactment of the National Health Insurance Administration of 1938 (hereafter the NHI Act). It covered those not eligible for EHI, including the self-employed (e.g. farmers, fishermen, and small shopkeepers), temporary workers, the unemployed population, and retirees (Fukawa 2002; Oberländer 2003; Sakamoto *et al.* 2018). It was modeled after Jyorei, which was 'a method of financing health care with the involvement of the community in its organization and pooling of the health risks of insured members' (Ogawa *et al.* 2003: 270). Being the oldest prototype of community health insurance (CHI), the Jyorei system relied on prepaid contributions by members in the form of rice and later in the form of cash to provide basic curative and preventive services for beneficiaries (Ogawa *et al.* 2003). It originated in Kamisaigo village in 1835. It was then extended to other villages in Munakata District, other neighboring districts such as Kurate and Asakura, and Kumamoto Prefecture (Ogawa *et al.* 2003: 271). In 1933, the government carried out a survey on Jyorei in Kyushu Island, which was followed by the establishment of 12 government-sponsored CHI programs based on the Jyorei system between 1934 and 1935 (Ogawa *et al.* 2003: 274). The NHI Act was passed in 1937 and enacted in July 1938 (Oberländer 2003: 91).

Under the NHI Act, three types of societies were organized by municipalities and employers to act as insurance carriers, including 'ordinary societies' to cover residents of local administrative units, 'special associations' to cover members of the same trade or business (e.g. barbers, grocers), and 'substitute associations' which were existing cooperatives (Oberländer 2003: 91). Insurance carriers were required to provide care for sickness and injury (Oberländer 2003: 92). But they were free to 'set their own contribution rates and methods of collection' (Oberländer 2003: 91), determine the scope and duration of medical care, and offer services and create their own medical facilities (Oberländer 2003: 92). Participation in NHI was voluntary, but government subsidies were granted to insurance carriers for the first year at a fixed rate per insured person to incentivize their participation (Oberländer 2003: 91–2). In 1939, the Salaried Employees Health Insurance Law was passed to extend the coverage of NHI to dependents of the insured (Fujii and Reich 1988: 11).

After the end of the Second World War, there was competition between the Liberal Democratic Party and the Japan Socialist Party over 'establishment of a welfare state, with health insurance for all as a popular and tangible goal' (Ikegami *et al.* 2011: 1108). The NHI system recovered from the chaos of war due to several policy measures undertaken by the government. These measures included the amendment of the NHI Act in 1948 that required each municipal government to organize and manage its own NHI society; the introduction of the NHI tax in 1951 to let the government assess and collect uniform levies according to the number of households and insured persons in each municipality; and the provision of government subsidies in 1953 to incentivize insurance carriers to maintain and upgrade NHI coverage (Oberländer 2003: 94–5). Economy recovery facilitated the re-establishment and expansion of NHI as well as the growth in EHI (Ikegami 2005: 132). During the post-war period, 'the growth of democratic movements and a commitment to social solidarity gave rise to the impetus to achieve universal insurance' (Sakamoto *et al.* 2018: 25). 'In addition, the nationwide municipal mergers in the 1950s facilitated the process of universal coverage' (Kobayashi 2009: 267).

In November 1955, the Five-Year Plan for Social Security released by the MHW proposed comprehensive medical care coverage by 1960 (Oberländer 2003: 95). In 1956, 'the government's Social Security System Council issued a landmark report that called for a more equitable health insurance system' (Fujii and Reich 1988: 11). In 1957, a four-year plan was set up by the government to achieve UHIC (Fujii and Reich 1988: 11). In 1958, the amendment of the NHI Act provided a legal basis for universal coverage by requiring all municipalities to implement a health insurance scheme and make participation mandatory for people not covered by the existing system (about 30 percent of the population) (Fujii and Reich 1988: 11). In 1961, Japan officially achieved UHIC (Sakamoto *et al.* 2018: 8). Both EHI and NHI covered a wide range of medical care, including medical treatment, medicines, surgery, hospitalization, nursing, dental care, and transportation (Liu 1987: 29). Medical costs were contained through the enforcement of the same fee schedule for all insurance plans (Ikegami *et al.* 2011: 1106). Both EHI and NHI were administered by the MHW (Liu 1987: 29).

Achieving UHIC in 1961 assured 'a basic level of health and medical care without imposing undue financial pressure on the individual or family' (Powell and Anesaki 1990: 92). It guaranteed universal access to healthcare and greatly improved the overall health of the Japanese people (Kobayashi 2009: 265). Nevertheless, persistent inequality in benefits and payments between EHI and NHI remained (Fujii and Reich 1988: 12). While EHI covered 100 percent of medical costs for subscribers and 50 percent for their dependents, NHI only covered 50 percent of medical costs for both subscribers and their dependents (Fukawa 2002: 2; Fujii and Reich 1988: 13). To redress inequality, the benefit levels were raised to 70 percent for subscribers of NHI in 1968 and dependents of EHI in 1973 while the benefit level of inpatient care for dependents of EHI was raised from 70 percent to 80 percent in 1980 (Fukawa 2002: 3). In 1984, a 10 percent copayment was introduced for subscribers of EHI (Fujii and Reich 1988: 18; Ikegami *et al.* 2011: 1108). As a result, the differences in benefits between EHI and NHI decreased (Kobayashi 2009).

Health insurance for the elderly

Health insurance for the elderly was implemented in 1983 after the passing of the Health Care for the Aged Law in 1982 (Liu 1987: 30–1). The new law introduced a cross-subsidization scheme among various health insurance schemes to cover the medical cost for the elderly (Peng 2003: 221) and required all elderly persons to pay a fee in exchange for medical coverage (Liu 1987: 31). Health insurance for the elderly covered those aged 70 years and above and disabled people aged 65 to 69 years, providing both preventive and curative healthcare services (Fujii and Reich 1988). Under the principle of national solidarity, a pooled fund was created to respectively receive 10 percent and 20 percent of financial resources from local governments and the national government (Fukawa 2002; Fujii and Reich 1988). The remainder came from fund pooling among all health insurance plans (Liu 1987: 31) 'based on a formula that took into account the plan's total number of persons insured and past medical expenditures for the elderly' (Fujii and Reich 1988: 14). Copayments by the elderly were introduced to make the elderly more aware of the costs of medical attention (Eto 2000: 23). 'This was feasible because improved pension benefits had increased the elderly's ability to pay' (Eto 2000: 28). The MHW 'had kept the amount of the copayment extremely small' (Campbell 1992: 291). Cost-sharing for outpatient care was 400 yen monthly for each medical facility, while cost-sharing for inpatient care was 300 yen daily for the first 50 days for the elderly and 60 days for their dependents (Fujii and Reich 1988: 14). The scheme was 'administered by cities, towns, and villages' (Powell and Anesaki 1990: 137).

The introduction of health insurance for the elderly was part of a government effort to contain health expenditures caused by an ageing population as well as elderly patients' overuse of medical services (Fukawa 2002: 3). From 1973 to 1983, healthcare expenditures for the elderly drastically increased about ten times from 430 billion yen to 4,369 billion yen (Liu 1987: 30). Such an increase was the result of instituting free medical care in 1973, which led to the use of public funds to pay the copayment that was previously paid by the elderly (Fujii and Reich 1988: 13; Tamiya *et al.* 2011: 1183). Since 1973, NHI had faced financial difficulties and received substantial government subsidies because it covered most of the elderly in the nation (Kobayashi 2009: 264–5; Liu 1987: 29). The introduction of health insurance for the elderly helped NHI redistribute its financial burden (Fujii and Reich 1988: 14). Meanwhile, a comprehensive preventive health program containing a regular health screening program and health education program was provided by each municipality for people aged 40 years and above to reduce the incidence of costly chronic illnesses in the future (Liu 1987: 31).

The long-term care (LTC) insurance reform

The problem stream

Japan faced the problem of a rapidly ageing population due to declining fertility and increasing longevity (Ng 2007: 37–8). Its fertility ratio fell sharply from 4.5 in 1947 to 2.1 in the 1960s, and to 1.42 in 1995 (Yashiro 1997: 248). From 1947 to 1995, the average life expectancy for males increased from 50.1 years to 76.4 years, while the average life expectancy for females increased from 54.0 years to 82.9 years (Yashiro 1997: 248). Hence, the share of older people in the total population had increased rapidly over time. From 1950 to 1960, Japan's population aged 65 years and over rose from 4.9 percent to 5.7 percent (Statistics Bureau 2018: 10). In 1970, Japan officially became an ageing society when its total population aged 65 years and over reached 7.1 percent (Statistics Bureau 2018). By 1995, Japan had officially become an aged society when its population aged 65 years and over doubled to become 14.6 percent (Statistics Bureau 2018). The pace of population ageing was considered very rapid because Japan only took 25 years to move from an ageing to an aged society, whereas France and Sweden, respectively, took 115 years and 85 years to make the transition (United Nations Economic and Social Commission for Asia and the Pacific 2017a: 3).

The shift in demography to older ages greatly affected disease structure. The Japanese elderly 'experience more chronic and multimorbidity, which require long-term care (LTC) and put pressures on health-care expenditure and use of resources' (Nomura *et al.* 2017: 1521–2). Health expenditures of the elderly drastically increased from 13.4 percent in 1975 to 25.4 percent in 1985, and to 33.1 percent in 1995 (Fukawa 2002: 7). In 1980, only 9 percent of NHI members were elderly but 'their medical expenses accounted for more than 30 percent of NHI expenses' (Powell and Anesaki 1990: 112). In 1994, elderly patients aged 70 years and above used more than five times more medical services than those below 70 years (Organization for Economic Co-operation and Development 1997: 133). This ratio was 'one of the largest amongst the seven major OECD countries' (Organization for Economic Co-operation and Development 1997: 133). This showed that the introduction of health insurance for the elderly in 1983 had little impact on containing health expenditures of the elderly.

Meanwhile, 'medicalization of elderly care' or social hospitalization was another reason for cofounding the problem of the rapid increase in health expenditures for the elderly (Estévez-Abe 2002; Ng 2007; Ozawa and Nakayama 2005). It referred to the phenomenon of weak or disabled elderly people occupying a hospital bed for a lengthy period of time, not because they had a critical medical condition but because they had no place to go (Eto 2001: 34; Ng 2007: 39–40). There were several reasons for social hospitalization, including changing family structures, higher labor force participation by women, the avoidance of stigma, and the inadequate provision of home care services and supply of nursing homes. In post-war Japan, society had 'grown increasingly oriented toward nuclear families' (Lai 2002: 9). The average number of persons in a household decreased from 4.97 in 1955 to 4.05 in 1965, 3.23 in 1985, and 2.99 in 1990 (Hashimoto and Takahashi 1995: 50). According to the National Census of 1990, nuclear family households accounted for 59.5 percent of all households in the nation (Hashimoto and Takahashi 1995: 50). From 1975 to 1990, the proportion of elderly people living with their children decreased from 71.9 percent to 58.5 percent (Peng 2005: 82). With the demographic trends of fewer children and the decline in co-residence, younger people found it difficult to perform caregiving work for elderly parents or parents-in-law (Lai 2002: 10). The traditional role of the family in caring for the elderly slowly became obsolete and difficult to maintain (Kimura 2002: 335–6). Women also found it difficult to provide full support for their elderly relatives because of their dual roles in the workplace and the family. They 'were more likely to work and continue working after marriage and childbirth' (Peng 2005: 82). The female labor force participation rate had increased and accounted for a larger proportion of regular employees in all age groups (The Japan Institute for Labour Policy and Training 2016: 23). From 1975 to 1995, the female labor force participation rate increased steadily from 46.1 percent to 49.3 percent (Statistics Bureau 2010). Hence, the availability of women and their capacity to take care of the elderly decreased (Ozawa and Nakayama 2005: 63; Curry *et al.* 2018: 2).

Due to changing public attitudes toward family responsibilities and the care burdens on families, family caregivers began to treat hospitals as a substitute to a nursing home and sent their elderly to hospitals with little medical justification

(Matsuda 2009: 34; Curry *et al.* 2018: 14). Besides, it was 'less stigmatizing to place older parents in a hospital than in a residential care facility' (Ng 2007: 40). The under-development of home care services (Ng 2007: 40) and the inadequate supply of nursing homes also aggravated the problem of social hospitalization (Olivares-Tirado and Tamiya 2014: 18). There were 'waiting lists for nursing home placements of two to three years in many localities' (Ozawa and Nakayama 2005: 67). 'Legally as well as administratively, the request for services or institutionalization was not regarded as a claim or right of an elderly person' (Kimura 2002: 337). The placement (*Sochi*) system which was used by local authorities to distribute scarce elderly services had stringent eligibility criteria (Hieda 2012: 104–5) and 'was generally targeted to low-income elderly people and those without other family members at home' (Ozawa and Nakayama 2005: 66). The needs of other categories of the elderly were neglected by the government (Eto 2001: 21). Middle-class frail elderly who were not qualified for means-tested services in public nursing homes had to pay expensive user fees for home-based or institutional care services out of pocket (Ozawa and Nakayama 2005: 66). This drove them to substitute hospitals for temporary nursing homes (Estévez-Abe 2002: 159–60). Meanwhile, hospitals and doctors had great incentives to keep elderly patients hospitalized longer (Estévez-Abe 2002: 160) and oversupply medical services because the provision of medical treatment was fee-for-service based and doctors enjoyed great autonomy in their medical practices (Hieda 2012: 117). Hence, the quality of LTC in hospitals was 'often poor – very little space, few opportunities for recreation or "human" services, too many drugs and tests' (Campbell and Ikegami 1998: 194).

The ten-year Strategy to Promote Health and Welfare for the Aged (commonly known as the Gold Plan) implemented in 1989 to increase home beds, home helpers, and adult daycare centers failed to alleviate pressures on the health service because access was limited to older persons with few means and no family support (Curry *et al.* 2018: 14). The provision of services failed to keep pace with the growing needs of the elderly (Eto 2000: 24–5). From 1963 to 1995, about half of all inpatients were 65 years and over, and about one-third of them had been hospitalized for more than one year (Ng 2007: 39). The problem of social hospitalization led to a serious waste of medical resources and tax dollars. In 1983, government subsidies to NHI reached 2 trillion yen (Fujii and Reich 1988: 16). The NHI scheme 'represented one of the three largest sources of deficit in the national budget' (Fujii and Reich 1988: 16). Hence, there was an urgent need to separate LTC from medical care (Izuhara 2003: 397) through reforming the health insurance and LTC systems.

The rapid increase in health expenditures negatively affected the stabilization and sustainability of health insurance funds. To make matters worse, money contributed to health insurance funds being decreased due to the shrinking workforce and a stagnating economy. The shrinking workforce was caused by an ageing population. The labor force participation rate decreased from 67.1 percent in 1970 to 64.1 percent in 1980, and to 63.4 percent in 1990 (Statistics Bureau 2010). Meanwhile, a prolonged period of economic stagnation caused by the bursting of Japan's asset price bubbles in the period from the late 1980s to the early 1990s (Fujii and Kawai 2010) led to a serious unemployment problem. From 1990 to 1995, the number of unemployed persons drastically increased from 1.91 million to 2.87 million (Statistics Bureau 2010). The increase in the number of retirees and unemployed persons meant that the number of NHI subscribers also increased. During the period 1992–994, the growth of the Gross Domestic Product (GDP) was close to zero (Ozawa and Kono 1997: 308). Since 1992, the government had been continuously running a substantial fiscal budget deficit (Cabinet Office 2001). In times of economic difficulty, the government was under heavy financial pressure to support the health insurance system.

The policy stream

In the 1980s, the government recognized that a new and comprehensive LTC system was needed to meet the growing demand for senior care as well as contain escalating healthcare costs caused by 'medicalization of elderly care'. But it was not until the mid-1990s that the government finally decided to fund LTC by social insurance. Welfare bureaucrats recognized that the placement (*Sochi*) system based on the general tax revenues was unable to provide the frail elderly with care services in a flexible way, and hence they sought an alternative to the placement system (Hieda 2012: 129). In the mid-1980s, welfare bureaucrats' research on the LTCI under study in Germany resulted partly from pressure from major business organizations and the Federation of National Health Insurance Associations to ease the financial burden caused by the cross-subsidization schemes (Peng 2003: 222). In 1988, a policy study group organized by young bureaucrats and protégé of top-level ministry officials launched a report titled *A Proposal for a New System of Health and Welfare Administration in the Reform Period*, which recommended using social insurance to fund comprehensive home care programs and replacing the eligibility system with freedom of choice (Eto 2000: 30).

In 1989, the first Gold Plan was introduced by Prime Minister Hashimoto Ryūtarō, who calculated that the popularity of expanded state-funded eldercare services would help the public forgive the ruling Liberal Democratic Party (LDP) for introducing a controversial new consumption tax (Schoppa 2006: 185). The 1989 Gold Plan 'firmly placed the issue of care for the frail elderly on the public agenda' (Rhee *et al.* 2015: 1324). It promised 100,000 home helpers and 240,000 beds in special nursing homes by 1999 and made local authorities responsible for implementing welfare services for the elderly (Eto 2000: 24). 'This infrastructure development of elderly care services paved the way for long-term care insurance' (Hieda 2012: 129). In 1990, LDP leaders intervened in the budgetary negotiation between the Ministry of Finance (MOF) and the MHW, thereby increasing the budget allocation to elderly care services more than the MHW requested (Hieda 2012: 128).

At the beginning of the 1990s, the Study Group of the Total Plan for the Elderly established by the MHW strongly criticized the tax-funded placement

(*Sochi*) system for being unable to respond to the growing demand for elderly care (Hieda 2012: 130). It proposed that the frailty of older persons should be regarded as a social risk in the aged society, and a social insurance system for the frail elderly should be established (Hieda 2012: 130). In August 1993, the LDP lost the general election due to the defection of its members (Hieda 2012: 130), and 'this ended nearly four decades of uninterrupted single-party political domi-nation' (Peng 2005: 85). A coalition government of seven parties that excluded the LDP was formed (Curtis 1999: 113–14). After becoming the new minister of the MHW, Keigo Ōuchi, who was the chairman of the Democratic Socialist Party (DSP) and keen on LTC for the aged, directed the officials of MHW to establish the Advisory Panel on Vision for Elderly Welfare (hereafter the Advisory Panel) (Hieda 2012: 130–1). In February 1994, the Advisory Panel was tasked with justifying the abolition of the consumption tax and the introduction of a new National Welfare Tax suddenly announced by Prime Minister Hosokawa Morihiro (Hieda 2012; Eto 2000). However, the governing coalition parties, which had not been consulted prior to the announcement of the welfare tax, attacked Hosokawa's proposal on procedural grounds (Eto 2000: 33). The gen-eral public was also strongly opposed to the 7 percent welfare tax rate because it would increase their financial burden under the post-bubble economic stagnation (Matsuda 2009: 34). This resulted in the immediate withdrawal of the tax reform plan (Eto 2000: 33).

In March 1994, the Advisory Panel produced a report titled *21st Century Welfare Vision: Toward an Aged Society with Fewer Children* (Osawa 2011: 60), which recommended changing the weight of public social welfare expenditures from the 5:4:1 (pension, healthcare, and other welfare services such as old-age care) to 5:3:2 in the future (Ozawa and Nakayama 2005: 67; Conrad 2017: 128). Social services supporting nursing care and child-rearing were identified as needing improvement, along with proposals for a 'New Gold Plan' and an 'Angel Plan' (Conrad 2017: 128; Osawa 2011: 60). The New Gold Plan was a revised and expanded version of the 1989 Gold Plan expanding the variety of services (e.g. home care support services) targeted for homebound elderly (Jenike 2003: 181; Masako 1999: 93). As regards Angel Plan, it was a ten-year strategic plan aiming to reduce family-work tension and encourage childbirth through the pro-vision of more public childcare, after-school programs, and community-based support centers for families with children (Peng 2008: 1041). Both plans were adopted in December 1994.

However, the coalition government of seven parties did not last long because deep policy differences and intense personal rivalries divided the parties in the coalition (Curtis 1999: 116). The coalition's collapse led to the formation of a three-party coalition government composed of the LDP, the Socialist Party, and the Sakigake in June 1994 (Curtis 1999). The new coalition government carried out the tax reform by combining an increase in the consumption tax from 3 to 5 percent and a personal income tax cut, which became effective beginning in April 1997 (Hoshino 1996). The tax increase by 2 percent was 'rarely enough to finance ever-increasing expenditures on health and personal social services for the elderly' (Hoshino 1996: 40). This left a social insurance system as a viable policy option to the MHW to fund the new LTC system (Hieda 2012: 132).

In September 1994, the Prime Minister's Advisory Council on Social Security, which occasionally provided ideological support for the MHW, published a report that proposed a social insurance system for LTC (Eto 2000: 33–4). In December 1994, the MHW-appointed Study Group on Elderly Care and Self-support System, which consisted of scholars and experts on economics, healthcare, social care, and social welfare, also published a report that proposed LTCI as a desirable option for the new elderly care system from the viewpoint of risk-sharing (Hieda 2012: 132). In January 1995, the prior initiation of LTCI in Germany 'legitimized the social insurance approach and demonstrated that a workable plan could be devised' (Campbell *et al.* 2009: 71). The policy direction toward an insurance-based scheme for LTC had become clear and led to the MHW's decision to draft the LTCI bill.

The political stream

The elite bureaucracy of Japan was central to policy-making (Powell and Anesaki 1990: 106), made most major decisions, drafted virtually all legislation, and was the source of all major policy innovations in the system (Johnson 1982: 20–1). The ministries, before making an important decision, first commissioned their various attached advisory councils or committees and, based on their recommendations or reports submitted to the ministries, formulated concrete policies or formed the core of new legal proposals (Bochorodycz 2010: 42; Pempel 1992: 23). Advisory councils were 'an important constituent element of the organizational apparatus of each ministry and agency for the making and carrying out of policy' (Wright 2002: 127). They were 'staffed with "expert" members invited from outside the government administration offices' (Kitazawa 2015: 128), including scholars, economic and industrial leaders, and members of the business community and professional associations (Peng 2002: 423). They were an important venue for the participation of a wide range of non-governmental interests, individuals, and groups necessary in a consensual model of policy-making (Wright 2002: 128) as well as the expression of diversified opinions (Mulgan 2000: 34). They helped 'consolidate differing opinions, and provide forewarning of probable conflict over government proposals' (Pempel 1974: 656).

Deliberations obliged council members to justify and clarify their respective positions while letting ministries sound out the interested parties and gauge the appropriate response to policy issue (Wright 2002: 128–9). Advisory councils allowed the ministry to reconcile its representation of the public interest with those of the private interests represented by the council members (Wright 2002: 128). Recommendations made by council members were not legally binding, and their implementation depended on the decisions of the ministries that established them (Bochorodycz 2010: 42). Advisory councils 'generally support[ed] ministry policies and legitimise[d] new policy directions drafted by ministry officials' (Mulgan 2000: 35). In the case of the LTCI bill, however, the MHW found it difficult to get support from members of the Council on Health and Welfare for the Elderly (CHWE) because council members were much more fractious and they wanted to represent the interests of their constituencies first (Peng 2002: 438).

Drafting the LTCI bill fell under the purview of the CHWE (Eto 2000: 34). In February 1995, the MHW launched discussions on the LTCI bill at the CHWE. The CHWE consisted of 26 members involved in health and welfare services for the elderly, including scholars and the representatives of medical profession groups (e.g. the Japan Medical Association, the Japan Dental Association), business groups, trade unions (e.g. Japanese Trade Union Confederation), health insurance associations (e.g. the Federation of National Health Insurance Associations), social welfare corporations, women's organizations, senior citizens' organizations, and local governments (e.g. the Japan Association of City Mayors, the National Association of Towns & Villages) (Eto 2000: 34–5; Hieda 2012: 135; Tsutsumi 2014: 8). Torii Yasuhiko, who was president of Keio University, served as chairman of the CHWE (Eto 2000: 34), while the MHW served as the secretariat of the CHWE (Tsutsumi 2014: 8). Meetings in the CHWE were open to the public (Tsutsumi 2014: 8).

From February 1995 to April 1996, the CHWE had meetings more than 20 times to discuss a list of key issues related to the LTCI, which included:

1   source of finance: whether an LTC system should be funded by social insurance or national tax revenues;
2   management of the LTCI scheme: whether the national government, local governments or a third party should be responsible for managing the LTC insurance scheme;
3   minimum ages of the insured and beneficiaries: whether premiums should be collected from those aged 20 years and above but beneficiaries would be limited to those aged 65 and above;
4   the employers' premium contribution: whether employers should pay 50 percent of an employee's insurance premium;
5   no cash benefits to families caring for disabled or frail elderly;
6   copayment rate: whether the copayment rate for service costs should be 10 percent;
7   types of services: whether there would be home-based services or community-care services;
8   care facilities: whether three existing types of facilities, namely, special nursing homes, geriatric hospitals, and facilities of healthcare services for the elderly, should be unified into the LTC facilities;
9   implementation date: implementing the LTC system on 1 April 1997.
                    (Eto 2000: 34–5; Hieda 2012: 135–8; Tsutsumi 2014: 8–9)

The LTCI system aimed to 'shift from the former principle of selective application to universal coverage for all elderly Japanese in need of care' (Eto 2001: 18) and place some financial burden on the elderly participants (Eto 2001: 18). It stressed 'the idea of insurance as a mutual assistance framework' (Kimura 2002: 338) and attempted to 'remove the stigma and reluctance of being a care recipient' (Kimura 2002: 338). In the first phase of the discussion, the MHW succeeded in securing majority support from council members for replacing the tax-funded, means-tested placement (*Sochi*) system in elderly care with an LTC system funded by social insurance. It got support from social welfare corporations and the Japan Medical Association by making compromises with these two interest groups. It gave up the idea of unifying three existing types of facilities into the LTC facilities and let social welfare corporations continue to 'monopolize ownership and management of special nursing homes under the new system' (Hieda 2012: 138). Meanwhile, it met the demand of the Japan Medical Association by allowing small and medium-sized hospitals to convert their beds into convalescent beds so that a new funding source for healthcare could be guaranteed under the new system (Hieda 2012: 134). This explained why 'medicalization of elderly care' was preserved under the LTCI system (Hieda 2012).

In the later phases of the discussion, however, the MHW failed to reconcile conflicting and competing interests among council members who represented different interest groups, especially on the issues of managing the LTCI scheme, minimum ages of the insured and beneficiaries, the employers' premium contribution, and cash benefits (Eto 2000; Hieda 2012). Who should manage the LTCI scheme was particularly controversial so that the MHW bureaucrats negotiated with representatives from local governments for a long time. Representatives from local governments, including a city mayor and a village head, were strongly opposed to the idea that local governments should manage the LTCI scheme (Eto 2001: 24). They feared that inadequate subsidies from the national government would force them to make up the deficit, as had occurred with NHI, and hence their financial burden would increase (Eto 2000: 35). They also feared that a shortage of service infrastructure at the local level could hardly meet demands for LTC services because enrollees would demand such services as a legal right when the law became effective (Eto 2000: 35–6). But the MHW bureaucrats argued that implementing LTCI could improve health insurance finances of local governments, and accessibility for citizens made local governments the logical entities to manage the LTCI scheme (Eto 2000: 36). Regarding minimum ages of the insured and beneficiaries, health insurance associations and business groups argued that minimum ages of the insured should be raised in order to reduce employers' premium contributions. Some of them were against the idea that employers should pay part of employees' premiums because it was unfair to ask employers to share costs for services they would not receive (Eto 2000: 36).

When it came to cash benefits, there were dividing opinions among local government representatives, medical profession groups, female council members, and caregiver organizations. Local government representatives argued that it was contradictory for the MHW to pay an outsider to provide care but not pay family caregivers (Eto 2000: 36–7) and suggested the MHW institutionalize the care allowance for family caregivers (Hieda 2012: 135). The Japan Medical Association, which espoused a German-style social insurance system that encouraged family caregiving, thought that family members could fill the gap in trained care workers, and hence they supported the provision of cash benefits for family members (Eto 2000: 37). However, caregiver organizations and female council members were against cash allowances to families (Hieda 2012: 205). The Women's Committee for the Improvement of the Aged Society (WCIAS), which served as a public voice for women (Peng 2003: 221), called attention to the problem of women's double burden (Peng 2003: 220) and argued that 'cash provision for carers would reinforce women's formal care role and institutionalize women's domestic care duty' (Peng 2005: 95). It demanded that the LTCI should primarily provide services rather than cash benefits (Osawa 2011: 66). Higuchi Keiko, who was the head of the WCIAS and a member of the CHWE (Peng 2003), vigorously argued along feminist lines that 'paying cash to female relatives would simply perpetuate the gendered division of labor' (Schoppa 2006: 188). 'Real help could come only through more social services in the community – plus greater access to institutional care' (Campbell 1997). The strong opinion given by Higuchi helped keep the option of cash allowances to families off the table for most of the process of deliberations (Schoppa 2006: 188).

The incapability of the MHW bureaucrats to adjust conflicting interests among council members was reflected in the content of the three reports published by the CHWE from July 1995 to April 1996. An interim report titled *the Establishment of a New Long-term Care Scheme for the Elderly* was published by the CHWE in July 1995 (Tsutsumi 2014: 9). While the interim report proposed the adoption of a social insurance system for LTC, it used a lot of vague terminology to obscure the specifics of the new system (Hieda 2012: 135). The second report published in January 1996 only juxtaposed the pros and cons of many issues, such as insurers and cash benefits, due to the inability of council members to reach a consensus on the skeleton of the LTC system (Hieda 2012: 135). The final report titled *Establishment of Long-term Care Insurance for the Elderly: A Summary of Deliberations* was published on 21 April 1996 (Eto 2000: 40). It was an inconclusive report merely identifying points in dispute and enumerating different opinions (Eto 2000: 40). The issue of who should manage the LTCI scheme remained unresolved because of the inability of the MHW bureaucrats to alleviate the fiscal concerns of local governments (Hieda 2012: 136). It showed that the CHWE failed to provide useful recommendations for the MHW to draft the LTCI bill.

Disagreement among council members had already derailed the MHW to complete the draft LTCI bill by December 1995 (Eto 2000: 35). But what made the MHW frustrated was that it was forced to give up submitting the LTCI bill to the Diet in June 1996 because the bill was not approved by local governments and therefore the Social Affairs Division of the Policy Affairs Research Council (PARC) (Hieda 2012: 136). The PARC was 'the party organ through which all legislative bills had to pass before being sent to the Diet' (Krauss and Pekkanen 2010: 8). Sharing the same understanding with the MOF that the LTCI was the key to public acceptance of the tax increase, the MHW had wanted to roll out the

LTCI when the increase in the consumption tax became effective from 1 April 1997 (Eto 2000: 38). Without submitting the bill to the Diet as it had originally planned, however, the MHW realized that rolling out the LTCI on 1 April 1997 became impossible. But the coalition government agreed to submit the LTCI bill to the next session of the Diet.

In fact, the three-party coalition government since early 1996 had stepped in to help the MHW reconcile diverse interests. Hashimoto Ryūtarō, who was the president of the LDP and former Minister of Health and Welfare, became the leader of the three-party coalition government in January 1996. When he gave a policy speech to the Diet, he said that his cabinet set the creation of a society where people could grow old happily as its second priority (Ministry of Foreign Affairs of Japan 1996). He promised that his administration would 'make every effort to create new systems of care for the aged using social insurance' (Ministry of Foreign Affairs of Japan 1996). The coalition government under the leadership of Hashimoto set up the Welfare Project Team to discuss the LTCI scheme in parallel with the deliberation of the CHWE (Eto 2000: 39; Hieda 2012: 136).

In mid-March 1996, the Welfare Project Team received help from the LDP Diet member and former Minister of Health and Welfare Niwa Yūya, who made two important private suggestions to revise the draft of the LTCI bill. To address the problem of lacking service infrastructure at the local level, Niwa suggested that the implementation of the LTCI scheme would start with home-care services followed by gradual implementation of institutional services (Eto 2000: 39). Besides, Niwa suggested raising the minimum age of the insured from 20 to 40 and over because people at the age of 40 may become caregivers to their parents and begin to anticipate their own senior years (Eto 2000: 39). Niwa's suggestions helped the MHW revise the draft bill. Nevertheless, the revised draft bill failed to win the support from local governments. Later, the coalition government set up the Working Team on the Establishment of Long-term Care Insurance to negotiate with local governments (Hieda 2012: 136). In summer 1996, the Working Team held special public hearings in several cities to facilitate public discussion of the LTCI bill (Hieda 2012; Kimura 2002). In order to reduce the financial burden of local governments as insurers of LTCI, the Working Team promised that the central government would subsidize the administrative costs of LTCI and allocate funds to compensate for financial deficits it may generate (Hieda 2012: 136).

Meanwhile, different public opinion polls conducted in summer and autumn 1996 indicated that a majority of people favored the introduction of LTCI (Eto 2001: 26). But the lack of responses from mayors and conservative LDP Diet members to the public's demand to socialize care for the elderly and their inaction to discuss the LTCI bill led to frustration among citizens and influential figures such as Higuchi. The introduction of a new electoral system combining single-member districts and proportional representation in 1994 led to nearly all Lower House members' districts corresponding to municipal jurisdictions (Eto 2000: 41). Due to electoral concerns, many conservative LDP Diet members stayed aloof from the LTCI bill to avoid losing mayoral support and upsetting voters who may regard LTCI as a new tax (Eto 2000: 41; Campbell and Ikegami 1998: 113).

In September 1996, Higuchi collaborated with Hotta Tsutomu, chief director of a nationwide welfare volunteer organization, and Sugawara Hiroko, the editor of a journal targeted at middle-class seniors, to establish a new citizen action group called Ten Thousand Citizens' Committee to Realize a Public Care of the Elderly System (hereafter the 10,000 Citizens' Committee) (Eto 2001: 26; Schoppa 2006: 188). The name '10,000 Citizens' Committee' was chosen to show that the majority of people was demanding socialized care for the elderly, as shown by a network bringing together 10,000 people (Eto 2001: 26). The 10,000 Citizens' Committee organized a work team consisting of experts in related fields to draw up the 'Citizens' Amendment', which proposed an amended version of the LTCI bill to meet citizens' expectations. The 'Citizens' Amendment' consisted of three pillars, stating that the law must (1) secure the right of citizens to participate in insurance management; (2) guarantee free access to diverse services; and (3) abolish age limitations (Eto 2001: 27). The 10,000 Citizens' Committee launched a nationwide political campaign to raise public awareness of its proposed version of the LTCI bill and to stimulate public discussion through engaging in different activities. These included holding high-profile meetings in Tokyo, publicizing opinion polls that showed wide public support for LTCI (Schoppa 2006: 188–9), lobbying government officials, politicians, and businesses, and undertaking extensive media promotion of the draft bill (Peng 2005: 92).

The general election of October 1996 brought the LDP back to a position of predominance (Inoguchi 1997: 48). The LDP formed a single-party government, with the Social Democratic Party and Sakigake supporting it from outside the cabinet (Eto 2001: 26). In November 1996, the LTCI bill was submitted to the Lower House of the Diet. But deliberation about the bill was soon interrupted by a scandal that involved the vice-minister of the MHW receiving bribes from a nursing home operator in return for helping the operator obtain lucrative government subsidies to build nursing homes (The Japan Times 1998; Wudunn 1996; Efron 1996). Deliberations about the LTCI bill continued in February 1997. The 10,000 Citizens' Committee actively lobbied the ruling and opposition parties and asked them to amend the LTCI bill by incorporating elements of the 'Citizens' Amendment' into it (Eto 2001: 27). Due to receiving little support from the LDP, the 10,000 Citizens' Committee formed an alliance with the opposite Democratic Party of Japan (DPJ) to push for its proposed version of the LTCI bill (Peng 2002: 424). In late March 1997, the DPJ presented its proposal for amendment to the Diet Committee, which consisted of the three main principles of the 10,000 Citizens' Committee's proposal (Eto 2001: 27). The three main principles were: (1) requiring a municipality to adopt some measures necessary to reflect the insured's opinions when it established a program for implementing LTCI; (2) establishing a third-party organ for examining claims; and (3) abolishing age limitations (Eto 2001: 27–8). While the LDP could not accept amendments which may affect the framework of the LTCI bill, it agreed to incorporate the first principle proposed by the DPJ into the bill so as to get support from the DPJ to pass the healthcare insurance reform bill (Eto 2001: 28; Peng 2003: 223). The LTCI bill was passed in the Lower House on 22 May 1997 and approved by the Upper House on 9 December 1997. The LTCI law was scheduled to take effect on 1 April 2000.

However, in November 1999, the central government decided to revise the LTCI system. It was because some conservative politicians from the LDP tried to derail the program by arguing that the LTCI system would threaten the sanctity of the Japanese family system, and the new premiums would be resented by employers, employees, and older people (Campbell 2014: 12). Meanwhile, the LDP desired to secure more votes in the upcoming elections (Talcott 2002). As a result, two important changes to the LTCI system came without formal revision of the law, but as budget items in a supplementary budget (Talcott 2002: 98). First, the government decided to suspend insurance contributions for the elderly aged 65 and above for six months, which would be followed by taking a 50 percent cut of premium contributions from this group for a further twelve months (Talcott 2002: 98). Second, the government decided to pay an annual cash allowance of up to 100,000 yen to family caregivers in low-income households (Eto 2001: 32). The government revision plan appeared to have weakened the effectiveness of the LTCI system to maintain a balance between premiums and benefits and to develop socialized care for the elderly (Eto 2001: 32). But under LTCI, LTC was no longer allocated by the state on the basis of need (Burau *et al.* 2007: 84), but rather becoming 'part of a social contract based upon a system of mandatory contributions, uniform entitlements, and consumer choice' (Izuhara 2003: 395).

Challenges to the current long-term care system

Implemented in 2000, the LTCI 'operates on social insurance principles, with benefits provided irrespective of income or family situation' (Tamiya *et al.* 2011: 1183). It covers every individual from age 40. It is financed through two sources. Half of the finance comes from premium contributions. Premiums are 'collected nationally and redistributed to municipalities' (Curry *et al.* 2018: 16). Half comes from general taxation (25 percent from the central government, 12.5 percent from the prefectures, and 12.5 percent from the municipalities) (Sakamoto *et al.* 2018: 136). Enrollees are divided into two categories: Category 1 enrollees are those aged 65 years and over, and Category 2 enrollees are those aged between 40 and 64. Category 1 enrollees who meet the eligibility criteria and Category 2 enrollees who have disabilities resulting from specified age-related diseases (e.g. stroke or Alzheimer's disease) can receive LTC services (Ikegami 2007: 425).

'Eligibility is assessed using a 74-item questionnaire based on activities of daily living' (Iwagami and Tamiya 2019: 68). A computer algorithm is used to group the applicant according to the seven levels of long-term care need certificates: support levels 1 and 2 (i.e. need support for daily activities) and care need levels

1 to 5 (i.e. need continuous care, with level 1 being the least disabled and level 5 being the most disabled) (Iwagami and Tamiya 2019: 68; Tamiya *et al.* 2011: 1185; Tsutsui and Muramatsu 2007: 1460; United Nations Economic and Social Commission for Asia and the Pacific 2015: 21). The result is then reviewed and finalized by a local expert committee (Tamiya *et al.* 2011: 1185). Once certified, the eligible person can go to any certified care management agency where a care manager would develop a care plan based on the assessment of need and individual preference (Ikegami 2007: 425–6).

The assigned level of LTC need 'determines the monthly notional budget individuals have available to them' (Curry *et al.* 2018: 18–19). The budget 'can only be used to purchase services and is not available as a cash allowance' (Curry *et al.* 2018: 19). Services commence upon approval of the care plan and the provider by the eligible person (Tamiya *et al.* 2011: 1185). Many services are covered under LTCI, including home-based (e.g. personal care), community-based (e.g. daycare, short-stay respite care) and institutional services (e.g. nursing homes, chronic-care hospitals, institutional rehabilitation) (Curry *et al.* 2018: 15; Tamiya *et al.* 2011: 1185). All services are subject to a copayment. The municipality governments are 'the insurers for LTCI and are responsible for setting budgets as well as premium levels for beneficiaries' (Rhee *et al.* 2015: 1324). They revise the premium rates every three years to maintain fiscal balance beneficiaries' (Rhee *et al.* 2015: 1324).

Japan's public spending on LTC is higher than other Western countries such as the United States (US) and Germany (Campbell 2011; Tamiya *et al.* 2011). It has relatively low thresholds for accessing LTC services to ensure that there are a large number of beneficiaries from the outset (Curry *et al.* 2018: 22). Its LTCI is generous in both its coverage and its benefits by world standards (Campbell 2014: 9; Tamiya *et al.* 2011: 1184). For example, 17 percent of the 65 and over population is eligible for LTC services in Japan compared with just 10 percent in Germany (Curry *et al.* 2018: 22). Besides, 'Japanese people can use about twice the amount of community-based services as can German people with similar levels of disability' (Tamiya *et al.* 2011: 1185). A study which analyzed national survey data showed that the introduction of LTCI has noticeably improved access to formal care in the community at a lower cost to households (Tamiya *et al.* 2011: 1186). By investing in community and prevention resources, the government aims to create supportive communities so that older people can remain active and independent in society (Curry *et al.* 2018: 4). The public has favored the LTCI system since its implementation. The percentage of the public giving a 'high' to 'moderate' approval rating of the LTCI system increased from 44 percent in 2000 to 61 percent in 2005 (Curry *et al.* 2018: 23). However, challenges to the current LTCI system include fiscal sustainability, the shortage of professional care workers for the elderly, and ways to provide necessary support for family caregivers (Tsutsui and Muramatsu 2007; Tamiya *et al.* 2011; Hirano 2017; Curry *et al.* 2018).

Fiscal sustainability of the LTCI system has been an area of concern because a drastic increase in the number of eligible people has led to a drastic increase in the cost of the LTCI system. In the first year of LTCI operation, only 2.3 million people were certified as eligible (Rhee *et al.* 2015: 1325). By 2005, however, the number certified as eligible had nearly doubled to 4.3 million, which accounted for 16 percent of the population aged 65 and over (Rhee *et al.* 2015: 1325). As of January 2015, the number certified as eligible was over 5 million, accounting for 17 percent of the population aged 65 and over (Japan Health Policy NOW, n.d.). At present, the number certified as eligible is 6 million (Curry *et al.* 2018: 4). From 2000 to 2017, the cost of the LTCI system 'increased from 3.6 trillion yen to 10.7 trillion yen' (Curry *et al.* 2018: 26).

So far, the government 'has managed to sustain the system by increasing insurance premiums and user copayments' (Curry *et al.* 2018: 4). Insurance premiums increased by 2.8 times on average for enrollees aged between 40 and 64 and by 2.0 times for those aged above 65 over financial year 2000–2018 (Organization for Economic Co-operation and Development 2019a: 138). The copayment rate increased from 10 percent to 20 percent for those with annual income (including pension benefits) greater than 2.8 million yen in 2015 and further increased to 30 percent for those with income greater than 3.4 million yen in 2018 (Organization for Economic Co-operation and Development 2019a: 139). Additionally, a 50 percent copayment for room and board expenses in special nursing homes was introduced in October 2005 to reduce the economic incentive for institutional care (Tsutsui and Muramatsu 2007: 1459). To contain costs and discourage nursing home placement, new preventive services were introduced in 2006 for those with lower needs (i.e. those with support levels 1 and 2 and those with care need levels 1) (Tsutsui and Muramatsu 2007: 1459). Services such as nutrition management, strength training, and education were provided to meet the goals of maintaining or enhancing the ability of older people to perform daily activities and preventing them from becoming dependent (Tsutsui and Muramatsu 2007: 1459–60).

Professional care workers for the elderly have been in short supply in Japan due to a shrinking work-age population and low wages of care workers. The average monthly salary of a care worker is lower than the all-industry average by more than 100,000 yen, leading to a higher turnover (The Japan Times 2018a). 'The manpower shortage is set to worsen as the number of elderly people requiring care is projected to increase' (The Japan Times 2018a). It is estimated that Category 1 enrollees of LTCI will increase from 34.75 million in 2017 to 36.1 million in 2025 (The Japan Times 2018a), and by 2025, there will be a shortage of 380,000 elder-care workers in Japan (Hirano 2017). The problem of manpower shortage may increase the workload for and levels of stress among existing care workers, resulting in a decrease in quality of care in nursing homes. To address the problem, the government in recent years has taken steps to expand acceptance of foreign care workers by extending the Technical Intern Training Program to care work and adding 'nursing care' to the list of residence status under the revised Immigration Control Act (2016) (Nokubi 2017). However, these policies are not effective enough to recruit and retain foreign care workers. Many foreign care workers encounter the language barrier because of having difficulties in reading and writing Japanese kanji characters (Sugi 2018). They end up leaving Japan and heading instead to other English-speaking nations such as Australia and the US (Sugi 2018). In order to fill the gap in the nursing workforce, the government has invested in nursing care robotic devices that help frail older persons get out of their bed and into a wheelchair or ease them into bathtubs (Hurst 2018). However, financial barrier and psychological resistance of those who receive care are factors hindering extensive application of robotic devices in nursing homes in Japan (Hurst 2018). Recently, an AI-powered care management platform known as CDI Platform MAIA has been used by health-care providers in Toyohashi City, Aichi Prefecture, to optimize patient care plans such as recommending physiotherapy or physical activity when needed so that seniors can maintain their independence for as long as possible (Forbes 2018).

Another issue that the government needs to deal with is finding ways to provide necessary support for family caregivers (Tamiya *et al.* 2011). The implementation of LTCI has yet to fully liberate family caregivers due to the lack of special nursing home for elderly people, resulting in long waiting lists (Tamiya *et al.* 2011: 1188). In 2013, about 520,000 elderly people across the nation were on waiting lists for special nursing homes (AsiaOne 2015). Of that number, about 29 percent have care need level 3 or higher (AsiaOne 2015). The current home help, daycare and community-based services are insufficient to relieve the burden of family caregivers when caring is regarded as a full-time duty (Tamiya *et al.* 2011: 1188). Scholars suggest that more specific services (e.g. night visits and respite care), professional counseling services for caregivers, and care leave from companies can be introduced to support family caregivers and ensure their wellbeing (Tamiya *et al.* 2011: 1188–9).

Conclusion

Japan has already become a super-aged society. In 2018, the number of Japanese citizens aged over 100 had risen to 69,785, marking the 48th annual increase in a row (McCurry 2018a). The National Institute of Population and Social Security Research estimates that the centenarian population is projected to exceed 100,000 in five years and 170,000 in a decade (The Japan Times 2018b). As the size of the centenarian population continues to rise, the demand for LTC is expected to grow significantly and costs of LTC is expected to increase sharply. Ongoing review and reforms are required to ensure the sustainability of the LTCI system in the long run.

5 Singapore

A compulsory long-term care insurance reform

Introduction

Singapore is experiencing rapid ageing population growth. By 2025, it will become a super-aged society. Longer life expectancy increases the risk of disability in older adults due to frailty and chronic illness. 'Disability limits the autonomy of older people, introduces dependence, reduces the quality of life and increases the risk of nursing home admission' (Heikkinen 2003: 7). For these reasons, the government in 2020 will introduce a compulsory long-term care insurance (LTCI) scheme called CareShield Life to provide higher and lifetime cash payouts for the severely disabled.

This chapter gives a detailed account of the process of LTCI reform in Singapore. The ElderShield Review Committee (ERC) appointed by the Ministry of Health (MOH) played an important role in designing CareShield Life. Members of ERC were policy entrepreneurs in this reform. CareShield Life was technically feasible because the ERC drew from the experiences of Japan, South Korea, Germany, Switzerland, and the United States and engaged the general public, community partners, and experts in designing the LTCI scheme. CareShield Life promoted the ideas of universal coverage and inclusivity, which were accepted by multiple stakeholders, especially those with a pre-existing disability and those from lower-income families. The unchallenged rule of the People's Action Party (PAP), its comfortable majority in Parliament, and the 'national survival' discourse put the PAP government in a very advantageous position to secure majority support for the LTCI reform.

The creation of a multi-layered health financing system

Medisave

When Singapore became independent in 1965, it inherited a British public health system funded by general taxes. Outpatient services were provided at a nominal fee of S$2.50 (about US$1.00) per consultation at public hospitals (Quah 1977: 337). The fee was waived if patients could not afford it (Quah 1977: 337). 'Most serious illnesses were treated in public hospitals, which were well equipped and offered technically sophisticated services' (Hsiao 1995: 261). From 1971 to 1980, the number of admissions to public hospitals drastically increased from 146,700 to 234,500, with the rate of increase averaged at 5.5 percent per year (Ministry of Health 1983: 15). Facing rapid healthcare cost inflation, the government was pressed to reform its health financing system based on the principles of self-reliance, self-accountability, consumer choice and market competition (Hsiao 1995: 261). In April 1984, Singapore became the first country introducing a universal, compulsory medical savings scheme called Medisave (Hurley and Guindon 2008: 127).

The concept of mandatory savings was not new for Singapore because, as early as 1955, Singapore had already instituted a mandatory social security savings scheme called the Central Provident Fund (CPF), which was funded by contributions from both employers and employees (Chia and Tsui 2005: 858). With the implementation of Medisave, an individual Medisave account was created within the CPF to which every employee who was a Singapore citizen and Singapore Permanent Resident (SPR) contributed a portion of his or her monthly wages (Chiu *et al.* 2012). Originally, the contribution rate for Medisave was 6 percent and was shared equally between employers and employees (Ministry of Health 1983: 10). 'Over the years, revisions have been made to the Medisave contribution rate' (National Library Board Singapore 2019a). In 2015, the contribution rate for Medisave ranged from 8 to 10.5 percent of monthly wages, depending on the age group (Ministry of Health 2015: 1). Starting from 1992, self-employed persons who earned an annual Net Trade Income of more than S$6,000 were also required to contribute to Medisave (Central Provident Fund Board 2019a). Contributions to Medisave are tax free (Barr 2005: 153) and 'are guaranteed to earn a fixed interest rate established by the CPF Board' (Haseltine 2013: 43).

Initially, Medisave could only be used to pay for acute hospitalization charges of an account holder or his or her immediate family members (i.e. spouse, children, or parents) in government hospitals or approved private hospitals (Ministry of Health 1983: 11). Over time, Medisave has been extended to pay for personal or immediate family members' day surgery or approved outpatient expenses (e.g. renal dialysis treatment, radiotherapy) in all public healthcare institutions and approved private hospitals and medical institutions, up to the respective Medisave Withdrawal Limits (Central Provident Fund Board 2019b). Medisave Withdrawal Limits are carefully set to ensure that account holders have sufficient savings in their Medisave account to pay for their medical expenses when they retire or no longer have a regular income (Ministry of Health 2018a). Medisave can also be used to pay for the account holder's or his or her immediate family members' health insurance premiums (Ministry of Health 2018a). An account holder has to 'name a beneficiary to whom the funds are passed upon death, or the funds will be distributed in accordance with intestacy laws' (Haseltine 2013: 43).

The ideology leading to the individual account system was based on 'the cultural approach to saving for unforeseen contingencies as a manifestation of self-reliance' (World Health Organization 2005: 28). The government thought that individuals of the current generation 'should save for their healthcare needs in old age instead of relying on uncertain tax revenues from future generations' (Abeysinghe *et al.* 2011: 123). The individual Medisave account was designed to increase cost consciousness of an individual, thereby minimizing the use of unnecessary medical services (World Health Organization 2005: 28). Meanwhile, Medisave also reinforced family as the building block of the Confucius society Singapore was building (Lim and Saxena 2015: 49). The government sent a clear signal that individuals should seek help first from their immediate family members by enabling family members to pay one another's health insurance premiums using Medisave balances (Graham and Bilger 2017: 364). It encouraged risk pooling among family members (Chia and Tsui 2005: 859) and acted as 'a financial incentive for the family together to remain fit and well' (Phua and Yap 1998: 128).

MediShield/MediShield Plus/Integrated Shield Plans/MediShield Life

In 1990, a low-cost, risk-pooling medical insurance scheme called MediShield was implemented to provide financial protection against long-term and catastrophic illnesses that Medisave was inadequate to cover. MediShield coverage was first 'automatically offered on an opt-out basis to Singaporeans at the point of first working (Medisave) contribution to CPF' (MediShield Life Review Committee 2014: 31). Later, coverage was extended to cover younger Singaporeans (MediShield Life Review Committee 2014: 31). Those who were over 92 years old or who had pre-existing health conditions were excluded from MediShield coverage (MediShield Life Review Committee 2014: 25). In 2013, MediShield covered 93 percent of the Singapore population (MediShield Life Review Committee 2014: 31). Premiums were set 'based on risk pooling within each specific age group, which results in higher premiums for the elderly' (Hanvoravongchai 2002: 13). For example, the annual premium in 2013 was S$55 for those aged between 1 and 20, S$66 for those aged between 21 and 30, S$105 for those aged between 31 and 40, S$455 for those aged between 61 and 65, and over S$1,100 for those aged between 81 and 90 (MediShield Life Review Committee 2014: 100). Premiums were deducted annually from the insured members' or their payers' Medisave accounts (Central Provident Fund Board 2015). MediShield covered hospitalization expenses (e.g. surgical operations, implants, intensive care) in the bottom two classes of wards (i.e. Class B2 or Class C ward) in public hospitals as well as selected subsidized outpatient treatments (e.g. renal dialysis, radiotherapy, and chemotherapy for cancer, immunosuppressant drugs for organ transplant) (Lim 2010: 115; MediShield Life Review Committee 2014: 31).

Avoiding a moral hazard on the supply and demand sides was essential in the implementation of MediShield. In order to avoid an oversupply of medical services arising from third-party payments, MediShield operated on a system of negotiated fee schedules to restrict the amount healthcare providers could charge the insurers (Chia and Tsui 2005: 860). In order to avoid an excessive demand on medical services, MediShield reimbursement was determined by a complicated system of deductibles, coinsurance, and claimable limits (Hsiao 1995: 262; Asher and Nandy 2006: 81). MediShield had a deductible of S$1,000 per policy year for Class B2 wards and S$500 per policy year for Class C wards, and a coinsurance of 20 percent (Ministry of Information and the Arts 1994: 6). From 1994 to 2014, the maximum claim limit per policy year increased from S$20,000 to S$70,000 while a lifetime claim limit increased from S$70,000 to S$300,000 (Ministry of Information and the Arts 1994: 6; MediShield Life Review Committee 2014: 32). MediShield covered, on average, 80 percent of the larger hospital bills for subsidized (B2 or C class) patients (Lim 2010: 116).

In 1994, the government introduced MediShield Plus, which was 'a more expensive version of MediShield targeted at high-income earners' (Barr 2005: 155). MediShield Plus offered a two-tier plan to provide higher coverage for those using the top two classes of ward (i.e. Class B1 or Class A ward) in public hospitals or private hospitals. MediShield Plus Plan A, which had a premium five times higher than the basic MediShield scheme, was designed to provide coverage for those using the Class A wards and to a lesser extent the private hospitals (Ministry of Information and the Arts 1994: 2–3). MediShield Plus Plan B, which had a premium three times higher than the basic MediShield scheme, was designed to provide coverage for those using the Class B1 wards (Ministry of Information and the Arts 1994: 2–3). Both Plans had a co-insurance of 20 percent as in the case of the basic MediShield scheme (Ministry of Information and the Arts 1994: 2). But they had higher deductibles, yearly and lifetime claim limits than the basic MediShield scheme. Plan A had a deductible of S$4,000 per policy year, a yearly claim limit of S$70,000, and a lifetime claim limit of S$200,000, while Plan B had a deductible of S$2,500 per policy year, a yearly claim limit of S$50,000, and a lifetime claim limit of S$150,000 (Ministry of Information and the Arts 1994: 6). MediShield Plus covered 80 percent of the amount in excess of the deductible (Ministry of Information and the Arts 1994: 2).

In 2005, private insurance plans called Integrated Shield Plans (IPs) were introduced to cover hospitalization expenses in the Class A and B1 wards in public hospitals and in private hospitals (MediShield Life Review Committee 2014: 34). Premiums could be paid by Medisave accounts. IPs followed mandatory design guidelines issued by the MOH in order to be CPF approved (Fu 2012). They consisted of two parts: the basic MediShield plan operated by the CPF Board and an additional private insurance coverage portion operated by an approved private insurer (MediShield Life Review Committee 2014: 35; Monetary Authority of Singapore 2015: 3). A variety of IPs were offered by five private insurers licensed by the Monetary Authority of Singapore (MAS), including AIA, Aviva, Great Eastern, NTUC Income, and Prudential (MediShield Life Review Committee 2014: 35). Some IPs removed limits on the amount that could be claimed each day for procedures and hospital stays, while others offered riders that paid for the deductible portions of the bill (Lim 2010: 114). About 60 percent of all

Singapore citizens and SPR had bought IPs (MediShield Life Review Committee 2014: 35).

In November 2015, MediShield Life was introduced by the government to replace the original MediShield scheme. It was designed based on the idea of inclusiveness and greater collective responsibility. It was a mandatory basic hospitalization insurance scheme providing universal and lifelong protection for all Singapore citizens and SPRs, including the very old and those with pre-existing health conditions (MediShield Life Review Committee 2014). It paid for large medical bills in subsidized wards (i.e. Class B2 and Class C wards) in public hospitals and selected expensive outpatient treatments, such as dialysis and chemotherapy for cancer (Ministry of Health 2018b). Premiums were actuarially calculated based on the principle of age-based risk pooling in order to avoid intergeneration cross-subsidy and ensure the sustainability of MediShield Life in the future (MediShield Life Review Committee 2014: 72–3). They were higher than MediShield because of providing coverage for all and better benefits, such as no lifetime claim limit, maximum claim limit of S$100,000 per policy year, and lower co-insurance rates. Premiums were higher for those with pre-existing conditions for the first ten years to reflect higher risks. But government had carried out several measures to keep premiums affordable. These included the provision of transitional subsidies over four years for all Singapore citizens; additional premium support for the needy and vulnerable who could not pay for premiums even after subsidies; the provision of substantial subsidies for lower-income and middle-income earners; and the provision of special MediShield Life premium subsidies and Medisave top-ups for the elderly (MediShield Life Review Committee 2014). Premiums could be fully paid by the Medisave account. Those who wanted to enhance MediShield Life coverage could purchase private IPs.

Medifund/Medifund Silver/Medifund Junior

In April 1993, a medical endowment fund called Medifund was set up by the government to provide a safety net for lower-income patients who were unable to pay their subsidized medical bills despite Medisave and MediShield. 'Medifund was given a start-up capital of S$200 million, which would be increased by S$100 million every year from budgetary surplus' (Phua and Yap 1998: 130). The capital sums for MediFund stood at S$3.13 billion at the end of Financial Year 2017 (Ministry of Health 2018c: 1). To keep Medifund sustainable, only the interest income from the capital sum was used (Chia and Tsui 2005: 861). Medifund assistance could be sought through consultation with medical social workers from Medifund-approved institutions at which a patient had treatment (Ho 2017; Ministry of Health 2018d). The eligibility to qualify for Medifund support would be determined by means testing (Lim 2010; Chia and Tsui 2005), and a home visit may be required (Ministry of Health n.d.). Approval authority was decentralized to the Medifund Committees in Medifund-approved institutions, including public hospitals, national specialty centers, polyclinics, intermediate and long-term care facilities (Ministry of Health 2018c: 1). In financial year 2017, there were 48 Medifund Committees administering Medifund for 139 Medifund-approved institutions (Ministry of Health 2018c: 1). The amount of assistance from Medifund depended on the health condition of an eligible patient, the financial circumstances of the patient and his/her family, and the size of medical bills incurred. In financial year 2017, MediFund provided a total of S$149.8 million to about 1.18 million patients for assistance with medical bills (Ministry of Health 2018e). In November 2007, the government converted a portion of Medifund into Medifund Silver to help the low-income elderly aged 65 and above with their medical bills. In March 2013, the government converted another portion of Medifund into Medifund Junior to help low-income patients under the age of 18 with their medical bills.

ElderShield/ElderShield Supplements

In 2002, a national severe disability insurance called ElderShield was implemented to provide monthly payouts for care of people who were unable to perform certain daily activities such as washing, dressing, or feeding themselves (Central Provident Fund Board 2019c). Singapore citizens and SPRs were automatically enrolled in ElderShield when they turned 40 years old. However, they could choose to opt out if they did not wish to be covered under the ElderShield scheme. People with a pre-existing disability were not eligible to join ElderShield (Elder-Shield Review Committee 2018: 23). ElderShield was available in two schemes. ElderShield 300 covered those who enrolled in ElderShield between September 2002 and August 2007 and offered a monthly payout of S$300 for a maximum of 60 months (Government of Singapore 2018). ElderShield 400 covered those who enrolled in ElderShield after September 2007 and offered a monthly payout of S$400 for a maximum of 72 months (Government of Singapore 2018). Premiums were affordable, were determined at the age of entry, and did not increase with age (Ministry of Health 2018f). They were payable annually until enrollees reached 65 years old or when enrollees were qualified to receive Elder-Shield payouts (HealthHub 2019). They could be fully paid by their Medisave or family members' Medisave accounts (Ministry of Health 2018f). Enrollees were insured for life and could make claims at any age if they became severely disabled (HealthHub 2019).

Aviva Limited, Great Eastern Life Assurance Company Limited, and NTUC Income Insurance Co-operative Limited were private insurers appointed by the MOH to manage ElderShield (Central Provident Fund Board 2019c). Policyholders were assigned to one of the ElderShield insurers randomly, but they could switch insurers before their cover commenced (Central Provident Fund Board 2019c). Starting from 2007, ElderShield enrollees could purchase Elder-Shield Supplements offered by the three appointed private insurers in order to enjoy higher monthly payouts, a longer payout period, less strict claims' criteria for disability, or any combination of the above (ElderShield Review Committee 2018: 23). They could pay the premiums of ElderShield Supplements using their

Medisave accounts or cash, up to a limit of S$600 per year per insured person (Government of Singapore 2018; Ministry of Health 2018g).

Introducing the new CareShield Life from 2020

The problem stream

Singapore is facing the problem of a rapidly ageing population due to low total fertility rate (TFR) and longer life expectancy. Since 1977, its TFR has been below replacement level of 2.1 children per woman (National Library Board Singapore 2019b; Singapore Department of Statistics 2018). In 2017, its TFR was 1.16 children per woman (Singapore Department of Statistics 2018: vii). Factors attributed to low TFR included rising proportions of women remaining single, higher ages at marriage and childbearing, and increased use of contraception and abortion (Gubhaju and Moriki-Durand 2003: 3). In Singapore, life expectancy at birth increased from 65.8 years in 1970 to 83.1 years in 2017 (Singapore Department of Statistics 2018: vii). The proportion of the resident population aged 65 years and over was 13.7 percent in 2018 (Singapore Department of Statistics 2018: 4). Singapore will soon move from an ageing society to an aged society when its resident population aged 65 years and over reach 14 percent. By 2025, it will become a super-aged society with 21 percent of its citizen population aged 65 years and over (Population.sg 2016). By 2030, it will have the same demographic profile as Japan has today, with the percentage of seniors aged 65 years and over reaching 27 percent while that of juniors aged below 15 years will decrease to 10.8 percent (Tan 2017).

Older people have a higher risk of disability because of declining health and vulnerability to chronic illnesses such as diabetes and cardiovascular diseases (Mahesh *et al.* 2016; World Health Organization 2011). According to *World Report on Disability*, the prevalence of moderate and severe disability in people aged 60 and over was estimated to be 46.1 percent in 2004 (World Health Organization 2011: 30). In Singapore, the MOH estimated that one in two healthy Singaporeans could become severely disabled in his or her lifetime, and three in ten would remain severely disabled for at least ten years (ElderShield Review Committee 2018: 16). Presence of chronic illnesses, specifically stroke, transient ischemic attack, heart problems, dementia, and depression, were strongly associated with disability in Singapore's elderly population (Mahesh *et al.* 2016: 288). Besides, there were gender differences in the prevalence of disability. A study based on a sample survey of 1,209 elderly Singaporeans living in Kampong Glam, Kreta Ayer, and Bukit Merah parliamentary constituencies found that more than half of the aged had a disability, and the rate of disability among the women was twice as high as that among the men (Yadav 2001: 360). It is expected that rapid population ageing would lead to the growth of the number of older persons with activities of daily living (ADL) limitations. A simulating study projecting the number of resident Singaporeans aged 60 and over with one or more ADL limitations would drastically increase from 31,738 in 2010 to 82,968 in 2030, accounting for 7 percent of the total population aged 60 and over (Thompson *et al.* 2014: 51).

An increase in the number of disabled elderly would bring a greater demand for long-term care (LTC) services. The study of Yadav (2001) indicated that even if the rate of disability in Singapore was to remain constant, there would be an almost five times increase in the demand for LTC services and facilities such as nursing homes, geriatric centres, rehabilitation, and daycare centers during the period 1990–2030 (366). Nevertheless, the provision of LTC would be burdensome and expensive to individuals and their families because the duration of need can be lengthy, which can last for years or even decades (Scanlon 1988: 7). An LTC study conducted by Aviva in 2011 showed that a severely disabled individual on average required an amount of S$2,150 per month to pay for a domestic helper, nursing home care, mobility aids and bills (Aviva 2015). Besides, supporting LTC needs through personal or family savings alone will become more difficult in Singapore due to shrinking family sizes and a declining old-age support ratio (ElderShield Review Committee 2018: 17). For these reasons, finding a better way to finance LTC needs has become an important task for the government.

The policy stream

In Singapore, ElderShield was implemented in 2002 as a basic LTCI scheme to provide the severely disabled with some financial assistance to pay for expenses such as hiring a maid or staying in a nursing home. But it needs to be improved because it does not cover everyone, and its payouts are limited to five or six years, depending on when policyholders joined the scheme. In March 2016, the People's Action Party Seniors Group (PAP.SG), which was headed by Speaker of Parliament Halimah Yacob, was among the first to propose changes to Elder-Shield (Neo 2017). Being a wing of the ruling party to champion causes for the elderly, the PAP.SG stated in its Budget 2016 recommendations that it wanted ElderShield to be made compulsory and administered by the CPF Board, have affordable premiums, the payouts of ElderShield to last until the end of the beneficiary's life, and be pegged to inflation or reviewed every three years (Chong 2016; The People's Action Party Seniors Group 2016).

In August 2016, Prime Minister Lee Hsien Loong announced at the National Day Rally that a committee would be formed to review the ElderShield scheme so that the scheme could be strengthened to cover more people and provide more protection while remaining affordable for all (Prime Minister's Office Singapore 2016). In October 2016, the MOH appointed a 14-member ERC to study ways to enhance ElderShield, as part of the national efforts to further strengthen the social safety nets for an ageing population (Huang 2016). The ERC was chaired by Mr. Chaly Mah, who is the Chairman of Singapore Tourism Board and the Singapore Accountancy Commission (ElderShield Review Committee 2018: 71). Committee members came from the public sector, the private sector, voluntary welfare organizations, and academia. Among them were Mr. Mohamed

Faizal Mohamed Abdul Kadir, Deputy Chief Prosecutor of Attorney-General's Chambers; Ms. Chan Chia Lin, Director of Holywell Pte Ltd; Dr. Ng Wai Chong, Chief of Clinical Affairs at Tsao Foundation; and Dr. Yusuf Ali, Assistant Professor at the Lee Kong Chian School of Medicine, Nanyang Technological University, Singapore (ElderShield Review Committee 2018: 71).

The ERC sought to understand from Singaporeans how ElderShield could be enhanced to better meet their needs (ElderShield Review Committee 2018: 31). From November 2016 to January 2018, the ERC engaged over 800 members of the public (e.g. ElderShield claimants and their caregivers), community partners (e.g. health ambassadors, grassroot leaders, unions, community organizations) and experts (e.g. health professionals, insurers, financial advisors, academicians) through 26 focus group discussions and other feedback channels such as email to gather a wide representation of views (ElderShield Review Committee 2018: 31). Meanwhile, the ERC studied overseas experiences to guide its deliberations (ElderShield Review Committee 2018: 29). Apart from studying the experiences of Japan, South Korea, Germany and Switzerland in designing their national LTCI schemes (ElderShield Review Committee 2018: 27), the ERC also 'studied the private LTCI market in the United States as it is relevant to Singapore's current private insurer administration model for ElderShield' (ElderShield Review Committee 2018: 29). In May 2018, the ERC completed the review and submitted the report to MOH. In the report, the ERC made the following recommendations to enhance ElderShield:

1   provide basic protection for all Singaporeans, starting from age 30, regardless of their health and financial status;
2   provide higher and lifetime payouts to severely disabled claimants;
3   keep premiums affordable and sustainable through regular premium adjustments and the use of Medisave to pay premiums;
4   spread premium payments over a longer duration during Singaporeans' working years, from age 30 to the current re-employment age of 67;
5   provide means-tested premium subsidies to lower- and middle-income Singaporeans;
6   simplify claims and a periodic re-assessment process;
7   administer the scheme by the government on a not-for-profit basis;
8   raise public awareness and understanding of the enhanced scheme; and
9   rename the enhanced scheme as CareShield Life to better reflect its objective to provide Singaporeans with lifetime protection for LTC.

(ElderShield Review Committee 2018: 6–12)

According to the ERC, the ElderShield scheme will be enhanced based on the principles of universality, inclusivity, sustainability, affordability, and collective responsibility. Enrollment in this enhanced scheme will be compulsory. The first cohorts to be enrolled will be Singapore citizens and SPRs aged between 30 and 40 in 2020, with all subsequent cohorts automatically enrolled when they turn 30 (ElderShield Review Committee 2018: 45). Those aged above 40 can opt to participate in the scheme from 2021. The enhanced scheme will be a pre-funded scheme collecting premiums during policyholders' working years and pooling the risks within each generation. It will help minimize intergenerational transfer and ensure the sustainability of the scheme (ElderShield Review Committee 2018: 42). It will complement government subsidies, personal savings, and family support to finance LTC and provide Singaporeans with greater peace of mind in affording their basic LTC needs (ElderShield Review Committee 2018: 20). Initial payouts of the enhanced scheme will be S$600 per month, which is a 50 percent increase from the current ElderShield payout of S$400 per month (ElderShield Review Committee 2018: 49).

In order to ensure the sustainability of the enhancement scheme, there will be an establishment of an independent council through legislation to regularly advise the government on premium and payout adjustments (Parliament of Singapore 2018). Using CareShield Life to provide cash payouts is better than using it to reimburse the use of specific LTC services because more flexibility will be given to claimants and their caregivers to decide on care arrangements appropriate to their needs (Parliament of Singapore 2018). Administration of the enhanced scheme by the government on a not-for-profit basis 'ensures that premiums paid are fully used to support policyholders' (ElderShield Review Committee 2018: 62). The government accepted the ERC's report and agreed with the key recommendations in enhancing the ElderShield scheme (ElderShield Review Committee 2018: 4). It promised to follow up on the recommendations and work out the implementation details (ElderShield Review Committee 2018: 4).

The political stream

On 10 July 2018, Parliament debated the motion on CareShield Life raised by the Minister for Health. Minister for Health Gan Kim Yong opened the debate on CareShield Life in Parliament by taking the Members of Parliament (MPs) through the key principles underlying CareShield Life and the features of it. He explained why it was important to introduce this universal LTCI scheme:

> Preparing for our old age need is often of low priority when we are young, as we tend to focus more on building our career and bringing up our children, and this is understandable. But starting to prepare only when we are old would be very challenging. Therefore, having a universal LTCI scheme for future cohorts is critical, and will ensure that our future generations will have [a] basic level of protection.
>
> (Parliament of Singapore 2018)

Although it was a debate, MPs discussed the white paper in a very calm and peaceful atmosphere, and they sought clarifications politely from the ministers. Most of the MPs welcomed and supported the introduction of CareShield Life. Some of them said that the introduction of CareShield Life was 'timely and significant', 'a step in the right direction for LTC support', and 'a step in the right direction to provide Singaporeans with an accessible, affordable means to plan out their long-term healthcare needs' (Parliament of Singapore 2018). Some MPs said that CareShield Life was 'a very thoughtful initiative' and 'superior to ElderShield in many ways' (Parliament of Singapore 2018). Many MPs praised that CareShield Life had the advantages of being a strong social safety net to provide an additional layer of social security for Singaporeans, providing greater assurance for claimants and their families and giving them peace of mind on their healthcare and LTC needs, empowering Singaporeans suffering from disabilities to maintain financial independence without being a burden to loved ones, cushioning the financial burden of caregivers on taking care of family members who required LTC, and being more sustainable and equitable for LTC (Parliament of Singapore 2018).

While supporting CareShield Life as a whole, MPs raised several concerns during the parliamentary debate that lasted for more than five hours. These included the compulsory nature of CareShield Life, gender-differentiated premiums, transparency in premium and payout calculations, and the rigidity of the three ADLs test. Regarding the compulsory nature of CareShield Life, some MPs asked if it was possible to make the scheme optional for future cohorts to avoid duplication and additional costs because younger Singaporeans might already have similar disability insurance coverage run by private insurers. Addressing the concerns raised by MPs, Senior Minister of State for Health Dr. Amy Khor explained that a scheme that was made optional may lead to healthy Singaporeans to opt out of the scheme while low-income people drop out of the scheme due to their inability to pay (Parliament of Singapore 2018). Premiums could only be kept affordable and the scheme sustainable if the size of the risk pool was maximized to include all future cohorts in the scheme (Parliament of Singapore 2018). Meanwhile, the government would also inject a total of S$100 million into the CareShield Life insurance fund to cover a significant portion of the costs of the future cohorts with pre-existing disabilities (Parliament of Singapore 2018). Dr. Amy Khor also explained that private disability insurance products such as total and permanent disability plans were different from CareShield Life in term of coverage because the former typically protected an individual against loss of income during his/her working years while the latter provided lifetime protection (Parliament of Singapore 2018).

As regards gender-differentiated premiums, some MPs from the ruling PAP and the opposing Workers' Party (WP) raised concerns about women having to pay higher premiums than men under CareShield Life. They wanted to know if premiums could be set on a unisex basis and whether additional premium support could be provided for women, especially those with lower incomes, considering that women earned less than men and had less savings in their Medisave accounts. Many women gave up their careers or earned less than men due to family commitments such as childcare, housework, and care-giving responsibilities (Parliament of Singapore 2018). Dr. Daniel Goh Pei Siong from WP said that the gender-differentiated premiums compromised inclusivity because 'women [were] being penalised for something that [was] not within their control, being born women' (Parliament of Singapore 2018). Nominated MP Ms. K Thanaletchimi said that women were more financially vulnerable due to the gender wage gap and asked if the government could consider reducing the difference in premiums or providing greater financial support so that women would not be penalized twice in having to pay for higher premiums (Parliament of Singapore 2018). Ms. Sylvia Lim from WP used the study of Professor Nicholas Barr on LTC to support her view that CareShield could not truly be inclusive and universal unless premiums were set on a unisex basis:

> Prof Barr agrees that to finance long-term care needs, using compulsory social insurance rather than optional private insurance will better cushion citizens from risk and uncertainty. On the issue of women living longer, however, Prof Barr argues that social insurance schemes for LTC should not take this into account. He offers several reasons for this: "first, if the insurance is mandatory, there is little or no distortionary effect from charging men and women a premium based on joint probabilities; second, there are obvious political difficulties from imposing on women a significantly higher contribution rate than men; and finally, the use of unisex tables can be defended as a simple value judgement".
>
> (Parliament of Singapore 2018)

In response to the concerns raised by the MPs, Senior Minister of State for Health Dr. Amy Khor said that the ERC debated on the gender-differentiated premiums extensively, and it was not an easy decision to make (Parliament of Singapore 2018). She explained that women were charged higher premiums because they lived longer than men and were more likely to spend more years in severe disability, thereby drawing on CareShield Life payouts for a longer period (Parliament of Singapore 2018). She said that researchers, based on a longitudinal survey of older Singaporeans in 2009 and the period 2011–2012, estimated that women aged 60 were expected to spend 7.8 years requiring assistance with any of the ADLs by the end of their lives compared to 2.6 years for men aged 60 (Parliament of Singapore 2018). Applying gender-differentiated premiums 'would more accurately reflect the differences in risks between men and women, and result in a more actuarially fair and sustainable scheme' (Parliament of Singapore 2018). Dr. Khor said that the government would continue to explore different ways to help women who faced difficulties and would ensure that premiums remained affordable for all (Parliament of Singapore 2018). She said that, in fact, government's means-tested subsidies had already provided a higher quantum of subsidies for women because it was based on a percentage of premium payables (Parliament of Singapore 2018). Meanwhile, to promote strong family values and support, Dr. Khor said that spouse or family members could help pay women's premiums by using their Medisave.

During the parliamentary debate, several MPs from the WP and Nominated MPs urged for greater transparency in premium and payout calculations and asked if raw data and assumptions in actuarial computations could be made available to the industry and academia. Some of them suggested that a pro-active approach to public education, open information, and effective communication of the policy would make citizens appreciate CareShield Life more and help ease unhappiness caused by the lack of choice (Parliament of Singapore 2018). Addressing the MPs' concerns, Senior Minister of State for Education and Trade and Industry Mr. Chee Hong Tat explained that premiums were calculated based on a complex actuarial model that was in line with internationally accepted standards. Factors that were incorporated in the model included disability incidence, prevalence rate, recovery rate, the disabled mortality rate, improvements to mortality rate, claims continuance rate, and risk profile for various cohorts (Parliament of Singapore 2018). Mr. Chee said that the government would 'discuss with the council and the actuaries on how best to share information on the details, and assumptions for CareShield Life meaningfully' (Parliament of Singapore 2018). Both mainstream and social media platforms would be used to engage the general public. Health Minister Gan Kim Yong also said that the government would initiate more communication and engagement efforts to increase the awareness of Singaporeans on CareShield Life and ways to support their LTC needs (Parliament of Singapore 2018).

Another concern raised by some MPs was about the rigidity of the three ADLs test. Similar to ElderShield, CareShield Life only provided payouts to those who suffered from severe disability, which was defined as the inability of a person to perform three or more ADLs independently, with or without mobility aids. Some MPs said that such payout criteria were too onerous and strict. It was because even the loss of just one ADL could already significantly affect one's mobility and earning ability while the loss of two ADLs such as eating and toileting would already require full-time assistance (Parliament of Singapore 2018). Hence, they recommended the adoption of a more inclusive definition of severe disability and the adoption of a two-ADL test or more flexible disability test for CareShield payouts (Parliament of Singapore 2018). They thought was that a more flexible criterion could also incentivize older cohorts currently on ElderShield to join CareShield Life. Meanwhile, one of the MPs suggested the government consider a lower payout for those who were unable to perform one ADL or two ADLs (Parliament of Singapore 2018). But Mr. Chee Hong Tat said that there was the trade-off between lowering the claims criteria and keeping premiums affordable. Premiums would increase by one-third if the claims' criteria were lowered from three to two ADLs (Parliament of Singapore 2018). He said that different types of financial assistance schemes were already available for Singaporeans with mild or moderate disabilities, including government's means-tested subsidies for homecare, nursing homes, and community care, Pioneer Generation Disability Assistance Scheme and the Senior's Mobility and Enabling Fund (Parliament of Singapore 2018). But the government would introduce a new ElderFund scheme to provide additional financial support for lower-income Singaporeans with severe disabilities for their LTC needs (Parliament of Singapore 2018).

At the end of the debate, the Minister of Health said that he was encouraged that MPs 'voiced support for the introduction of CareShield Life to provide better protection and greater assurance, compared to the current ElderShield' (Parliament of Singapore 2018). The government intended to introduce a Bill in 2020 to establish the CareShield Life fund and an independent council to regularly review and recommend premium and payout adjustments to the government in accordance with an actuarially sound adjustment framework (Parliament of Singapore 2018).

Unanimous support offered by MPs for the introduction of CareShield Life can be explained by the PAP's 'longstanding position of centrality in the state' (Tan 2010: 1) and its dominance in Parliament. In political science, scholars describe Singapore as an illiberal democracy (Bell *et al.* 1995; Mutalib 2000; Peou 2014), a 'soft' authoritarian regime (Zakaria 1994; Mohamed Nasir and Turner 2013), bureaucratic authoritarianism (Law 2017), competitive authoritarian regime (Ortmann 2011; Abdullah 2016), electoral authoritarianism (Case 2006; Schedler 2006; Siaroff 2009) or hegemonic electoral authoritarian regime (Diamond 2002). These terms are used to indicate that Singapore's political regime is a hybrid regime combining both democratic and authoritarian elements (Diamond 2002: 23). Singapore has a dominant party system (Rodan 1993: 78; Mauzy and Milne 2002: 38). It has been ruled by the PAP since its independence in 1965. 'Through unchallenged and continuous rule, the PAP has become closely identified with the government' (Ho 2010: 71).

Singapore is vulnerable because of its small size, having no national resources, and 'being a Chinese-majority nation in a predominantly Malay-Muslim region' (Abdullah 2018: 476). This vulnerability led to the development of a 'national survival' discourse by the PAP government (Mauzy and Milne 2002; Abdullah 2018). The discourse has been utilized by the PAP government to 'legitimise and justify their domestic policies and its stance towards the outside world' (Lee 1978: 230). It has also been used by the PAP government to instrumentally justify a set of governing principles, which include pragmatism, elitism, meritocracy, and multiracialism (Mauzy and Milne 2002: 52–6). Pragmatism means non-adherence to any dogma and instead to do 'what works' (Abdullah 2018: 476). Elitism is a belief that 'only a few of the best and brightest are capable of leading well' (Mauzy and Milne 2002: 53). Meritocracy is the idea that an individual's social and occupational position is determined by his or her achievement rather than race, class, parentage, political, or economic influence (Mauzy and Milne 2002: 55). Multiracialism means 'respect for and tolerance of all the ethnic groups and cultures represented in the society, and equality under the law' (Mauzy and Milne 2002: 56).

The 'national survival' discourse emphasizes 'the inseparability of economic and political survival and the necessary subservience of all other considerations' (Rodan 1989: 88). Most importantly, survival demands 'the internalisation of an entirely new set of social attitudes and beliefs which embodied self-sacrifice for the national interest' (Rodan 1989: 88). For this reason, Singaporeans largely sacrifice their personal freedoms (Abdullah 2017: 492) and accept the PAP government's sole right to determine the national interest (Rodan 1989: 88). The relationship between the PAP government and the people is built on a subtle consensus of social stability and tangible material welfare in return for acceptance of a paternalistic regime (Yeo 2009: 183–4). For example, substantial expenditures on public housing and education helped build working-class electoral support for the PAP (Rodan 1993: 82). The centralized power structure and elitist policy-making structure together with pragmatism are seen as important factors contributing to the PAP government's efficiency and ability to continuously deliver social stability and economic growth (Yeo 2009: 183). Meanwhile, punitive actions have been taken by the PAP government against opposition and public dissent in general (Mutalib 2000: 325) that result in a depoliticized civil society. Besides, there is no free press in the nation. 'All domestic newspapers, radio stations, and television channels are owned by companies linked to the government' (Freedom House 2018). 'Editorials and news coverage generally support state policies' (Freedom House 2018). Political liberalization is selective and carefully managed (Yeo 2009: 184). Since the mid-1980s, the PAP government 'has opened up avenues for greater, albeit conditional, public consultation in the policy process' (Rodan 1993: 93). Nevertheless, openness is seen as a way to help the government make better policies rather than allowing citizens to challenge the fundamental grip on power by the PAP (Yeo 2009: 184).

Singapore 'is a parliamentary republic with regularly held elections' (Sim and Krishnasamy 2016: 42). Elections 'are free from irregularities and vote rigging' (Freedom House 2015) and can be contested by opposition parties (Case 2006: 96). 'Because of their tight calibration of competitiveness, however, governments were unlikely to lose' (Case 2006: 96). 'The electoral system, featuring a first-past-the-post system and multi-member constituencies, favours the dominant party' (Tan 2010: 1). On the other hand, the PAP government's tactics of frequent electoral boundary changes and short notice of newly created constituencies disadvantage the opposition because such tactics hinder the opposition from planning and organizing campaigns and identifying suitable candidates in advance of the new election (Tan and Grofman 2018: 278). Nevertheless, Singaporeans have voted for the PAP time and again (Abdullah 2017: 492) because they are thought to be satisfied on the whole with the PAP government's performance over the decades, particularly in the areas of economic development, security, the living environment, and social harmony (Tan 2010: 2).

Since 1968, the PAP has won super-majorities in each of the 12 general elections (Abdullah 2018: 473–4). Opposition party candidates were unable to win any seats in Parliament until 1984 (Wong 2018: 719). In the 2015 general election, the PAP had a landslide victory, sweeping 83 out of 89 seats in Parliament. The WP is the only opposition party possessing seats in Parliament (Abdullah 2018: 480). But it legitimizes the PAP's governance and governing ideologies by unequivocally stating that the PAP is the best party to govern the nation and it wishes the PAP government would remain in power for the foreseeable future (Abdullah 2017: 502). Being a 'moderate' opposition party, the WP serves only to act as a check and balance against the PAP (Abdullah 2017: 502) and 'seeks to implement incremental change to the system, and usually in areas where the PAP allows contestation' (Abdullah 2018: 480).

The introduction of CareShield Life is part of the government's effort to deal with health problems and greater demand for LTC arising from its rapidly ageing population. Driven by the crisis-survival mentality, the PAP government has been planning ahead for its population so that timely and appropriate actions can be taken to deal with profound problems caused by the rapidly ageing population. It uses the term 'silver tsunami' to describe the growing wave of older adults in the population, implying that the government is alert to serious threats posed by this demographic shift. When Prime Minister Lee Hsien Loong delivered a speech at the debate on the President's Address in 2011, he had already pointed out that healthcare and LTC services were two important areas that required a national effort so that society as a whole could best prepare for a rapidly ageing population:

> The third aspect of making an inclusive society is to enable Singaporeans to age with dignity and grace. We are going to have a silver tsunami coming and we need a national effort to plan ahead to be ready for it so that it does not wash us away. . . . To prepare for the silver tsunami, we need to contain and share healthcare costs. This, also, the Ministry of Health is doing. Mr Gan Kim Yong has been focusing on that. We need to build up care services so that there will be more hospitals, many more nursing homes but, beyond hospitals and nursing homes, also community facilities and home care. Because for old folks, if you can stay at home, it is always much better than if you have to go to a nursing home or have to be at a hospital, because you want the elderly to enjoy their care and the love of the family and to be near friends and the community.
>
> So these are major national initiatives which will be necessary over the next 10 years. I say national because it cannot be done just by the Government. You will need VWOs, you need community groups, you need households, parents, families all to participate and do their part. We can help to orchestrate this but it is something which has to be a national effort.
>
> (Prime Minister's Office Singapore 2011)

Indeed, the introduction of CareShield Life is a new scheme to ensure that LTC remains accessible and affordable in a rapidly ageing context. Although the ERC was formed to study ways to enhance ElderShield, over 800 young and old Singaporeans were invited by the ERC to join focus group discussions to offer ideas on ways to improve inclusivity and affordability of the current ElderShield scheme and share their personal experiences on LTC (ElderShield Review Committee 2018). Through these focus groups discussions, the general public 'were called forth to feel responsible for matters that are important not only for themselves but for the larger national community' (Tan 2010: 3). A wide range of information, ideas, and insights obtained from these focus group discussions could help the ERC provide useful recommendations that could better meet the needs and concerns of Singaporeans. With a comfortable majority in Parliament, the ruling PAP has no problem garnering support from MPs for the introduction of

CareShield. Meanwhile, MPs from the opposition WP thought that recommendations made by the ERC were 'a step in the right direction' and supported the rationale for CareShield Life (Parliament of Singapore 2018). CareShield Life will be launched in 2020.

Conclusion

To conclude, unchallenged rule of the PAP, its comfortable majority in Parliament, and the 'national survival' discourse put the PAP government in a very advantageous position to secure majority support for the LTCI reform. The introduction of CareShield Life represents the government's commitment towards a more resilient and inclusive society. It is expected that CareShield Life can enhance financial protection for the severely disabled in times of need.

Acknowledgement

This chapter is supported by the Start-Up Grant (SUG) of Nanyang Technological University, Singapore (Grant number: M4082137.SS0.).

6 Taiwan

The National Health Insurance reform

Introduction

This chapter gives a detailed account of the process of the National Health Insurance (NHI) reform in Taiwan. The problems of a large uninsured population, a severe deficit in insurance funds, and partisan competition set the NHI reform agenda on a universalist trajectory. The NHI was a product of nearly five years of planning efforts (1988–1993) and a two-year legislative marathon (Lu and Chiang 2011: 94). Scholars and technical experts of the NHI Research and Planning Task Force were policy entrepreneurs in this reform. The NHI was technically feasible because the Task Force learnt from the single-payer system in Canada, and the premium model it proposed had long been used by the government to fund healthcare before the reform. The NHI promoted the ideas of redistributive equity, cost containment, and systemic efficiency, which were endorsed by the government and the public, especially the uninsured and those who faced high medical expenses. The ruling party's full control of the planning and policy decision-making process, its sizable majority in the Legislative Yuan, internal factionalism of the opposition party, and fragmented societal groups facilitated the passage of the NHI Bill. The NHI was finally implemented in 1995. At present, there is high level of public satisfaction with the NHI. But the problems of an ageing population, insurance coverage for patients with catastrophic illnesses, and the waste of medical resources pose serious challenges to the fiscal sustainability of the NHI system in the long run.

Pre-reform era

Before the introduction of the NHI in 1995, Taiwan provided free medical services to military personnel at national defense hospitals and clinics (Tang 1997: 97) and established a government-managed, occupation-based social health insurance system consisting of 13 different schemes under the administrative aegis of three insurance programs: the Labour Insurance (LI), the Government Employees Insurance (GEI), and the Farmers Health Insurance (FHI) (Wong 2004). Insured persons only had to pay a very small registration fee when seeking medical treatment at designated medical institutions. 'Thereafter, the central bureau of social insurance, as a third party, reimburse[d] the hospitals or doctors for the medical care costs' (Tang 1997: 78).

There were both political and economic considerations behind the implementation of these insurance programs. Politically, the ruling party Kuomintang (KMT) wanted to achieve political legitimacy through the implementation of the LI and the GEI in the 1950s. The KMT, which retreated from the mainland to Taiwan, was regarded by many native Taiwanese as an alien regime that did not represent them (Tang 1997: 82–3). It 'had no substantial roots and no clear affiliation with any of the various widespread Taiwanese interest groups' (Tang 1997: 85). Under the leadership of Chiang Kai-shek, the KMT imposed authoritarian rule on the island (Wu and Dai 2014: 61). It placed Taiwan under martial law, which 'provided a legal framework for repressing dissent, censoring publications, and outlawing new political parties' (Rigger 2001: 6). Social insurance programs were implemented to tie the loyalties of the individual directly to the central state of authority (Tang 1997: 83). Particularly, the LI was widely regarded as 'an appeasement measure to avoid potential worker revolts' (McGuire 2010: 200). Economically, the government wanted to maintain the harmonious relationship between employers and employees and build a healthy and productive workforce to facilitate industrialization and economic development (Fu 1995: 43).

In the 1980s, the implementation of the FHI 'could be seen as the government's response to the changed political situation in Taiwan' (Son 2001: 48). As political liberalization and democratization deepened from the early 1980s onwards and martial law was lifted in 1987, 'Taiwan entered a new era of competitive party politics' (Tien 1996: 11). A number of oppositional leaders criticized the KMT's social policy for favoring urban wage workers while neglecting rural residents who lacked a regular income (Son 2001: 48). Implementing the FHI represented the KMT's efforts to win support from the crucial, forthcoming electorate of the masses of farmers, as well as to compete more effectively in elections against the newly formed Democratic Progressive Party (DPP) (McGuire 2010: 201).

The Labour Insurance (LI)

Established in 1950, the LI was the earliest and the largest social insurance program in Taiwan (Chiang 2008: 48). However, the government did not promulgate the Labour Insurance Act until 1958 and then put it into practice in 1960 (Yen and Lin 2015: 193). The LI provided the insured with a comprehensive benefits package, including maternity benefits, injury or sickness benefits, medical care benefits, disability benefits, old-age benefits, and death benefits (Chiang 2008: 49). But medical care benefits did not become part of the LI until inpatient services were covered by the LI in 1956 (Wu 1996: 175). Outpatient services were also covered by the LI in 1970 (Wu 1996: 175). Participation in the LI was compulsory. Initially, the LI was 'only for wage earners who worked in certain types of occupations' (Tang 1997: 78). It covered workers in public factories and mines, salt fields, public transport enterprises, or public utilities

(Bureau of Labor Insurance 2010: 13). Over time, it had been expanded to cover a wide cross-section of workers above 15 and below 65 years of age, including those in private factories and mines or fisheries, sugarcane planters, members of an occupational union who had no definite employers or who were self-employed (Bureau of Labor Insurance 2010: 16–24), non-military engineers in weapons factories, technicians in public and private schools, workers in a firm which employed more than five employees, and those who were not entitled to the GEI (Son 2001: 47–8). Workers in a firm with four employees or less could participate in the LI on a voluntary basis (Chiang 2008: 49). The premium was equivalent to 7 percent of an insured person's monthly salary, with 4 percent of it for health insurance (Wu 1996: 172). Eighty percent of the premium was to be contributed by the employer and the rest by the worker (Wu 1996: 172). For workers who had no definite employers or who were self-employed, the contribution to the premium was 60 percent while the government contributed 40 percent (Chiang 2008: 49). As of the end of December 1989, the total number of LI participants was 6.55 million, which accounted for 33 percent of Taiwan's population (Chiang 2008: 49).

The Government Employees Insurance (GEI)

In 1958, the GEI was established after the promulgation of the Government Employees Insurance Act. It was a compulsory insurance program providing civil servants with seven kinds of benefits, including medical care benefits for maternity, sickness, and injury; and cash benefits for disability, old-age, and death, as well as funeral allowances for dependents (Ministry of Culture 2011). The premium was equivalent to 7 percent of a civil servant's monthly salary, with 3.71 percent of it going to health insurance (Wu 1996: 176). It was raised to 8 percent in 1977 and then 9 percent in 1980 (Department of Government Employees Insurance and Bank of Taiwan 2011). Thirty-five percent of the premium was to be contributed by a civil servant while the rest was contributed by the government (Wu 1996: 176). Insured civil servants could seek diagnosis and treatment at outpatient centers established by the insurer or designated medical institutions (Wu 1996: 176). Sickness benefits of the GEI covered childbirth, disease prevention, physical examination, and medical treatment for injury and illness (Bureau of National Health Insurance 2010: 7). Insured civil servants only needed to the pay registration fee when seeking medical care (Chiang 2008: 50).

Subsequently, the government respectively introduced an insurance scheme for retired civil servants in 1965, private school teachers in 1980 (Hill and Hwang 2005: 150), and retired private school teachers in 1984 (Fu 1995: 44). For retired civil servants, it fully paid their premium. For private school teachers, the contribution to the premium was 35 percent while the school and the government paid 32.5 percent (Chiang 2008: 50). As for retired private school teachers, the contribution to the premium was 50 percent, while the school and the government paid 25 percent (Department of Government Employees Insurance and Bank of Taiwan 2011).

Since the 1980s, a series of sub-schemes had been established within the GEI to provide health insurance coverage for family dependents of civil servants, retired civil servants, private school teachers, and retired private school teachers. These included spouses, parents, unmarried children with a disability, and other unmarried children of civil servants; the spouses of retired civil servants; the spouses, parents, and unmarried children of private school teachers; and the spouses of retired private school teachers (Fu 1995; Department of Government Employees Insurance and Bank of Taiwan 2011). As of the end of December 1989, the total number of GEI participants was 1.04 million (Chiang 2008: 50), which accounted for about 5.2 percent of Taiwan's population. About 49 percent of the GEI participants were incumbent civil servants (Chiang 2008: 50).

The Farmers Health Insurance (FHI)

In October 1985, the experimental FHI began in certain areas to improve basic livelihood and medical care of farmers (Yen and Lin 2015: 194). Participation in the experimental FHI was restricted to farmers who were members of farmers' associations according to Article 12 of the Farmer's Association Law (Bureau of Labor Insurance 2013). Farmers' associations were the insured units of the FHI. The premium rate was 5 to 7 percent of the monthly insured amount of the insured person (Bureau of Labor Insurance 2013). In October 1987, the experimental program was expanded to Taipei City, Kaohsiung City, Kinmen County, and Lienchiang County (Bureau of Labor Insurance 2013). The premium rate was 6.5 to 8.5 percent of the monthly insured amount of the insured person (Bureau of Labor Insurance 2013).

In October 1988, the experimental program was fully implemented in Taiwan. During the experimental period, farmers contributed 40 percent of the premium, with the government and farmers' associations paying 50 percent and 10 percent respectively (Bureau of Labor Insurance 2013). In July 1989, the Farmer Health Insurance Act became effective, which required farmers who were members of farmers' associations as referred to in Article 12 of the Farmer's Association Law and farmers who were over 15 years old and who engaged in agricultural work to participate in the FHI (Bureau of Labor Insurance 2013). The premium rate was 6 to 8 percent of the monthly insured amount of the insured person (Bureau of Labor Insurance 2013). Thirty percent of the premium was to be contributed by a farmer while the rest would be paid by the government (Bureau of Labor Insurance 2013).

The FHI provided five types of benefits to the insured, including maternity benefits, injury benefits, sickness benefits, disability benefits, and death benefits. Sickness benefits covered both outpatient and inpatient services such as diagnostic (including examination and consultation), pharmaceutical, treatment, and surgical services (Ministry of the Interior 2013). The insured persons had to pay only 10 percent of the outpatient expenses and 5 percent of the inpatient expenses when seeking medical care at designated medical institutions (Ministry of the Interior 2013). As of the end of December 1989, the total number of FHI participants was 1.34 million (Chiang 2008: 51), which accounted for 6.75 percent of Taiwan's population.

The process of National Health Insurance (NHI) reform

The problem stream

The occupation-based social health insurance system created two main problems. One of the problems was having a large uninsured population. Another problem was the deficit in the insurance funds. The occupation-based social health insurance system was discriminatory in nature. It led to large segments of the population being left without any insurance protection. Children, the elderly, the disabled, housewives, and the unemployed were uninsured (Cheng 2010; Chiang 2008) despite the fact that they were vulnerable people having high demands for medical care but lacking financial independence (Bureau of National Health Insurance 2010: 6). As of the end of December 1989, the occupation-based social health insurance system only provided health coverage for about 45 percent of Taiwan's population.

In July 1990, a health insurance scheme was introduced to provide maternity, injury, and sickness benefits for low-income households, with the premium fully subsidized by the government (Lin 2006: 295). As of the end of February 1995, the percentage of the population covered by the occupation-based social health insurance programs increased to about 56.4 percent while the percentage of people covered by Low-Income Household Insurance was only about 0.56 percent (Wu 1996: 178). Over 40 percent of Taiwan's population remained uninsured.

The healthcare delivery system was heavily dominated by privately owned medical centers and hospitals (Tang 1997: 76). Most of the outpatient clinics that numbered more than 15,000 by 1995 were privately run (McGuire 2010: 196–7). People without health insurance coverage 'relied on private-sector pharmacists for medical advice' (McGuire 2010: 197) and may face financial ruin or incur substantial amounts of medical debt due to paying out-of-pocket payments for healthcare, especially those who needed to have surgeries or suffered from hereditary diseases. Some of them may discontinue medical treatment, put off medical treatment, or do not seek needed healthcare services because they cannot afford out-of-pocket payments for healthcare. This could jeopardize their health. In sum, the occupation-based social health insurance system deterred the uninsured from seeking necessary medical services and created unequal access to healthcare (Lu and Hsiao 2003: 78).

The deficit in insurance funds had been a serious problem for many years. The LI was insufficient to provide medical benefits for the insured and operated at a loss in some years (Chiang 2008: 54). But the financial situation of the GEI was even worse because there was a deficit in the second year of its inception (Chiang 2008: 55). As of 1992, the accumulated deficit of the GEI fund reached NT\$13.2 billion (US\$428 million), depending entirely on the clearance through the fund granted by the Ministry of Finance (Chiang 2008: 55). For the FHI, as of the end of 1989, there was a shortfall of NT$1.4 billion (US$45.4 million) (Chiang 2008: 55).

There were three reasons attributed to the deficit in insurance funds. The first reason was that there was a drastic increase in medical expenses that quickly depleted insurance funds. In the 1980s, healthcare spending rose faster than Gross Domestic Product (GDP) (McGuire 2010: 197). This was because doctors heavily over-prescribed medicines in order to earn more income from the sale of these medicines (McGuire 2010: 197). 'In the early 1990s, nearly half of total health spending went to drugs and injections' (McGuire 2010: 197). From 1985 to 1994, the amount of medical care benefits covered by the LI drastically rose from NT$17.9 billion (US$580.2 million) to NT$73 billion (US$2.37 billion) (Wu 1996: 179). During that period, the average outpatient expenses rose from NT$248 (US$8.04) to NT$412 (US$13.40), while the average inpatient expenses rose from NT$20,577 (US$667.90) to NT$26,170 (US$849.44) (Wu 1996: 179). In 1994, medical care benefits accounted for about 57 percent of the LI funds (Wu 1996: 179).

For the GEI, the amount of medical care benefits it covered drastically rose from NT$2.5 billion (US$82 million) in 1985 to NT$5.8 billion (US$188 million) in 1994 (Wu 1996: 181). During that period, the average outpatient expenses rose from NT$310 (US$10.05) to NT$504 (US$16.34) while the average inpatient expenses rose from NT$17,078 (US$554) to NT$26,297 (US$853) (Wu 1996: 181). For the FHI, the amount of medical care benefits it covered drastically rose from NT$760,000 (US$24,633) in 1985 to NT$27 billion (US$800 million) in 1994 (Wu 1996: 182). During that period, the average outpatient expenses rose from NT$155 (US$5.03) to NT$397 (US$12.88) while the average inpatient expenses rose from NT$5,899 (US$191.39) to NT$28,613 (US$928.33) (Wu 1996: 182).

The second reason was that people who were originally ineligible for health insurance enrollment enrolled illegally by 'making fraudulent claims of employment by a firm or self-employment' (Wong 2004: 77). This led to a very odd situation so that by 1993, 'the number of people claiming health insurance benefits amount to 120 percent of the employed population' (Wong 2004: 77). The third reason was that there was a shortfall in insurance funds due to employers' perpetual underreporting of income to reduce operating costs and low premium rates (Wong 2004: 77).

Starting from 1980, the implementation of universal health insurance became a political issue in electoral competition. Candidates of opposition parties included the implementation of universal health insurance in their election manifestos in order to canvass for votes (Fu 1995: 44). Being the first organized opposition party in Taiwan, the DPP 'claimed to represent the middle and lower classes' (Tang 1997: 87) and declared that it 'stood for a welfare society built on the Western European model' (Copper 1989: 13). It used welfare policy as a major slogan in every election during the 1980s (Tang 1997: 86). It criticized the KMT for 'neglecting social policies and advocated national health insurance as a critical indicator of a good government and a modernized nation' (McGuire 2010:

201). It succeeded in appealing to voters and resulted in winning 12 seats (16.44 percent) in the Legislative Yuan election in 1986 (Mengin 2015: 115). Partisan competition subsequently led to the KMT's organization of a committee devoted to national health insurance (Son 2001: 49).

Meanwhile, the increasing number of native Taiwanese obtaining politically influential positions and a change in party leader of the KMT led to the party and politicians of Taiwan origin showing a keener interest in improving social conditions in Taiwan itself (Son 2001: 49). In the 1970s, a policy of indigeniza-tion pursued by former president Chiang Ching-Kuo led to Taiwan-born tech-nocrats and local politicians obtaining some important positions in the KMT (Tien 1996: 11). As of 1994, 19 out of 31 members of the Central Standing Committee, which was the highest decision-making body in the KMT, were native Taiwanese (Tien 1996: 12). Social policies became the focus of attention (Tang 1997: 86). Lee Teng-hui, who was a native Taiwanese with a PhD from the United States, became vice president in 1984, and president of Taiwan and chairman of the KMT in 1988. He consolidated his power over the military, the party, and the government following three rounds of power struggles and leader-ship reshuffling (Tien 1996: 12). Realizing that there was still a large segment of the population being left without any health insurance protection, Lee wanted to provide medical protection for all citizens through the introduction of NHI. As Professor William Hsiao, who served as a healthcare adviser to the Taiwan government in the 1990s, said during a newspaper interview,

> Only a portion of the people were insured, including civil servants, employees of large firms and farmers. The military had its own system of coverage. But 45 percent of the population did not have insurance, and they faced financial barriers to access to health care. President Lee Teng-hui felt strongly that he wanted to do something concrete and visible for all the citizens. He thought of introducing national health insurance to touch the lives of all the people. There was a sense in Taiwan that health care is needed by everyone and a country has to assure everyone equal access.
>
> (Underwood 2009 November 3)

The policy stream

It was the logic of political competition and the change in party leader of the KMT that set the NHI reform agenda in Taiwan on a universalist trajectory (Son 2001: 49; Wong 2004: 77). To protect against the legitimacy crisis, the government in 1984 charged the Council for Economic Planning and Development (CEPD) under the Executive Yuan (Taiwan's Cabinet) with establishing a comprehensive planning task force to study Taiwan's social welfare programs (Chiang 1997: 228). In 1986, the planning task force completed an integrated planning report and concluded with a recommendation for integrating the existing fragmented social insurance programs and inaugurating a universal health insurance scheme by the year 2000 (Wang 2017: 129). In February 1986, former Premier of the

Executive Yuan Yu Kuo-hwa, in consideration of the year-end legislative election (Wong 2004: 76), announced the government's intention to 'achieve the ideal of national health insurance by 2000' in the Legislative Yuan for the first time (Lin 2012: 569). In fact, the year 2000 was also the same target year that the World Health Organization suggested to countries to attain healthcare for all (World Health Organization 1981). It seemed that the KMT government wanted to win respect and recognition in the international arena through the implementation of the NHI in 2000 (Tang 1997: 72). Consequently, the implementation of the universal health insurance became one of the economic development plans in an official document called *Long-term Economic Perspectives in Taiwan, 1986–2000* (Lin 2012: 569).

Nevertheless, 'widespread social movements and the inability of the KMT to restore social order for capitalist production' (Ku 1997: 238), strong political pressure caused by mounting criticism from the younger Taiwanese parliamentarians within the KMT, and the major opposition from the DPP pushed former Premier Yu to demonstrate government goodwill in the NHI and speed up its implementation by setting 1995 as the new target year (Chiang 1997: 228; Chiang 2008: 75; Ku 1997: 238; Ku 1998: 121; Lin 2012: 570; Son 2001: 50; Tang 1997: 71; Wong 2004: 76). The NHI was 'regarded by the KMT as a means of retaining support both from capitalists and the public in a more democratic political environment' (Ku 1997: 238).

The first stage of policy planning of the NHI was assigned to the NHI Research and Planning Task Force (hereafter the NHI Task Force), which was established in 1988 under the CEPD (Huang *et al.* 2012: 27). With the support of senior cadres of the KMT government (Lin 2002: 333), the CEPD initially appointed three Taiwanese professors of public health – Yang Chih-liang, Wu Kai-shiun, and Chiang Tung-liang – and later Dr. Lo Joan C., a research fellow from Institute of Economics, Academia Sinica to lead the NHI Task Force of technical experts to set a basic framework for the development of the NHI (Huang *et al.* 2012: 27; Ku 1998: 122; Lu and Chiang 2011: 94; Underwood 2009 November 3). But the four scholars all had different ideas, with each going in a different direction (Underwood 2009 November 3). Recognizing the importance of international experiences, Minister of CEPD Frederick Chien in 1989 decided to appoint William Hsiao, a professor of economics at the Harvard School of Public Health, as chief advisor to the NHI Task Force of four scholars and 16 other technical experts (Lu and Chiang 2011; Underwood 2009 November 3).

The NHI Task Force was asked to design an NHI plan for Taiwan based on international experience (Underwood 2009 November 3). Government officials wanted to know how other advanced countries organized and funded healthcare and if they could offer valuable lessons to Taiwan (Underwood 2009 November 3). Hence, the NHI Task Force began by approaching academic leaders in six advanced nations, including the United States (US), Canada, the United Kingdom (UK), Germany, France, and Japan, and asking them to write a paper on the strengths and weaknesses of the healthcare system in their home country (Reid 2009a: 169). After that, the NHI Task Force held a three-day conference in Taipei and invited these academic leaders to the conference to debate each other (Reid 2009a: 169). Meanwhile, cabinet ministers in Taiwan, such as the minister of finance and the minister of health, were asked by Professor Hsiao to chair the various sessions of the conference so that they could understand different viewpoints of academic leaders (Reid 2009a: 169–70). Considering different healthcare systems in six nations, the NHI Task Force rejected the market-driven healthcare system in the US because such a system only provided healthcare for those who could afford it (Reid 2009a: 170). It also rejected the publicly funded national healthcare system in the UK because Taiwan had mostly private hospitals (Reid 2009a: 170). The NHI Task Force did not favor Japan's and Germany's healthcare financing models because they used many different types of funds to pay the bills (Reid 2009a: 170). At the end of the study, the NHI Task Force concluded that 'the Canadian model of a single insurance carrier would be the most effective in controlling health care costs and should therefore be adopted' (Son 2001: 50). As Professor William Hsiao said during the newspaper interview:

> Canada has a single-payer system with universal insurance coverage. It offers people free choice of doctors and hospitals, and it has competition on the delivery side between public and private hospitals. The quality of health services is very high, and people were very satisfied with the system from the 1980s through the mid-1990s.
>
> (Underwood 2009 November 3)

In another interview, Profession Hsiao highlighted the strength of a single-payer system:

> When you have a single payer . . . for the doctors and hospitals, then you can identify who's really abusing the system. That also allows you to put a global budget in place. When you have a single payer, you can say, 'I'm only going to spend X percent of my GDP for health insurance', and you can enforce that.
>
> (Reid 2009a: 170)

Nevertheless, unlike the Canadian model that was funded through general taxation, the NHI model proposed by the NHI Task Force would be funded by the mandatory premium contributions from both employers and employees (Reid 2009a: 171). As former Health Minister Ching-Chuan Yeh said in an interview, there were three main reasons why the premium model rather than the general tax model was chosen:

> Three reasons: first, previously existing social insurance schemes such as Labor Insurance, Government Employees Insurance, and Farmers Insurance were all premium based, so the public was familiar with that model. Second, the general tax model would not work in Taiwan, because the government's ability to levy taxes is poor – total tax revenue as a percent of GDP is

currently 13 percent, down from a historical high of 18 percent. Finally, the Department of Health would have to compete for government budget allocation against other government departments such as defense, finance, education, and transportation; this may lead to unstable and insufficient funding for the NHI because the government's priorities may shift.

(Cheng 2009: 1038)

In 1990, the NHI Task Force submitted a formal planning report to the government (Ku 1998: 121). It identified three principle goals and nine strategies as follows (Ku 1998: 121–2):

Goals

1 Provide proper health service for everyone;
2 Keep medical expenditures within a reasonable range;
3 Make efficient use of medical resources.

Strategies

1 The new NHI system must cover the entire population through a model of compulsory social insurance;
2 The new NHI system should be separated from other social insurance programs;
3 Premiums for the new NHI should be set with each insured person as a unit regardless of the number of their insured dependents;
4 Total medical expenses should be set at a level below a definite ratio of total national resources;
5 Under the principle of 'neither waste nor loss', cost sharing and financial accountability should be introduced into the new NHI scheme;
6 A single unified 'pipe' payment system for medical treatment should be designed and a global budget should be introduced;
7 A referral system should be implemented, and the availability of medical resources in remote and rural areas should be promoted;
8 A sound NHI administrative system should be set up in order to make efficient use of medical resources;
9 Public knowledge about NHI should be improved through education and propaganda.

Three principle goals and nine strategies reflected that the ideas of redistributive equity, cost containment, and systemic efficiency were endorsed by the NHI Task Force (Wong 2004: 78). The integration of the fragmented social insurance schemes into a government-run, single-payer NHI scheme would 'maximize the redistributive impact of social insurance by expanding the common pool of resources and spreading the costs of medical care more equitably' (Wong 2004: 78). Regarding cost containment, the introduction of a global budget system was expected to 'control the growth of overall expenditures by setting a cap on total reimbursements to providers' (Chou *et al.* 2014: 2). It could improve efficient production of health services (Berenson *et al.* 2016: 3) and discourage over-prescription, unnecessary tests, and treatments. Meanwhile, the introduction of a copayment or user fee system could increase the cost consciousness of patients and 'curtail the overutilization of medical facilities' (Wong 2004: 78). The imple-mentation of both supply-side and demand-side cost containment mechanisms was expected to achieve systemic efficiency.

Meanwhile, the new NHI system was affected by policy legacies in aspects such as the type of insurance model chosen and the administrative organization. The NHI still adopted a social insurance model, which helped increase public acceptance because the general public was familiar with the model used to finance healthcare. Besides, the administrative arrangement of the NHI was still based on the earlier social insurance programs (Tang 1997: 80). This helped to reduce administrative costs because it 'inherited most of the bureaucracy and skills it needed to implement its programs' (Tang 1997: 80).

In June 1990, former Premier of the Executive Yuan Hau Puo-tsun announced that the NHI 'would be initiated one year earlier than expected, which meant that the NHI would be put into practice in 1994' (Tang 1997: 99). At that time, consultants in the NHI Task Force strongly expressed the view that the NHI pro-posal was not mature enough to have early initiation, which may lead to bureau-cratic chaos and economic crisis (Tang 1997: 99). But their warning was ignored by Premier Hau, who wanted to use early initiation of the NHI to placate public criticism that his military background was not suitable for the position of top administrator and help the KMT gain popularity (Tang 1997: 98–9).

The political stream

In June 1990, the CEPD officially endorsed the NHI Task Force's health insur-ance reform proposal (Wong 2004: 79). Due to a cabinet reshuffle in the middle of 1990, the NHI Task Force was dismissed (Lu and Chiang 2011: 94). The second stage of planning was then given to the Department of Health (DoH) to develop 'a politically viable and administratively tenable legislative proposal' (Wong 2004: 79) aiming to ensure the smooth implementation of the NHI (Huang *et al.* 2012: 32). The DoH set up a planning committee as the highest decision-making unit to determine the policy direction of NHI (Huang *et al.* 2012: 32). The planning committee consisted of the health minister, deputy ministers from 13 ministries, secretary-general of provincial and municipal gov-ernments, experts, and scholars (Huang *et al.* 2012: 32) to ensure a wide range of views were considered. Both foreign and local scholars took on advisory roles in the planning committee (Huang *et al.* 2012: 33). Under the planning com-mittee, a planning group was set up to handle tasks in different policy divi-sions, such as financing, provider payment, medical care delivery and legal affairs (Huang *et al.* 2012: 33; Wong 2004: 79). '[T]he KMT leadership played a supervisory role, insulating the bureaucratic policy process from outside influ-ence' (Wong 2003: 63). After more than two years of work, the DoH submitted both the drafts of the *Important Points in Establishing a NHI Act* and the NHI Bill to the Executive Yuan (Lin 2002: 335). On 27 October 1993, the draft of the NHI Bill was subsequently presented to the Legislative Yuan for deliberation (Lin 2002: 335).

Passage of the NHI Act presented by the DoH was not easy (Son 2001: 50). It was because legislators also submitted five different versions of reform bills to the Legislative Yuan for deliberation, representing the interests of medical groups, consortia that invested in and operated hospitals, Western physicians, and Chinese medicine practitioners (Fu 1995: 62). In January 1993, ahead of the DoH's draft, the Health, Welfare and Environment Foundation formed by legislators with a medical background submitted its own version of the NHI bill with the signatures of 23 legislative members (Lin 2002: 339; Pei 2002: 3). In March 1993, Shen Fu-hsiung of DPP submitted his version with the signatures of 70 members (Lin 2002: 339). Legislator Wu Dong-sheng, Lin Cheng-chieh, and Chen Che-nan also submitted their own versions to the Legislative Yuan (Lin 2002: 339; Pei 2002: 3). 'The content of the various members' bill ranged from slight modifications to the government's proposal to systematic overhauls' (Wong 2004: 80). Much contention of each version of reform bills centered on the premium rate, the proportional breakdown of premiums, and whether the administrative organization should be publicly or privately operated (Pei 2002: 3–4). But among all the versions of reform bills, the DoH's version was, for the most part, well planned (Wong 2004: 80).

During the legislative process, the KMT held several rounds of negotiations with opposition parties due to differences on some controversial issues. One of the controversies centered on the premium rate. While the DoH's reform bill proposed the premium rate range to be 4.5 to 6.0 percent of the wage earner's payroll, some legislators felt that the bottom range should be 2.8 to 4.0 percent (Wong 2004: 188). Legislators finally agreed on setting the premium rate at 4.25 percent (Wong 2004: 80). Another controversy centered on the proportional breakdown of premiums (Wong 2004: 80). Labor unions were strongly opposed to the DoH's proposal that the distribution of premiums between employers and their employees should be 6:4 (Yu *et al.* 2016: 86). Some legislators thought that the distribution of premiums between employers and their employees should be 7:3 (Yu *et al.* 2016: 86). During the negotiation process, some legislators proposed that the government should shoulder a portion of the insurance premium and later even initiated a signature campaign demanding the distribution of premiums among the government, employees, and employers to be 2: 2: 6 (Yu *et al.* 2016: 86). But the government, which had faced fiscal deficits for several years, had reservations about sharing a portion of insurance premiums (Son 2001: 50). When the negotiation entered a deadlock, the government softened its stance on its share of premiums (Yu *et al.* 2016: 86). Eventually, the legislature adopted a compromise formula of 1: 3: 6 (government/employee/employer) (Son 2001: 51; Yu *et al.* 2016: 86).

Although legislators demanded more time to discuss the details of the DoH's reform bill and settle their differences, President Lee Teng-hui instructed that the

Legislative Yuan should pass the NHI Act by the end of a session in July 1994 out of political considerations (Yu *et al.* 2016: 86). He was eager to help the KMT maintain a lead in the coming elections and anticipated that the passage of the NHI Act could help the KMT win votes in upcoming gubernatorial elections in late 1994, Legislative Yuan legislation in 1995, and founding direct presidential election in early 1996 (Wong 2004: 81). In 1994, the NHI Bill passed the first reading on 23 June and entered into the second reading on 14 July (Lin 2012: 573). When the NHI Bill entered into the third reading, President Lee Teng-hui instructed that the Legislative Yuan should work around the clock to ensure the bill's passage (Wong 2004: 81).

'The Legislative Yuan worked for thirty hours straight between July 18 and 19' (Wong 2004: 188). During the process of article-by-article voting, the Legislative Yuan plunged into uncontrollable disorder (Lin 2002: 339). Protests regarding some specific issues of the reform bill led to cases of revolts among members of both the KMT and the DPP (Lin 2002: 339). Article 12 that stipulated mandatory participation in the NHI was unexpectedly rejected due to the last-minute decision taken by KMT legislators to join the DPP to oppose the Article (Lin 2002: 339; Yu *et al.* 2016: 87). Originally, the DPP was 'not really against the compulsory rule but only sought to disrupt the discussion about the NHI at that time' (Tang 1997: 93). But having KMT legislators join the DPP to vote against the compulsory component of the NHI led to the amendment of the Article that participation in the NHI should only be voluntary (Yu *et al.* 2016: 87). The spirit of providing medical protection for every citizen was totally lost (Yu *et al.* 2016: 87). In the midst of the clamor, the NHI Bill was swiftly passed on 19 July 1994 (Lin 2002: 339). 'There was an immediate public outcry' (Hill and Hwang 2005: 154). All labor organizations strongly protested that the passage of the NHI Bill without the requirement for compulsory coverage 'would inhibit access to medical care for the lower classes and widen the income gap between the rich and the poor' (Tang 1997: 93). After negotiations between the KMT and the DDP, both camps agreed to deal with the amendment of the NHI Act on a priority basis when a new session of the Legislative Yuan commenced (Yu *et al.* 2016: 87). In September 1994, the NHI Act was amended so that participation in the NHI became mandatory for every citizen (Son 2001: 50). But the price was that a 'sunset clause' requiring a review of the law after two years was included in the NHI Act (Hill and Hwang 2005: 154). The NHI was finally implemented at the beginning of March 1995.

The NHI was a product of nearly five years of planning efforts (1988–1993) and a two-year legislative marathon (Lu and Chiang 2011: 94). It was a political strategy used by the KMT to sustain its ruling legitimacy and compete with electoral pressure from the opposition (Tang 1997: 70; Wong 2003: 62). There are several reasons why the KMT succeeded in implementing the NHI within the constraints of democracy (Son 2001; Wong 2004; Yu *et al.* 2016). First, the KMT 'was in full control of the process of establishing the NHI' (Tang 1997: 100) and 'dominated the actual policy decision making process' (Wong 2005a: 58) under the strong political leadership of Lee Teng-hui. It 'ensured that the health policy network was small and exclusive' (Wong 2005a: 59) by only putting the CEPD NHI Task Force and the DoH Planning Committee in charge of the NHI planning process without societal and legislative inclusion (Wong 2005a: 59). It insulated the planning process so that 'societal groups and legislators were limited in their access to important policy information and data' (Wong 2004: 82). It only informed the general public of the reform process rather than soliciting societal opinions (Wong 2005a: 59). 'The complexity and newness of the bill' (Wong 2003: 63), the asymmetry of reform information, and expertise limited the ability of the general public or legislators to effectively carry on a political debate during the later legislative stage (Wong 2004, 2005a).

Second, the KMT 'was the major power resource in the legalization process because it held the most seats in the Legislative Yuan' (Tang 1997: 93). In the 1992 Legislative Yuan elections, the KMT won 53 percent of the popular vote and won 96 of the 161 seats (59.6 percent), including 73 seats in Regular Districts, 19 'non-regional' seats and four Overseas Taiwanese seats (International Committee for Human Rights in Taiwan 1993: 5). In the same election, the DPP won 31 percent of the popular vote and won 50 seats (31.1 percent) (International Committee for Human Rights in Taiwan 1993: 5). The KMT's sizable majority in the Legislative Yuan ensured the passage of the NHI Bill, with limited amendments (Fell 2012: 195).

Third, the DPP lacked cohesion due to internal factionalism (Copper 1989; Fulda 2002; Wong 2004) and power struggles (Fulda 2002). The party 'was plagued with factionalism from the start' (Copper 1989: 19) because it consisted of diverse support groups such as Taiwanese nationalists and politicians who believed in greatly differing political philosophies (Fulda 2002: 324–5). It included six different party factions: Centrist Faction, the pragmatic, moderate Formosa Faction, the activist New Tide Faction, Justice Alliance, Welfare State Alliance, and Taiwan Independence Alliance (Rigger 2001: 73). Factionalism not only damaged mutual trust among party members (Rigger 2001: 83) but also led to competition for party leadership (Fulda 2002: 326). The party 'lacked a strong and widely accepted leader' (Copper 1989: 19). The ongoing power struggle among different factions led to the selection of the four different party chairmen between 1986 and 1991 (Fulda 2002: 326). Faction leaders spent time and energy composing strategies for promoting their supporters' political careers rather than setting out the party's policy direction (Rigger 2001: 83). Hence, the DPP 'was in no position during the early 1990s to offer a tenable and cohesive alternative to the government's NHI proposal' (Wong 2004: 82).

Fourth, societal groups, including the medical profession and labor organizations, 'were organized along particularistic lines in the early 1990s, undermining intergroup operation' (Wong 2004: 82). The medical profession had serious conflicts of interest among themselves regarding the payment standard set for them (Tang 1997: 91). There were also conflicts between physician associations of the teaching hospitals and physician associations of the small local hospitals over competition for patients under the transferal process for the NHI (Tang 1997: 91–2). As a result, the medical profession 'failed to present a united front in fighting for their rights' (Tang 1997: 91). Within the labor movement, enduring conflicts among different labor organizations such as the Taiwan Labor Front and the Committee for Action on Labor Legislation inhibited the forma-tion of working-class coalitions that could influence the outcome of the NHI Law (Wong 2004: 82). Meanwhile, labor organizations failed to form coalitions with the medical profession because they continuously criticized the govern-ment for favoring the medical profession at the expense of workers (Tang 1997: 94). In sum, the highly fragmented societal groups failed to serve as a political counterweight to the governing regime during the NHI reform process (Wong 2004: 82).

Challenges to the National Health Insurance: the current situation

The NHI was implemented in March 1995. It is administered by the National Health Insurance Administration, which is under the Ministry of Health and Welfare. It is a universal scheme providing health coverage to all citizens based on egalitarian, financial self-sufficiency, and pay-as-you-go principles (National Health Insurance Administration 2017: 15–17). It has been gradually extended to cover new immigrant residents, foreign white-collar workers, overseas Chinese and foreign students, military personnel, and inmates at correctional facilities (National Health Insurance Administration 2017: 15). By June 2017, the NHI had covered about 23.8 million people.

The NHI is primarily funded by premiums paid collectively by enrollees, employers, central and local governments (Bureau of National Health Insur-ance 2010: 13). The premium rate was kept at 4.25 percent from the scheme that was implemented until the end of August 2002 (National Health Insur-ance Administration 2017: 21). It was then raised to 4.55 percent in Septem-ber 2002 and 5.17 percent in April 2010 (Bureau of National Health Insurance 2010: 13). In January 2013, the premium rate was lowered to 4.91 percent when the Second Generation NHI Reform introduced a new 2 percent sup-plementary premium charged on six sources of non-payroll income, including high bonuses, part-time income, income from professional practices, dividends, interest, and rental income (National Health Insurance Administration 2017). In January 2016, the premium rate was lowered to 4.69 percent and the supple-mentary premium rate was lowered to 1.91 percent (National Health Insurance Administration 2017: 21). To augment social solidarity, the government provides several financial assistance programs for those who are unable to pay premiums (e.g. members of low-income households, the unemployed, and those with a severe disability), including premium subsidies, relief loans, sponsorship refer-rals and installment payment plans (Bureau of National Health Insurance 2009: 31–2; National Health Insurance Administration 2016a, 2016b). Being a single-payer system, the NHI has a single risk pool and this 'enables cross-subsidization among diverse groups with not only different socioeconomic status but also different health status' (Cheng 2009: 1044).

The NHI provides a comprehensive and uniform benefit package covering some preventive services (e.g. pediatric and adult health examinations, prenatal checkup) (Bureau of National Health Insurance 2010: 17), inpatient, outpatient, and dental care, childbirth, traditional Chinese medicine, physical rehabilitation, chronic mental illness care, and home nursing care (National Health Insurance Administration 2017: 31). Patients can freely choose their providers and rarely face long waiting times for health care services (Cheng 2015: 503). They are required to pay a copayment for outpatient services, drugs, and inpatient care in order to promote prudent health spending and better utilization of healthcare services. 'A progressive copayment rate is applied to hospitalization according to the type of wards (acute or chronic) and length of stay' (Bureau of National Health Insurance 2010: 19). Patients who have a longer inpatient stay have higher copayments. But copayment exemption is given to children under the age of 3, centenarians, veterans, members of low-income households, outpatients, or emergency care patients from outlying islands, and those suffering from a catastrophic illness, or living and being treated in remote mountain areas (National Health Insurance Administration 2018a: 59–60). 'In short, the population covered by the NHI is well protected against uncertain large medical expenses' (Lu and Hsiao 2003: 81). In recent years, public satisfaction with the NHI has been over 80 percent (National Health Insurance Administration 2017: 79). Low premiums, free choice of providers, easy accessibility, virtually no waiting times, comprehensive benefits, and low copays explain high levels of public satisfaction (Cheng 2015: 507).

While the major achievements of the NHI have been praised and recognized by local and international communities, a major challenge needs to be addressed in order to maintain the success of the NHI. The major challenge facing the NHI is ensuring its financial sustainability in the long run. Medical expenditures have outstripped premium revenues for many years. From 1996 to 2008, for example, NHI revenues increased at an annual rate of 4.34 percent while medical expenditures increased at an annual rate of 5.34 percent (Department of Health, Executive Yuan n.d.). As of August 2009, there was an accumulated deficit of about NT$45 billion (Department of Health, Executive Yuan n.d.). In February 2012, the cumulative budget shortfall was shifted to a surplus after an increase in the premium rate in 2010 (National Health Insurance Administration 2018b: 25). As of June 2018, there was an accumulated surplus of NT$227.6 billion after the introduction of supplementary premiums in 2013 and an increase in the government's minimum contribution to premiums to at least 36 percent (National Health Insurance Administration 2018b: 25). However, the NHI had a shortfall of NT$9.8 billion in 2017 and NT$10 billion as of June 2018 (National Health Insurance Administration 2018b: 27). It will have a shortfall of NT$47.3 billion in 2021, according to the estimate made by Dr. Po-chang Lee, Director General of the National Health Insurance Administration (Lim 2018). While the financial status of the NHI is currently stable (National Health Insurance Administration 2018b: 21), the problems of an ageing population, insurance coverage for patients with catastrophic illnesses, the coverage of new drugs and new treatment items, and the waste of medical resources will continuously drive up medical expenditures and put financial pressure on the NHI system in the long run (Department of Health, Executive Yuan n.d.; Leong 2018).

According to Department of Health, Executive Yuan (n.d), medical expenses of the elderly are 3.3 times higher than that of the general population. In 2011, the elderly population aged 65 and over accounted for 11.2 percent of the total population in Taiwan, but they accounted for 33.5 percent of total healthcare costs (Lee 2013). In 2008, patients with catastrophic illnesses only accounted for 3.1 percent of the total population, but they accounted for 26.2 percent of total healthcare costs (Department of Health, Executive Yuan n.d.). The average per capita medical expenses of cancer patients, kidney dialysis patients, and hemophilia patients are, respectively, 5.3 times, 22 times, and 119.3 times higher than those of an individual (National Health Insurance Administration 2016c: 105).

The NHI has continuously been expanded to cover new drugs and new treatment items to reflect real clinical needs and technological progress, which escalates medical expenditures (Department of Health, Executive Yuan n.d.; National Health Insurance Administration 2018b). In 2007, for example, the NHI spent NT\$31.3 billion for 607 new drugs (Department of Health, Executive Yuan n.d.). 'As of June 2017, the fee schedule covered a total of 4,436 treatment items' (National Health Insurance Administration 2018b: 39). Huge waste of resources is caused by supplier-induced demand for medical services to increase the hospital's revenue and the doctor's pay when fee-for-service is the predominant payment method (Cheng 2003: 67–8; Cheng 2015: 508). Hospitals 'provide as much medical care as they could to compete for reimbursement within the fee-for-service mechanism under the global budget program' (Hu *et al.* 2015: 678). Besides, many hospitals use the professional fee system to compensate doctors based on the number of patients seen, procedures performed, and lab tests ordered (Cheng 2003: 68).

Meanwhile, '[t]he easy access that patients have to physicians drives up visit rates' (Cheng 2015: 508). Each patient averages 15 annual visits to the physician in Taiwan, compared with five annual visits in OECD countries (Leong 2018). The lack of a gatekeeper system also results in patients with mild illnesses consulting specialists at large hospitals and unnecessary or duplicated medical exams and drug prescriptions (Leong 2018). According to Dr. Po-chang Lee, Director General of the National Health Insurance Administration (NHIA), 20 percent of patients who underwent magnetic resonance imaging (MRI) or a computerized tomography (CT) scan never returned for the results and that such wastage costs NT\$1.7billion (Leong 2018). To reduce waste of medical resources, the government introduced the Taiwanese version of Diagnosis-Related Groups (Tw-DRGs) payment system in January 2010. Under this prospective payment system, 'hospitals are paid a fixed fee for treating patients in a single DRG category, regardless of the actual cost' (Hu *et al.* 2015: 679). A patient referral system was introduced in 2016 to encourage patients to first seek care at primary care-level clinics and hospitals (National Health Insurance Administration 2017: 33). If needed, they would be referred to another appropriate healthcare provider for further care (National Health Insurance Administration 2017). At present, patients without a referral are required to pay higher copayments, ranging from NT$30 to NT$250 (National Health Insurance Administration 2018b: 32). But such a copayment is fairly negligible to discourage patients from seeking outpatient treatment at large hospitals (Leong 2018).

In recent years, the government has made use of digital technologies such as cloud computing to address the problem of supply-induced demand. The Medi-Cloud system was introduced to 'enable healthcare providers to query patients' medical records within the NHI system' (Chen 2019). It can identify potentially fraudulent claims or raise an alert when a patient takes the same medical exam at two different hospitals (Rickards 2019). To avoid unnecessary medication, the NHI PharmaCloud system was introduced to enable various medical institutions contracted with the NHIA to view drugs prescribed to a patient over the previous three months (Rickards 2019). Through digital cloud tools, community-based primary care providers can receive prescription information and retrieve test reports (e.g. X-rays, MRIs, CT scans, ultrasounds, gastroscopies) from secondary and tertiary institutions (Chen 2019). The use of digital technologies can enhance the patient's experience by saving patients time and money and decreasing potential health risks arising from repeated examinations (National Health Insurance Administration 2018b: 57). Additionally, a "Central Intelligence System" was introduced to monitor medical claims through the integration of the medical information system and automated random checks (National Health Insurance Administration 2016c: 53). It 'automatically flags anomaly cases, which are then sent for professional review' (Rickards 2019). It has developed about 100 anomaly-screening indicators based on four dimensions, namely, NHI outpatient care, NHI inpatient care, NHI drugs, and NHI-specified diagnosis and treatment (National Health Insurance Administration 2016b: 47). To bolster the finances of the NHI, the government may have to institute third-generation reforms, although it has yet to have a formal discussion of a third-generation NHI system (Rickards 2019).

Conclusion

At present, Taiwan is an aged society. It will become a super-aged society by 2026, according to the National Development Council (Strong 2019). The government needs to implement third-generation reform or delivery and payment system reform to ensure the fiscal stability and sustainability of the NHI system so as to meet the growing healthcare needs of an ageing population.

7 The Republic of Korea

Integration reform

Introduction

This chapter examines the process of integration reform in the Republic of Korea (ROK). In 1989, the ROK achieved universal health coverage through a highly fragmented, occupational-segmented social health insurance system. But the health insurance system was plagued by the problems of insufficient risk and income pooling among the insured, serious inequality in premium contributions, and high out-of-pocket medical expenses. Changes in the political leadership and the 1997 Asian financial crisis created a window of opportunity to push forward the administrative and financial integration of all health insurance societies into a single-managed health insurer. President Kim Dae-jung, pro-integration officials in the Ministry of Health and Welfare (MHW), members of the Health Insurance Finance Committee, the Fees and Payment Systems Committee, the Executive Integration Committee, and the Health Solidarity Coalition were policy entrepreneurs in this reform. The alliance between President Kim and progressive labor and civic organizations helped enhance the legitimacy of the regime and win broader societal support for integration reform while the formation of a legislative coalition by President Kim ensured the passage of the integration reform bill in February 1999. But a series of anti-integration actions following the passage of the integration reform bill, and electoral concerns delayed the administrative and financial integration. The administrative integration was completed in July 2000, and the financial integration was completed in July 2003.

The current single-payer system has yet to solve the problems of high out-of-pocket expenses, high spending per capita, and a deterioration of quality care in the country. Low economic growth and a shrinking workforce also led to an increasing concern over the financial sustainability of the single-payer system. The government can consider developing a stronger community-based primary care system to lower healthcare costs.

Pre-reform era

Before the introduction of the National Health Insurance (NHI) reform in 2000, the ROK had a highly fragmented, occupational-segmented social health insurance system (Hwang 2006: 80; Nam 2015: 31). The government 'adopted an approach of pluralistic insurance societies when it extended health insurance incrementally, minimizing its own role in healthcare financing' (Kwon 2003: 76). Following the Korean War (1950–3), the ROK was one of the poorest countries in the world. 'Per-capita national income was a meager 1,000 US dollars' (Moon 2011: 223). 'Economic growth remained sluggish from 1953 to 1961, averaging only about 1 percent per year' (McGuire 2010: 205). The nation's shift from an agrarian workforce to an industrial one raised new concerns about workers' healthcare (Nam 2015: 31–2). In December 1963, the Health Insurance Act, as part of a plan for a series of five-year Economic Development Plans (Jo 2013: 396), was enacted to allow enterprises with over 300 employees to provide health insurance for their employees on a voluntary basis (Hwang 2006: 83). However, little was accomplished due to a very low participate rate (Yang 2002: 66). In 1976, the voluntary health insurance scheme only covered 0.46 percent of the population (Kim 2017: 52).

In 1977, the Second Health Insurance Amendment Act was enacted to mandate large enterprises with 500 or more employees to provide medical insurance for their employees and their dependents (Nam 2015: 32; Hwang 2006: 87). Large enterprises set up financially independent health insurance societies as the administrative organizations (Hwang 2006: 87; Lee 2003: 49) to collect and manage premiums and reimburse health service providers on the basis of fee-for-service (Nam 2015: 32). 'Each insurance society operated on the principle of self-supporting accounting systems' (Lee *et al.* 2017: 250), enjoying both administrative and financial autonomy (Chun *et al.* 2009: 140). The premium rate was set at 3.84 percent of the employee's salary (Nam 2015: 32). Employers and employees equally shared the premiums, (Nam 2015: 32) and 'the government bore only administrative costs' (Lee *et al.* 2017: 250). In 1979, the compulsory health insurance scheme was extended to cover medium-sized enterprises with more than 300 employees (Nam 2015: 32). In the 1980s, it was gradually extended to cover small-size enterprises: 100 or more in 1981; 16 or more in 1983; and five or more in 1988 (Jeong 2011: 137). Besides, coverage was also extended from employees' first-line dependents (e.g. spouses and children) to second-line dependents (e.g. parents-in-law) (Chun *et al.* 2009: 20). It shows that employment-based health insurance made smooth progress down the road of expansion (Moon 2011: 224).

In January 1988, the compulsory health insurance scheme was further extended to cover people in rural farming and fishery areas (Yang 2002: 66). Participants were mainly farmers and self-employed workers who had low and irregular incomes (Chung 1992: 332). Regional insurance societies were set up in cities and counties to collect and manage premiums from participants (Chung 1992: 332). They could exercise considerable discretion in determining the amount of premiums based on a flat-sum system consisting of two components: the basic rate component and the ability rate component (Chung 1992: 332). While the former 'was an equal contribution to the fund in proportion to the number in the household' (Chung 1992: 332), the latter 'was the payment in proportion of income and wealth' (Chung 1992: 332). Hence, the amount of premium contributions varied widely among regional insurance societies. In January 1989, the compulsory health insurance scheme was extended to cover self-employed workers in urban areas (Wong 2004: 71). The government 'subsidized from general revenues the health insurance societies for the self-employed to cover their administrative costs' (Hwang 2006: 94) and part of the contributions of the self-employed (Kwon 2015: 7).

In addition to the compulsory health insurance scheme for workers, a separate health insurance scheme was implemented to cover government employees and private school teachers in January 1979 (Chun *et al.* 2009: 20; Yang 2002: 66). This health insurance scheme was managed by an independent corporation, the Korean Medical Insurance Corporation (KMIC) (Nam 2015: 33). The government paid 50 percent of the premiums for its own employees and 20 percent of those for private school teachers (Hwang 2006: 94). In 1980, the health insurance scheme was expanded to cover military personnel and pensioners (Yang 2002: 66). In 1977, the Medical Aid Program, which was a public assistance program funded by general taxation and managed by local governments, was implemented to 'free medical services and the same benefits included within the NHI scheme' (Chun *et al.* 2009: 49) for the destitute such as the homeless elderly, the elderly poor, elderly people without supportive family members, and individuals whose income fell below the minimum standard of living (Nam 2015: 33; Yang 2002: 66). In 1989, universal health coverage was achieved in the ROK (Jeong 2011: 137) to provide health protection for enterprise employees and their dependents, government employees and private school teachers, and self-employed workers. As of 1997, the health insurance system covered 95.7 percent of the population while the Medical Aid Program covered the remaining population in the ROK (Yang 2002: 66).

There were both political and economic considerations behind the implementation of these insurance programs. Political legitimacy sought by the military and authoritarian regimes and rapid economic growth in the 1970s and 1980s contributed to the expansion of health insurance coverage (Kwon 2015: 5). Health insurance was implemented and then expanded to cover people with different employment statuses under the authoritarian regimes of Park Chung-hee (1963–1979) and Chun Doo-hwan (1980–1988) (Nahm 2014: 43). 'In the 1970s, the Park regime exercised a high degree of state autonomy and supreme state power' (Lee *et al.* 2017: 250). It 'overpowered all social forces, including capitalists, laborers, farmers, and doctors' (Lee *et al.* 2017: 250). The implementation of compulsory health insurance for company employees in 1977 was used by the Park regime as a means of boosting its political legitimacy (Nahm 2014: 43; Nam 2015: 32). The public was strongly discontent with the promulgation of a new Constitution in 1972 that increased President Park Chung-hee's authoritarian powers (Nam 2015: 32) and political oppression of democratic movements (Nahm 2014: 43). Meanwhile, the compulsory health insurance scheme was implemented to 'distribute the fruits of economic development to workers' (Kwon 2009: 64), 'stabilize the labor market by keeping skilled workers in the workforce' (Na and Kwon 2015: 10), and build a healthier and more productive workforce to facilitate industrialization and economic growth (Nahm 2014; Nam 2015).

In the 1980s, achieving universal health insurance coverage was an important political project for the Chun Doo-hwan regime (Hwang 2006: 89). President Chun Doo-hwan suffered from a legitimate deficit owing to his seizure of power in a military coup d'état (Barany 2012: 180). Socioeconomic inequality intensified worker protests (Wong 2004: 66). The Chun regime 'strongly suppressed the labor movement in the early 1980s, but the working class continually resisted and grew stronger through political struggle' (Lee *et al.* 2017: 251). Meanwhile, civic groups consisting of students, intellectuals, and democratic leaders challenged the military dictatorship and 'led public calls for a constitutional amendment allowing for direct presidential elections' (Lee *et al.* 2017: 251). In order to increase its political legitimacy, the Chun Doo-hwan regime established the Joint Commission for Medical Insurance, which laid a foundation for health insurance expansion (Wong 2004: 69). Subsequently, the idea of integrating all of the insurance funds was discussed among officials in the Ministry of Health and Social Affairs (MHSA) (Wong 2004: 69). However, such an idea was scrapped in 1982 due to opposition from business interests (Wong 2004: 69). Later, after the ruling Democratic Justice Party (DJP)'s debacle in the 1985 National Assembly elections, 'President Chun renewed his promise to initiate significant welfare reform, notably with the universalization of health insurance' (Wong 2004: 69). Nevertheless, the idea of expanding health insurance to self-employed workers came to no avail in 1986 (Wong 2004: 69).

In 1987, South Korea made a political transition to democracy. In December 1987, President Chun's hand-picked successor Roh Tae-woo (1988–1993) won the direct presidential election, though with just over one-third of the vote (Wong 2004: 68). President Roh immediately expanded health insurance to rural self-employed workers who represented a critical base of electoral support for the ruling party in the upcoming 1988 legislative elections (Wong 2004: 70–1). The government distributed health insurance cards to farmers and paid part of the premiums for the farmers (Wong 2004: 70–1). The expansion of the health insurance scheme covered approximately 6.7 million farmers and fishermen (Lee *et al.* 2017: 251).

After the 1988 legislative elections, President Roh expanded health insurance to urban self-employed workers because of opposition parties joining forces to push for the complete universalization of health insurance and grassroots movements in the cities (Wong 2004: 72). Meanwhile, the nation's booming economy with annual growth rates of about 12 percent between 1986 and 1988 improved the capacity of self-employed workers to pay premiums and the capacity of the government to subsidize health insurance for self-employed workers (Na and Kwon 2015:10–11). The expansion of the health insurance scheme covered approximately 12.6 million urban residents (Lee *et al.* 2017: 251). As a result, universal health insurance coverage (UHIC) was achieved in South Korea within 12 years (1977–1989) (Lee *et al.* 2017: 251; Moon 2011: 225).

The process of integration reform

The problem stream

The highly fragmented NHI system contained several problems. First, there was insufficient risk and income pooling among beneficiaries because 'many health insurance societies were too small in terms of the number of enrolees' (Kwon 2009: 67). As of December 1997, 373 health insurance societies were established on an occupational or a regional basis to independently manage contributions and finances (Nam 2015: 22; Yang 2002: 68). All of them 'provided the same statutory benefits package to enrollees and the same reimbursement to health-care providers' (Kwon 2015: 7). Multiple health insurance societies led to the creation of small, fragmented risk pools, which severely impeded income cross-subsidization between salaried workers and the self-employed, and between the healthy and the sick. The risk pools were small because a majority of health insurance societies covered only a small fraction of the population (Yang 2002: 68). In 1980, about 75 percent of health insurance societies pooled less than 3,000 members while only about 5 percent of health insurance societies pooled more than 10,000 members (Chun *et al.* 2009: 23). In 1997, over two-thirds of health insurance societies pooled less than 1,000 members (Nam 2015: 34).

The risk pools were also fragmented because there were over hundreds of enterprise-based and region-based funds in the nation (Nam 2015: 31). Health insurance societies did not compete to attract the insured because the insured were assigned to them based on employment or residential area (Kwon 2003: 77; Kwon and Reich 2005: 1005). The absence of competition did not provide any incentives for health insurance societies to merge so that their ability to pool risks could be enhanced (Kwon 2015: 9). In 1997, there were 145 health insurance societies managing the health insurance scheme for salaried workers, and 227 health insurance societies managing the health insurance scheme for the self-employed (Nam 2015: 22). Only the health insurance scheme for government and school employees had a single insurance fund, covering 4.6 million enrollees in 1990 (Wong 2004: 88). In sum, the principle of social solidarity was undermined due to structural decentralization in the organization of health insurance (Wong 2004: 88). Multiple health insurance societies also led to inefficiencies, both in management and in healthcare expenditures (Chun *et al.* 2009: 21).

The small, fragmented risk pools endangered the financial stability and sustainability of health insurance funds over time. Often, health insurance societies with a poor fiscal base faced higher expenditures because of having a greater proportion of sick and high-risk enrollees (Organization for Economic Co-operation and Development 2003: 70). From 1997, 'the total expenditure[s] of all health funds began to exceed the total revenue, causing a serious financial deficit' (Hwang 2008: 429). About one-third of the health insurance societies reported financial deficit, with some facing imminent insolvency (Nam 2015: 34–5). There were two main causes of this financial deficit. The first was the rapid increase in healthcare expenditures driven by a privately dominated healthcare system. Total health expenditures per capita drastically rose from US$401 in 1990 to US$870 in 1997 (Huber 1999: 104). Since healthcare providers were reimbursed by a regulated fee-for-service system, they had incentives to increase the volume and intensity of services and choose treatments with a greater profit (Kwon 2007: 166). The second was 'the outbreak of the [1997] economic crisis, which made a huge number of people redundant' (Hwang 2008: 429). 'The official unemployment rate reached 8.1 percent in March 1998, and the number of the unemployed exceeded well over 1.7 million' (Choi and Chung 2002: 5). Massive layoffs led to severe financial instability of health insurance funds. Meanwhile, managing the small, fragmented risk pools involved very high administrative costs. Many health insurance societies did not achieve economies of scale in management (Kwon 2015: 9). The proportion of administrative costs in the total expenditure was 9.5 percent in the health insurance scheme for the self-employed, while the proportion of the administrative cost in total expense was only 4.8 percent in the health insurance scheme for government and school employees (Na and Kwon 2015: 13). These figures indicated a high degree of inefficiency compared to 1.5 percent in Canada and 2.6 percent in the United Kingdom (Yang 1996: 234).

Second, there was serious inequality in premium contributions between the self-employed and regular workers and among regular workers due to the absence of equalization payment among different health insurance societies (Wong 2005b). Since health insurance societies functioned as quasi-autonomous bodies, they could use different methods to set their own premium contribution rates (Wong 2004: 89). While they only used income to set the contributions of regular workers, they used income, property, and the number of dependents to set the contributions of the self-employed (Kwon 2003: 80; Kwon and Reich 2005: 106). This led to the self-employed paying higher contributions than regulated workers. For example, estimates calculated by the MHW in 1998 indicated that 'the average contribution of a self-employed worker was about 30 percent higher than that of a regular worker' (Nam 2015: 36–7). Inequalities also existed among regular workers because health insurance societies were given considerable discretion in defining workers' earnings for contribution liability (the contribution base) (Kwon 2003: 80). While some health insurance societies used monthly wages as the only basis for the contributions of regular workers, some used overall compensation that included both monthly wages and annual bonuses as the basis for the contributions of regular workers (Nam 2015: 36). The lack of standardization led to horizontal inequity (Nam 2015: 36). Workers with similar earnings paid different contributions, depending on which health insurance societies in which they were enrolled (Kwon 2003: 80), 'while benefits for them were similar' (Hwang 2006: 101). Meanwhile, inequalities were reinforced by the small, fragmented risk pools. While health insurance societies of large enterprises pooled contributions from higher-income workers, regional health insurance societies pooled contributions from the self-employed (Nam 2015). It failed to redistribute income between higher-income workers and the self-employed so that inequality remained high in the health insurance system.

Third, there was the problem of high out-of-pocket medical expenses. This was mainly caused by low contributions and supplier-induced demand (SID). The government adopted a policy of low contributions and low benefits in order to first achieve universal coverage (Chun *et al.* 2009: 150; Jeong 2011: 137). The average contribution rate until 2000 was 5.6 percent of wage income for government and school employees and 3.75 percent for industrial workers (Kwon 2009: 65). 'Consequently, many services that were necessary for the treatment of certain diseases were excluded from coverage' (Chun *et al.* 2009: 150). The NHI mainly covered diagnosis, outpatient and inpatient treatment, most prescription pharmaceuticals, and dental care (Chun *et al.* 2009: 50). Although the NHI later also covered some high-technology services such as computed tomography (CT) scans (Chun *et al.* 2009: 49–50) and extended the number of days allowed for treatment from 180 in 1994 to 365 in 2000 (Jeong 2011: 137), its coverage was not comprehensive. Due to low contributions, the insured were required to pay out of pocket for insurance-covered services, including 20 percent of inpatient expenses, 30 percent of clinic outpatient expenses, and 55 percent of general hospital outpatient charges (Yang 2002: 68).

For uninsured services, the insured were required to pay the full cost out of pocket. Uninsured services were usually new or expensive high-technology medical services such as magnetic resonance imaging (MRI) and ultrasonography (Yang 2002: 68). Since uninsured services fell outside the state-regulated fee schedule, healthcare providers enjoyed free reign in setting market prices for uninsured services (Wong 2004: 88). In the ROK, private healthcare providers, including private hospitals and clinics, accounted for over 90 percent of the total number of medical institutions (Jeong 2011: 136). They had financial incentives to provide more uninsured services, mainly new technology (Kwon 2009: 66). 'A significant jump in the rate of technology adoption is observed in 1989 and 1990, when the NHI was fully implemented' (Yang 1996: 242). The rapid adoption of advanced medical technology resulted in the ROK having more MRI machines per million population than Western countries, including France, Germany, and Canada, and more lithotripsy machines per million population than the United States, France, Germany, and Canada (Yang 1996: 243). This led to the insured having high out-of-pocket payments.

In the 1980s, out-of-pocket expenditures 'averaged 55 percent of total health expenditures' (Nam 2015: 39). They accounted for 58.2 percent of total health expenditures in 1990 and 54.5 percent of total health expenditures in 1995 (Chun *et al.* 2009: 45). In 2000, out-of-pocket expenditures accounted for about 46 percent of total health expenditures (Nam 2015: 19). Although the percentage of out-of-pocket payments had decreased in the ROK over time, the ROK still reported the highest share of out-of-pocket medical expenditure across Organization for Economic Co-operation and Development (OECD) countries (Huber 1999: 113; Yang 2002: 70; Organization for Economic Co-operation and Development 2016). The NHI system, characterized by low contributions, limited benefit coverage, and high cost-sharing by patients (Hwang 2006: 101) failed to alleviate the financial burden of the insured and provide financial security for them, especially those who suffered from catastrophic illnesses (Chun *et al.* 2009: 151). There was a pressing need to reform the NHI.

The policy stream

One way to solve the problems of high out-of-pocket expenses and health insurance fund deficit was raising contributions (Hwang 2006: 102). However, this was obviously an unpopular solution because of the poor economic condition after the 1997 Asian financial crisis. Raising contributions would only increase both the financial and psychological burdens of the insured because many of them faced salary freezes while some faced the risk of becoming unemployed (Hwang 2006: 103). In 1998, nominal wages and real wages, respectively, dropped by 8.1 percent and by 14.2 percent in the ROK (Ahn 2009: 236). There was a hollowing out of the middle class due to wage cuts, job losses, and asset deflation (Yang 2017: 128). There was also the problem of growing poverty, with the headcount urban poverty index rising drastically from 9.6 in 1996 to 19.2 in 1998 (Yang 2017: 128). Raising contributions only increased the economic hardship of the general public.

Another suggested solution that became central to policy debates was to integrate the decentralized, multiple health societies into a single publicly administered insurance carrier (Wong 2004: 89–90). But the integration debate was nothing new in the nation. The first integration debate began in September 1980 when Minister for Health and Social Affairs Chun Myung-Kee publicly announced the intention of the MHSA to integrate the entire medical insurance system after the MHSA had merged several small insurance societies to increase the risk-pooling and redistributive effects of health insurance (Wong 2004: 90–1). However, opposition from business organizations, the National Association of Medical Insurance Societies, the Federation of Korean Industries and the Office of the President made it politically costly for President Chun Doo-hwan to endorse such a radical change (Wong 2004: 92; Chun *et al.* 2009: 141–2). Consequently, President Chun rejected the MHSA's reform proposal in 1982 (Wong 2004: 92) and dismissed the minister and several high-ranking bureaucrats in the MHSA in 1983 (Hwang 2006: 105; Yang 2017: 102). The MHSA 'was restaffed with bureaucrats who were either opposed to or neutral about the integration reform' (Wong 2004: 92).

The second integration debate began in 1988 when there were nationwide farmers' protests against high-premium contributions (Yang 2017: 104). In June 1988, a broader alliance known as the National Committee for Medical Insurance Integration (NCMII) was formed to call for the integration of all health insurance societies (Wong 2004; Yang 2017). The NCMII consisted of 48 social movement groups, including farmers' associations, urban poor organizations, religious groups, social security professionals, the Association of Physicians for Humanism, and the Korean Pharmacists for Democratic Society (Nam 2015: 141; Wong 2004: 93; Yang 2017: 104). It drafted an integration reform bill and pressured legislators in the opposition parties to support the bill (Nam 2015: 141).

In 1989, three main opposition parties – the Reunification and Democracy Party (RDP), the Party for Peace and Democracy (PPD), and the New Democratic Republican Party (NDRP) – lined up to support the bill (Nam 2015: 141–2). In March 1989, the National Assembly, where opposition parties held the majority, passed the integration reform bill (Wong 2004: 93; Yang 2017: 104). Nevertheless, President Roh Tae-woo vetoed the new law by claiming that the new law violated private property laws (Wong 2004: 93). The idea was that the government had no legal claims to health insurance funds, which were considered as the private property of health insurance societies held in trust for enrollees (Wong 2004: 93; Yang 2017: 104–5). The presidential veto brought to a decisive close the integration debate (Nam 2015: 143).

In the early 1990s, the cross-class coalition among workers, farmers, and civic activists proposed integration reform (Kim 2017: 116–17), but it failed to have any impact. 'President Kim Young-sam, who took office in 1993, was the ROK first civilian president in three decades (Ahn 2001: 457–8). His ruling Democratic Liberal Party (DLP), which merged the DJP, RDP, and NDRP, 'controlled three-quarters of the National Assembly's seats' (Wong 2004: 94), so that gave the 'coalition little room to motivate opposition legislators into challenging the ruling party's position' (Nam 2015: 149). But the disintegration of the DLP in late 1995, the corruption scandals surrounding Kim's immediate family, and the economic downturn weakened Kim's presidential power and legitimacy (Nam 2015: 149). In November 1996, two opposition parties – Kim Dae-jung's National Congress for New Politics (NCNP) and Kim Jong-pil's United Liberal Democratic Party (ULD) – joined forces to propose an insurance integration bill that largely replicated the one drafted by the NCMII in 1989 (Nam 2015: 152). 'Their proreform stance compelled ruling party legislators, particularly those dependent upon rural constituents, to respond' (Nam 2015: 152).

When approaching the 1997 presidential election, ruling party legislator Hwang Seong-gun, representing a rural electoral district (Wong 2004: 97), proposed a partial integration reform bill which called for the administrative consolidation of 227 regional self-employed health insurance societies with the KMIC, the unit that managed insurance funds for government employees and private school teachers (Nam 2015: 152). The partial integration reform faced little opposition because it mainly dealt with the operating inefficiencies of the self-employed insurers without touching upon contentious issues such as the financial consolidation of all of the insurance societies (Nam 2015: 152). Most of the ruling party legislators from rural constituencies supported Hwang's proposal (Kim 2017: 132). Business organizations were not opposed to the bill because the bill did not affect the enterprise-based health insurance societies (Wong 2004: 97; Kim 2017: 133). With votes from ruling party legislators and opposition party legislators, the Medical Insurance Act was passed in November 1997, just one month before the presidential election (Nam 2015: 152). In October 1998, 227 regional self-employed health insurance societies and the KMIC were integrated into a new authority known as the National Health Insurance Corporation (NHIC) (Hwang 2006: 104; Yang 2017: 143). The partial integration reform paved the way for the complete administrative and financial integration of all health insurance societies into a single, state-managed health insurer during the Kim Dae-jung era.

The political stream

The year 1997 marked a new milestone in the ROK's party politics because there was a genuine transfer of power between the ruling New Korea Party (formerly the DLP) and the opposition NCNP for the first time in the ROK's 50-year constitutional history (Lew 2006: 10). Kim Dae-jung, who was the opposition leader of NCNP, was elected president by winning 40.3 percent of the votes (Lew 2006: 10). President Kim had a strong political will to implement the integration reform. 'His opposition party career since the late 1960s made him a figure symbolic of support for democracy and human rights' (Lee 2016: 117). He was 'a proponent of greater equity and equality in the interests of social solidarity' (Hwang 2006: 104). During President Kim Young-sam's period, Kim Dae-jung, being the leader of the opposition NCNP, favored the integration reform and proposed an integration bill together with the ULD in 1996. He proposed the integration of all health insurance societies into a single insurer system as part of his campaign platform during the presidential election (Wong 2004: 97; Chun *et al.* 2009: 143).

In December 1997, amidst the Asian financial crisis, Kim Dae-jung was elected to the presidency (Kwon 2007: 157). Carrying out chaebol and financial restructuring that was required as a condition for emergency loans from the International Monetary Fund (IMF) became the Kim Dae-jung government's major task (Hundt 2009: 113). In early 1998, President Kim convened the Tripartite Commission that brought together representatives from government, the Korean Federation of Business, and two hostile national trade unions – the Federation of Korean Trade Unions (FKTU) and the Korean Confederation of Trade Unions – representing diverse views of labor to push through economic reform with social consensus (Kwon 2001: 219, 2007: 157–8). He believed that the Tripartite Commission could provide a foundation for political stability and overcoming the economic crisis by reaching a grand compromise through dialogue (Shin 2003: 189–90). The establishment of the Tripartite Commission represented a significant breakaway from the symbiotic alliance between government and business (Chun *et al.* 2009: 29; Shin 2003: 189) and 'marked the official inclusion of Korean labor organizations in politics' (Kim 2005: 385).

Under this new institutional setting, 'the three parties negotiated the Tripartite Agreement for Fair Burden Sharing' (Hundt 2009: 108) to increase the flexibility of the labor market. There were intense debates and confrontations among the three parties. But the bargaining position of business in the Tripartite Commission was weakened by its precarious financial situation, and hence it became more willing to concede some of the demands from trade unions in return for measures that could reduce their operating costs (Nam 2015: 158). After a series of 23 meetings, the Tripartite Commission announced the nation's first Social Pact (Nam 2015: 158), the contents of which reflected concessions made by both trade unions and businesses (Bridges 2001: 45). Trade unions accepted the legalization of extensive corporate layoffs in the case of 'emergency managerial needs' such as sell-offs and mergers in return for the expansion of labor rights and the entitlement of unemployment benefits (Bridges 2001: 45). They 'were allowed to engage in political activities and public workers and teachers were for the first time allowed to unionize' (Bridges 2001: 45). A special 6 trillion won unemployment fund was established (Bridges 2001: 45). Unemployed workers 'could receive unemployment benefits for at least 60 days at a rate of at least 70 percent of the minimum wage' (Bridges 2001: 45). Meanwhile, corporations had to make every available attempt to avoid layoffs and increase the transparency of operations (Bridges 2001: 45).

The Tripartite Commission also agreed to legislate for the full integration of health insurance societies by the end of 1998 (Chun *et al.* 2009: 143), which became one of the 100 major reform measures to be pursued by the Kim Dae-jung government (Shin 2003; Chun *et al.* 2009; Yang 2017). This was due to the fact that the Asian financial crisis of 1997 led to a growing demand for a more redistributive health insurance system (Shin 2003: 191–2). The financial crisis affected broad sections of society irrespective of social class, wage group, and region (Wong 2005b: 105), thereby heightening the timeliness and relevance of a redistributive healthcare insurance system (Nam 2015: 156). Hence, President Kim made use of this window of opportunity to push forward the integration reform with a broad base of support from both blue- and white-collar workers (Wong 2004: 97).

Traditionally, health policy in the ROK 'was characterized by the dominant role of bureaucrats and a top-down policy process' (Kwon and Reich 2005: 1014). Major health insurance policy decisions were in the hands of the MHW (Chun *et al.* 2009: 33). President Kim facilitated the drafting of a new integration reform bill by shuffling the MHW. Anti-integration reform officials were demoted or shuffled out of the MHW while pro-integration reform officials were appointed to key positions in the MHW. In early 1998, influential anti-integration reform officials Moon Kyung-tae and Yun Sung-tae were shuffled out of the MHW (Wong 2004: 192). In 1999, Kim Jong-dae, who was a 27-year veteran in the MHW and a staunch critic of integration reform, was demoted and then excused from the MHW (Wong 2004: 103). Cha Heung-bong, who was dismissed by then President Chun for supporting integration reform in the early 1980s, became the Minister for Health and Welfare (Hwang 2006: 104–5; Yang 2017). He 'pushed forward with the integration on the conviction that social policy should be something integrating the entire society' (Yang 2017: 144). President Kim's ally Lee Sang-yong was appointed head of the health insurance division in the MHW (Wong 2005a: 97). The MHW received strong political backing from the presidential Blue House (Wong 2004: 103).

President Kim also facilitated the drafting of the integration reform bill by establishing new committees. The Health Insurance Finance Committee and the Fees and Payment Systems Committees were established to review health insurance policy and draft the plan for insurance integration (Nam 2015: 155).

The Executive Integration Committee was also established within the MHW as 'the principal body in charge of implementing the integration reform' (Wong 2004: 102). The president of the Korean Institute of Health and Social Affairs (KIHASA), which was the unofficial think tank of the MHS, served as the chairman of the Executive Integration Committee (Wong 2004: 103). The alliance between President Kim and progressive labor and civic organizations to enhance the legitimacy of the regime (Kim 2005: 385–6) led to the invitation of social movement actors to serve on the Executive Integration Committee. These social movement actors were advocates of the integration reform and had rich expertise in health insurance integration. For example, both Kim Yong-ik and Yang Bong-min were professors from Seoul National University (Wong 2004: 101). While Professor Kim was one of the leaders in the Health Solidarity Coalition, Professor Yang was a standing member of the central policy research committee of the Citizen's Coalition for Economic Justice (CCEJ) (Wong 2004: 101).

The Health Solidarity Coalition was 'a key ally in the reform coalition assembled by President Kim' (Wong 2004: 99). It was originally named the National Solidarity Alliance, which was formed by 80 social movement groups in 1994 to seek the integration of health insurance and helped Kim Dae-jung's NCNP draft the insurance integration bill in 1996 (Wong 2004: 99). It unified disparate social activist networks and pooled together expert resources to facilitate the sharing of ideas and technical skills and strengthen its position vis-à-vis policymakers (Wong 2005b: 104). The CCEJ was the first civic organization founded in 1989 to pursue social reform in the nation (The Hankyoreh 2009) and was considered to be the most trustworthy and influential civic group in policy matters (Wong 2005b: 101). Labor movement leader Huh Young-gu also served on the Executive Integration Committee to provide useful advice on integration reform (Wong 2004, 2005b). The inclusion of social movement actors in the reform process was conducive to winning broader societal support for integration reform because 'they were seen as better able to speak up for citizens' concerns and desires' (Yang 2017: 131). In August 1998, the MHW introduced the integration reform bill to the National Assembly (Wong 2004: 98). The bill was immediately tabled to the Health and Welfare Committee (HWC) of the National Assembly in August 1998 (Wong 2004: 104).

In the ROK, most legislative decisions are de facto made in committee (Wong 2004: 104). Legislators who lack time and expertise to fully comprehend all the bills 'rely heavily on the outcomes of committee deliberations to inform their votes on the floor' (Wong 2004: 105). Partisan politics determined the HWC's decision to endorse the bill. The HWC had 16 members. Eight of them were from the ruling NCNP-ULD coalition while the remaining members were from the opposite Grand National Party (GNP) (formerly the ruling New Korea Party). Without an official party line, some GNP members, such as Hwang Seong-gun and Kim Hong-shin, fully supported the integration reform bill, while others were against the bill (Wong 2004: 98). Nevertheless, opponents of the bill remained silent during committee discussions for fear of alienating the GNP's electoral support among farmers, workers, and middle-class civic groups (Wong 2004: 98).

After four months of deliberations, the HWC in December 1998 endorsed the bill, which proposed the complete administrative and financial integration of all health insurance societies into a single, state-managed insurer (Nam 2015: 160). The administrative integration was to be completed by December 1999; the full financial integration was to be completed by December 2001 (Nam 2015: 160).

Before the bill was introduced on the floor of the legislature, the Legislative and Judiciary Committee of the National Assembly raised objections to integrating the funds of the self-employed with those of enterprises' health insurance societies because this potentially violated the latter's property rights (Nam 2015: 160). However, it failed to address the issue because the opposite GNP boycotted the National Assembly in a protest over the National Intelligence Service's intervention in parliamentary affairs (Nam 2015: 160). 'In a move that was to raise subsequent questions about procedural regularity' (Nam 2015: 160), the Assembly's speaker referred the bill to the plenary session anyway without the agreement of the Legislative and Judiciary Committee (Chun *et al.* 2009: 144). To ensure the passage of the bill, President Kim used his institutionally derived power as party leader to impose strict party discipline on ruling party legislators throughout the legislative process (Wong 2004: 106). His power to nominate electoral candidates ensured ruling party legislators' loyalty to him and their support for the integration reform bill (Wong 2004: 106–7).

Besides, President Kim formed a legislative coalition to ensure the passage of the integration reform bill in the National Assembly. Since his ruling NCNP got only 79 of the 299 seats (26 percent) in the legislature, President Kim cobbled together a legislative majority through forming an ad hoc alliance with the conservative ULD that held 50 seats in the legislature and embarking upon an aggressive campaign to woo legislators from the opposite GNP that held the largest number of seats (139 seats) in the legislature (Wong 2004, 2005b; Nam 2015). As a result, he succeeded in controlling 153 seats in the legislature (Wong 2005b: 97).

President Kim also benefitted from the help of his key ally, the Health Solidarity Coalition, which drew upon its organizational skills to raise public awareness and understanding of the benefits of integration reform and pressure legislators to support the reform through a thorough public advocacy campaign in late 1998 (Nam 2015: 159). This encompassed distributing pamphlets, writing editorials, making guest appearances on radio and television talk shows, putting together public panels, and organizing rallies to remind the GNP leader of his campaign pledge to support integration reform (Nam 2015: 159). In early January 1999, the National Assembly swiftly passed the integration reform bill known as the National Health Insurance Administration (NHIA). The NHIA came into force in February 1999.

Nevertheless, the passage of the NHIA did not lead to a smooth implementation of integration reform. In late February 1999, the opposite GNP cited that procedural oversight had rendered the passage of the NHIA illegal and submitted an amendment to the NHIA, which proposed delaying the administrative integration of health insurance societies for two years and repealing the financial integration (Nam 2015: 161). Meanwhile, the FKTU, which was an important base of support for President Kim and initially supported the integration reform during the Tripartite Commission negotiations, used various means to oppose the financial integration of health insurance societies after the unions of large enterprise insurance societies became affiliated with it (Nam 2015: 161–3). The FKTU asserted that the problem of self-employed workers underreporting their incomes led to many higher-income self-employed workers such as doctors and lawyers paying less in premiums (Wong 2004: 108). If this problem remained unsolved, whatever redistribution the integration accomplished would come at the expense of employees of medium and large enterprises (Nam 2015: 162) and would inhibit integration reform from achieving greater socioeconomic equity (Wong 2004: 107–8).

The FKTU formed alliances with employers to challenge integration reform in high courts, claiming that the financial integration of health insurance societies violated private property laws (Wong 2004: 108). In May 1999, the FKTU was allied with some workplace councils that governed medium-sized enterprises to form a coalition known as the National Citizens' Response to Reform (NCRR) (Nam 2015: 161). The NCRR initiated a signature campaign in July 1999 to request that the government delay integration reform (Wong 2004; Nam 2015). It also asked policyholders to oppose integration reform by refusing to pay their premiums (Nam 2015: 162). The NCRR demanded that the financial integration should be postponed until the government could find ways to enforce transparent income reporting and accurately assess the income of self-employed workers (Hwang 2006: 105; Nam 2015: 162).

Facing a series of anti-integration reform actions, President Kim and his administration worried that a poorly implemented integration would undermine government competence in the eyes of the general public and affect the April 2000 general election results (Nam 2015: 162–3). Accordingly, the Kim administration suggested postponing the administrative integration until after the April 2000 general elections and the financial integration for another two years (Nam 2015: 163). In September 1999, the MHW proposed an amendment of the NHIA to the National Assembly (Chun *et al.* 2009). In December 1999, the NHIA was revised to postpone the administrative integration of health insurance societies until July 2000 and the financial integration until January 2002 (Yang 2017: 145).

In June 2000, the Supreme Court decided in favor of integration reform, ruling that integrating the reserve funds of different health insurance societies did not violate private property laws (Wong 2004: 193). In July 2000, the administrative integration was implemented as scheduled (Chun *et al.* 2009: 144). All health insurance societies were merged into a single health insurer, the NHIC. But insurance funds for enterprise employees and self-employed workers remained separated from each other. Since the GNP was still opposed to the financial integration and the government had difficulty in developing a single criterion to set the premium rate (Chun *et al.* 2009: 144), both parties agreed to postpone the financial integration for a year and a half (Kim 2017: 141). In January 2002, the

Special Act for the Financial Stability of National Health Insurance was passed to extend the duration of the two-tiered insurance fund until 30 June 2003 (Kim 2017: 141). In December 2002, the ruling party candidate, Roh Moo-hyun, won the presidential election (Chun *et al.* 2009). The financial integration was finally completed in July 2003.

Advantages of the single-payer system

'With integration, the multiple health insurance funds were transformed into a single-payer system' (Chun *et al.* 2009: 24). The National Health Insurance Service (NHIS) is the single insurer responsible for operating and managing the NHI (National Health Insurance Service 2014). The NHI is a compulsory social insurance scheme primarily funded by contributions from employers, employees, and the self-employed. 'NHI contributions are levied on the basis of ability to pay' (Chun *et al.* 2009: 53). For employees, their premiums 'are proportional to wage income and shared equally between the employee and employer' (Kwon *et al.* 2015: 38). For the self-employed, their premiums are calculated based on income, the value of property (e.g. house, vehicle) and other factors (e.g. age, gender) (Kwon *et al.* 2015; Song 2009). The NHI is also funded by government subsidies. Government subsidies consist of general tax and tobacco surcharges (National Health Insurance Service 2015: 25). In 2014, 82 percent of the NHI revenues came from premium contributions, with the rest coming from government subsidies (National Health Insurance Service 2015: 25). In 2015, the NHI covered 97 percent of the population, with the rest being covered by the Medical Aid Program (National Health Insurance Service 2015: 24).

All of the insured have access to a uniform NHI benefit package. 'The benefits are granted both in-kind or in cash' (Song *et al.* 2014: 397). In-kind benefits include preventive care, dental care, diagnoses, treatments, drugs, medical materials, tests, surgery, hospitalization, rehabilitation, nursing, and transfer services (National Health Insurance Service 2015: 35). They also include health checkups such as the cancer screening program (National Health Insurance Service 2015: 35). Cash benefits are only available for refunding medical expenses spent on home oxygen therapy, peritoneal dialysis, and childbirth at a place other than a medical institution; refunding copayments exceeding 1.2–5 million won per year; and equipment purchases (e.g. wheelchair, hearing aids, canes) for the registered disabled (National Health Insurance Service 2015: 36). 'The pricing of services in the benefits package is negotiated annually between the NHIS and provider associations' (Kwon *et al.* 2015: 40). 'Health care providers in both inpatient and outpatient settings are mainly reimbursed on a fee-for-service basis' (Kim and Cheng 2018: 1223). About 90 percent of them are in the private sector (Kwon *et al.* 2015: 35).

The copay is applied at providers where the insured individual receives outpatient and inpatient care in order to increase his/her cost-consciousness toward the use of medical services. A 30 percent to 60 percent copayment is required for outpatient care, depending on the level of healthcare provider. The copayment rate for outpatient services is lower at clinics than at hospitals. A 5 percent to 20 percent copayment is required for inpatient care, depending on the types of diseases. The copayment rate for inpatients with rare or serious diseases is lower than the copayment rate for inpatients with general diseases. Meanwhile, copayment ceilings are set by income levels to avoid excessive financial burden on the insured due to catastrophic illnesses (National Health Insurance Service 2015: 38). Those covered by the Medical Aid Program are exempted from copayment at the point of service (Kwon *et al.* 2015: 42). Full payment is required for uncovered services on an out-of-pocket basis by those who can afford them (Kwon *et al.* 2015: 35).

Transforming a multiple payer system into a single-payer system has several advantages. First, it improves management efficiency and reduces administrative costs (National Health Insurance Service 2015: 20). Administrative costs decreased from 8.8 percent of total NHI expenditures in 1999 to 7.3 percent in 2000 and 4 percent in 2006 (Organization for Economic Co-operation and Development 2003: 73; National Health Insurance Service 2015: 20). Administrative integration led to heavy dismissals. By July 2000, the number of staff had been reduced by 4,320, which accounted for about 29 percent of the NHI staff (Organization for Economic Co-operation and Development 2003: 73). But laid-off staff were then absorbed into the National Pension Service (Organization for Economic Co-operation and Development 2003: 73). Second, it greatly improves the efficiency of risk pooling when risk is spread across a large number of individuals (Organization for Economic Co-operation and Development 2003: 73). Third, it improves equity in premium contributions. Horizontal equity is achieved for both employees and the self-employed because 'a uniform method for levying contribution is now applied nation-wide' (Organization for Economic Co-operation and Development 2003: 71). For employees, the contribution base is standardized on overall compensation (Organization for Economic Co-operation and Development 2003: 71). The contribution rate was first fixed at 3.63 percent (Organization for Economic Co-operation and Development 2003: 71) but has increased every year since 2005, except in 2009 and 2017 (Korea Herald 2017). It was set at 6.24 percent in 2018 (Yonhap News Agency 2018). For the self-employed, a single-payer system increases equity in contributions to health insurance due to the adoption of a uniform nationwide contribution formula (Kwon 2015: 15). Fourth, it improves income transfer effects (Moon 2012: S4). Income redistribution is achieved because wealthier individuals experience an increase in premium contributions, while lower-wage individuals experience a decrease in premium contributions (Organization for Economic Co-operation and Development 2003: 71). Official statistics showed that about 62 percent of households nationwide experienced a decrease in monthly contributions by 4,574 won on average after the reform, while the rest of households experienced an increase in contributions by 6,749 won on average (Kwon 2015: 15). Fifth, a single insurer has greater bargaining power relative to healthcare providers due to its monopsony power (Kwon 2015: 14). For example, there is rapid improvement in the technical and bargaining capacity of the NHIS with respect to pharmaceuticals after its introduction of the policy of positive listing of medicines based on economic evaluation in 2006 (Kwon 2015: 18).

Challenges to the current single-payer system

However, a single-payer system has yet to address the problems of high out-of-pocket expenses, high spending per capita, and a deterioration of the quality of care in the country. Out-of-pocket expenses remain high in the ROK. According to OECD Health Statistics 2015, the share of out-of-pocket expenses accounted for 37 percent of health spending in the ROK, which was second only to Mexico (45 percent) among OECD countries and was twice the overall OECD average (19.5 percent) (Organization for Economic Co-operation and Development 2015: 2). A major reason for high out-of-pocket expenses is that 'providers are inclined to substitute services that are not covered for those that are, in order to increase their revenue' (Jeong 2011: 143). High out-of-pocket medical expenses can weaken an individual's purchasing power and cut his/her expenses on basic household items. It can even contribute to the impoverishment of households (Kwon *et al.* 2015: 41). A study showed that unemployed households in the ROK were 2.8 times more likely to experience catastrophic health expenditure (CHE) (Choi *et al.* 2016), which is defined as 'out-of-pocket spending for health care that exceeds a certain proportion of a household's income' (Li *et al.* 2012: 664). The inability to pay medical expenses 'results in poor health if treatment for diseases is not received at appropriate times' (Choi *et al.* 2016).

Since 2002, health spending per capita in the ROK has already been growing at about 8 percent a year, which is the fastest among OECD countries and more than double the OECD average of 3.6 percent a year over the same period (Organization for Economic Co-operation and Development 2012: 9). But more health spending does not necessarily lead to a higher quality of care (Organization for Economic Co-operation and Development 2012: 6–7). In the ROK, quality of care deteriorates due to 'a weak primary care system and gatekeeping mechanism' (Kim and Cheng 2018: 1223), an over-continuing expansion of acute services and the incentives for over-provision of hospital services (Organization for Economic Co-operation and Development 2012). Since the government sets the service fees below market prices, many healthcare providers running on a profit motive are not interested in providing services that are most appropriate for patients' long-term health (Organization for Economic Co-operation and Development 2012: 10). Instead, they are keen on increasing the volume and intensity of services provided and choosing medical treatments with a greater profit (Kwon 2007: 166). In 2013, the ROK had the longest average length of inpatient stays across OECD countries (Organization for Economic Co-operation and Development 2016). The average length of inpatient stays was 16.5 days in the ROK, which was more than double the OECD average of 8.1 days (Organization for Economic Co-operation and Development 2016). From 2004 to 2015, the average annual growth rate of health expenditures among the total population for inpatient care was higher (12.4 percent) than that for outpatient care (8.2 percent) (Jeon and Kwon 2017: 216). High avoidable hospital admissions for chronic conditions (e.g. asthma, diabetes) in the ROK indicate that unnecessary use of expensive hospital care is a serious problem (Organization for Economic Co-operation and Development 2016). For example, hospital admission rates for asthma in the ROK were over twice the OECD average in 2015 (Organization for Economic Co-operation and Development 2017: 104).

How to reduce the over-utilization of hospital services and build better incentives for appropriate care are important tasks for the government, especially when the country is facing a rapidly ageing population and growing chronic disease burden (Organization for Economic Co-operation and Development 2012). Elderly people often require more medical services than younger adults due to 'additional functional decline, physical illness, and psychosocial needs' (Kim *et al.* 2018: 98). According to Korea Centers for Disease Control and Prevention (2017), medical expenses for the elderly topped 1.8 billion won, accounting for 35.5 percent of total medical expenses. Medical expenses for chronic diseases were 3.8 billion won, accounting for 80 percent of total medical expenses (Korea Centers for Disease Control and Prevention 2017). 'Burden of chronic diseases is expected to grow due to an aging population' (Korea Centers for Disease Control and Prevention 2017), posing a threat to the financial sustainability of the NHI in the long run. In 2018, the NHI had a shortfall of 177.8 billion won (US$158 million) (Yonhap News Agency 2019). It is expected to 'remain in the red due to increased expenditures, with the cumulative surplus likely to shrink to about 11 trillion won after 2022' (Yonhap News Agency 2019).

In August 2017, President Moon Jae-in announced a new 'Mooncare' plan, which had an objective of reducing the financial burden for citizens in need of medical care (Chu 2018) and focused on three major changes. First, the NHI will cover all forms of medical treatment except plastic surgery and cosmetic procedures (Yoon and Lee 2017). Coverage will be provided for an additional 3,800 medical services, raising the share of coverage from 63 percent to 70 percent (Chu 2018). Such coverage will require the government to spend 30.6 trillion won (US$28.1 billion) over the next five years (Chu 2018). Second, the cap for out-of-pocket expenses will be lowered so that low-income individuals would only have to pay a maximum of 1 million won per year for their medical care (Yoon and Lee 2017). Third, there will be an increase in emergency financial support for those in the lower 50 percent of the income bracket, providing them with medical coverage of a maximum of 20 million won in case of a major health crisis (Yoon and Lee 2017; Gibson n.d.). But the Mooncare plan is not welcomed by doctors and healthcare providers. More than 10,000 doctors protested in the streets and called for an overhaul of the new plan (Chu 2018). Doctors think that they will have fewer medical services to earn profit when Mooncare will cover all forms of medical treatment (Chu 2018) and face heavy financial losses unless the reform plan comes with a raise in medical service fees (Chu 2018; Lee, K. 2018). Healthcare providers argue that the reform plan would lead to overcrowding in emergency rooms (Lee, C. 2018). The reform plan will accelerate the transfer of patients to general hospitals (Lee *et al.* 2019: 50) so that shutdowns of smaller clinics and hospitals will be inevitable (Lee, K. 2018).

At present, many people raise concerns over the financial sustainability of the NHI. Including uninsured services into insurance benefit packages and reducing the financial burden of the low-income population 'may lead to moral hazards and increase instability and inefficiency in the system' (Lee *et al.* 2019: 52). Financial sustainability of the NHI is also undermined by low economic growth and a shrinking workforce (Kang *et al.* 2012: S22). Low economic growth 'threatens funding to NHI as the contribution rate is tied to the income of the beneficiaries' (Kang *et al.* 2012: S22). A shrinking workforce will reduce the revenue of the NHI because the number of employees or the self-employed contributing to the NHI decreases. The proportion of the working-age population was 73.1 percent in 2015 and is projected to drop to 63.1 percent in 2030 (Eck 2018). To increase the NHI revenue, an increase in the premium rate becomes inevitable. It is estimated that the premium rate will have to increase by 3.2 percent by 2025 or the NHI system will be in deficit (Lee, K. 2018). But another way to ensure the financial sustainability of the NHI is to ensure the delivery of appropriate care to patients through an effective primary care system. Driving more appropriate care requires the government to make primary care the core financing priority and investments to scale up primary care a distinct component of NHI expenditures (Organization for Economic Co-operation and Development 2012: 21). The development of a stronger community-based primary care system can provide care at a lower cost and deliver better value for the money (Organization for Economic Co-operation and Development 2012: 21–2).

Conclusion

The ROK is an aged society and will become a super-aged society by 2026 (Kim and Jang 2017). The government needs to strengthen the primary care system and gatekeeping mechanism so that healthcare costs and hospitalizations can be reduced and the quality of care can be improved. It also needs to promote healthy ageing to reduce the burden of chronic illnesses, which can lower the financial pressure placed on the NHI system.

8 Healthy ageing in Asia

Introduction

Life expectancy has been increasing in all countries of the world over the past two centuries (Roser 2019). In 1800, no country had a life expectancy above 40 years (Roser 2019). In 1955, average life expectancy at birth was only 48 years; in 1995 it was 65 years (World Health Organization 1998: 39). From 2000 to 2016, global average life expectancy increased by 5.5 years, the fastest increase since the 1960s (World Health Organization 2019c). 'Globally, in 2017, life expectancy was 73 years, but healthy life expectancy was only 63 years' (The Institute for Health Metrics and Evaluation 2018: 14). This means poor health resulted in a loss of ten years of healthy life, on average globally (The Institute for Health Metrics and Evaluation 2018: 14).

'Health is central to our experience of older age' (World Health Organization 2017a: 1). Living longer does not necessarily mean that these extra years are spent in good health (World Health Organization 2017a: 1). As stated by the World Health Organization in 1948, health is not merely the absence of disease or infirmity but a state of complete physical, mental, and social well-being (World Health Organization 2014: 1). Hence, achieving healthy ageing requires the adoption of a holistic approach to address both physical and mental health, as well as a cross-sectoral approach to improve the social determinants of health (EuroHealthNet *et al.* 2012), such as income level, education, housing, and recreational activities. It requires a range of actions at the individual and societal level to achieve this outcome (EuroHealthNet *et al.* 2012). A fundamental attitudinal and policy shift on ageing and old age is therefore needed to enable older adults to lead healthy, productive, and self-determined lives and promote their contributions to society (United Nations Development Programme 2017: 17). This chapter uses examples in some Asian places to examine how healthy ageing can be achieved through maintaining and improving physical wellness, social wellness, and financial wellness of older adults, creating dementia-friendly communities (DFCs) and adopting new care models.

Physical wellness

Throughout much of the 20th century, 'hospitals, with their technology and sub-specialists, have gained a pivotal role in most health systems throughout the world' (World Health Organization 2008: 11). The problem of hospital centrism, which refers to a disproportionate focus on resolving health problems through hospital care, 'has become a major source of inefficiency and inequality' (World Health Organization 2008: 11) and has generated 'considerable costs related to medication and iatrogenesis' (Padoveze and de Figueiredo 2014: 1132). While acute hospital care still plays an important role in responding to life-threatening health conditions and exacerbations of chronic illness, primary care also plays an important role in reducing avoidable hospital admissions through effective health interventions, 'particularly health promotion and disease prevention programmes that target the main causes of morbidity and mortality' (Rechel *et al.* 2009: vi).

In recent years, some governments in Asia have renewed their commitment to primary care in order to meet the healthcare needs of an ageing population in a more efficient and equitable manner, guarantee fiscal sustainability of health systems, and achieve better value for the money. They introduce regular health screening and check-up programs for their populations, especially older adults, so that diseases can be detected and treated in an early stage to reduce the chance of developing serious complications and thus improving health and the quality of life. For example, the Singapore government introduces the Enhanced Screen for Life, which is a national screening program offering all Singaporeans aged 40 years and over subsidized health screenings. Eligible Singaporeans pay SG$5 or less to screen for diabetes, high blood pressure, high cholesterol levels, cervical and colorectal cancers (Khalik 2017). In Taiwan, the government provides free health checkups every three years for people aged 40 to 64 and annually for people aged 65 and over (Lee 2019). In Hong Kong, the Elderly Health Assessment Pilot Programmes is introduced by the government in collaboration with non-governmental organizations to provide voluntary, protocol-based, and subsidized health assessment as well as one to two follow-up consultations to older adults aged 70 and over (Community Medical Support Network n.d.).

At a biological level, 'ageing is characterized by a gradual, lifelong accumulation of molecular and cellular damage' (World Health Organization 2015: 52) that leads to an increased risk of multimorbidity, frailty, disability, and death (World Health Organization 2015). There is growing evidence that the burden of disability and mortality in older age can be reduced by enabling healthy behaviors, such as engaging in physical activity and maintaining adequate nutrition (World Health Organization 2015: 69–70). In Asia, some governments carry out health promotion activities to enable people to take greater responsibility for their own health through improving their health literacy as well as positively impacting their attitudes and health behavior. They actively promote healthy diets and regular physical activity, which helps reduce the morbidity and mortality from many chronic diseases (World Health Organization 2003). For example, the Singapore government in 2016 produced *The Recipe for Healthy Ageing*, which was a toolkit comprising a nutrition guide, recipe book, and an educational poster and was available in four languages, to help older adults understand the importance of good nutrition and provide them with tips to prepare healthy and tasty meals at home (Health Promotion Board 2016; Khew 2016). It also launches the National Steps Challenge™, which is a national physical activity program encouraging 'Singapore residents to be more physically active every day, anytime and anywhere' (HealthHub 2017). To take part in the challenge, participants track their steps with a free step tracker and the Healthy 365 mobile application. As participants accumulate steps, they earn Healthpoints, which will allow them to redeem rewards such as shopping and grocery vouchers (Teo 2017). In Japan, the number of pieces of elderly workout equipment installed in parks had almost tripled since 1998 to over 15,000 in 2007, according to a report by the Ministry of Land, Infrastructure and Tourism (Osaka 2009). Besides, local governments funded 50 elderly workout classes conducted by the Association of Physical Fitness Promotion and Guidance (Osaka 2009). Studies find that exercising together increases exercise frequency due to getting more emotional support and encouragement from an exercise companion (ScienceDaily 2016).

Additionally, governments in Asia make use of digital technologies such as artificial intelligence (AI), Internet of things (IoTs), and robotics to improve diagnostic accuracy and safety, enhance productivity in healthcare, provide more personalized medical care for patients, and resolve manpower shortage in the medical sector. For example, the government in the Republic of Korea (ROK) has designated the promotion of AI-based healthcare innovation and drug development as a national priority (Haynes 2018). In 2018, the government approved the first AI-based medical device which determined a patient's bone age by recognizing patterns on an X-ray image and helped doctors diagnose precocious puberty and slow growth (Lee, H. 2018a). In the same year, the government approved two additional AI-based medical devices that, respectively, helped doctors diagnose pulmonary nodules through X-ray imaging and offer appropriate treatment options for patients with cerebral infarction through the patient's magnetic resonance imaging (MRI) (Lee, H. 2018b). In Singapore, the government has embarked on a national diabetes database project that uses 'predictive modelling to identify diabetic patients for early intervention programs, [and] support research to design improved care pathways for different cohorts of patients' (Basu and Rohaidi n.d.). In Taiwan, the Ministry of Health and Welfare, which utilizes AI and cloud computing to access massive databases, launched the MediCloud system to let healthcare providers query patients' medical records within the National Health Insurance (NHI) system as well as the PharmaCloud system to provide doctors and pharmacists with prescription drug information (Chen 2019).

Social wellness

Social wellness which refers to one's ability to effectively interact with people around him or her can contribute to a sense of belonging (Melnyk and Neale 2018) and is critical to one's physical and psychological health (AgeWell Cincinnati 2018). Social wellness is important for people of all ages. For older adults, staying socially active helps them navigate changes and transitions such as retiring (AgeWell Cincinnati 2018), reduces the risk for developing Alzheimer's disease and depression, and strengthens their immune system so that they can live independently longer (American Senior Communities 2016). Nevertheless, older adults 'are especially vulnerable to loneliness and social isolation' (The NHS website 2018) due to leaving the workplace, the deaths of spouses and friends, broken relationships, illness or disability, living alone (Independent Age 2016; The NHS website 2018), and lack of emotional support and companionship (Sorkin *et al.* 2002). Loneliness in older adults has become a public health concern in some Asian countries. For example, a study found that loneliness was associated with higher mortality risks among Singaporean elderly (Chan *et al.* 2015: 1362). In Japan, loneliness and poverty are two main reasons for the rapidly growing proportion of crimes committed by people aged over 65 (BBC News 2019). The promise of company in jail prompts many older adults to become repeat offenders (BBC News 2019). In the ROK, around one in five elderly persons were socially inactive, increasing the risk of depression and dementia and thus a potential for suicide or dying alone (Yang and Son 2019).

To ensure social wellbeing of older adults, governments, researchers, and different organizations introduce intergenerational programs that bring 'seniors and children or young adults together through planned, mutually beneficial activities' (Tumpane 2017). These programs help older adults combat feelings of isolation, slow cognitive decline, promote overall wellbeing, alleviate social anxieties and communication problems, foster regular social connections with other people, and provide them with much-needed stimulation (Tumpane 2017). In Singapore, the ARTISAN intergenerational arts program was developed by a researcher at Nanyang Technological University in partnership with the National Arts Council and the National Museum of Singapore to build resilience and social connectedness among the young and the old through storytelling, guided art-making and creative-writing, and curated art spaces illuminated by social artifacts (Ho 2019). In Japan, researchers from the Geriatric Care Project at St. Luke's College of Nursing, Tokyo, implemented a weekly, community-based intergenerational day program (IDP) called St. Luke's *Nagomi-no-kai* ("harmony and relaxation") to bring older adults and elementary-school children together through communication facilitation games, card (karuta) games, and handicrafts (Kamei *et al.* 2011). The IDP reduced the depressive symptoms of older adults and improved the health-related quality of life (HRQOL), specifically in relation to mental health (Kamei *et al.* 2011: 104–5). In Hong Kong, Project CARE brought older adults and primary school students together through designing and creating a mural artwork made from LEGO bricks (Singapore International School (Hong Kong) 2019). It helped 'break down barriers and stereotypes through effective communication, enhancing mutual respect and understanding between generations' (Singapore International School (Hong Kong) 2019). Another way to improve social wellness of older adults is to help them foster connections and interactions with their counterparts. For example, the government in Seoul funds a new daytime disco club to help older adults aged over 65 fight loneliness, isolation, and dementia as well as tackle poor health (Corbley 2019).

Financial wellness

Financial wellness refers to one's ability to fully meet current and ongoing financial responsibilities, absorb a financial shock, and enjoy the financial freedom to make choices that allow enjoyment of life (Consumer Financial Protection Bureau 2015). It is especially important for older adults because consumption by older adults is financed mostly through their own savings, social programs (Hurd 1990: 565), or financial support from family members. Older adults are at a higher risk of financial insecurity due to job loss, limited financial resources, the rising costs of basic living needs (e.g. food), and unexpected medical bills and long-term care costs. Compared to their male counterparts, older women are more susceptible to financial vulnerabilities because 'they tend to live longer, live alone, have lower lifetime earnings, and have higher uninsured disability risk' (U.S. Treasury Department Office of Economic Policy 2017: 2). Old-age poverty leads to material deprivation. Older adults are forced to go without essential items like food or cut back on household bills through reducing the use of gas and electricity, leisure activities, holidays, and transportation costs (Dominy and Kempson 2006). Material deprivation in turn may lead to a higher risk of physical and mental dysfunction (Groffen *et al.* 2007).

In some Asian countries and cities, old-age poverty is a serious problem. For example, one-third of older adults in Hong Kong live in poverty (Keegan 2018), while almost half of the elderly population aged over 65 in the ROK live in poverty (Lam 2017). The phenomenon of elderly waste collectors or cardboard grannies is a reflection of old-age poverty and inadequate social welfare and pension policies in these two places. Elderly waste collectors collect and sell discarded cardboard boxes, papers, and other scrap every day in order to make a living for themselves (Keegan 2018; Lam 2017). Adopting effective policy responses to old-age poverty and helping older adults live with dignity are essential components of healthy ageing.

Financial literacy is the knowledge and understanding of financial concepts and risks, and the ability to apply such knowledge and understanding to make sound and effective decisions about one's financial affairs, such as personal savings, retirement planning, living arrangements, and wealth distribution (MacLeod *et al.* 2017; Organization for Economic Co-operation and Development 2019b). It is a critical life skill that 'can contribute to individual and families' wellbeing as well as to financial stability in our economies' (Asia-Pacific Economic Cooperation 2012). Financial wellbeing in old age 'depends largely on decisions and savings behaviour much earlier in life' (The Financial Consumer Agency of Canada 2017: 6). It is important to 'strengthen the financial literacy of current and future seniors by increasing their knowledge, skills and confidence to make responsible financial decisions' (The Financial Consumer Agency of Canada 2017: 7). Financial education programs are introduced to increase an individual's financial literacy, while financial incentives are used by the government to attract the public to study these programs. For example, Singaporeans can use their S$500 SkillsFuture Credit from the government to pay for courses such as Financial

Planning for Retirement to assess personal needs and lifespan budgeting (Hartung 2017). In Hong Kong, the government introduced the *Hong Kong Strategy for Financial Literacy 2015* and the *Financial Literacy Strategy 2019* to empower the youth, working adults, the elderly, and vulnerable groups (e.g. low-income families, the disabled) to take control of their finances through a territory-wide awareness campaign and financial education (The Investor and Financial Education Council 2019). In China, the financial literacy pilot program was rolled out in schools in Shenzhen, Guangzhou, and Shanghai a few years ago (McGregor 2019). In 2019, the Ministry of Education and the Chinese Regulatory Securities Commission agreed to include financial knowledge on national curriculum in the future to equip primary and middle school students with practical investment and money management skills (McGregor 2019; Xie 2019). Chinese tech firms have developed mobile applications, videogames, and digital devices to teach children basic financial skills in an interesting way (McGregor 2019).

In some Asian countries, retirement age has been raised to let older adults work longer, save more money before retiring, and reduce pressure on the pension system. In the ROK, the law raising the retirement age from 58 to 60 came into effect in 2017 (Kim 2019). In Japan, the government will raise the retirement age from 65 to 70 to solve the problem of labor shortages and stabilize social security revenues (Takahashi 2019). In Singapore, the government will raise both the retirement age and the re-employment age to let older workers work longer and become more financially independent (Seow 2019a). The retirement age in Singapore will be raised to 63 in 2022 and eventually to 65 by 2030, while the re-employment age will be raised to 68 in 2022 and eventually to 70 by 2030 (Seow 2019a). Mature workers are encouraged to 'upskill and re-skill themselves in order to safeguard employability at old age' (Workforce Singapore 2019). Meanwhile, employers are encouraged to tap on the Job Redesign Grant to create physically easier, safer, and smarter jobs for older workers (Seow 2019b).

The creation of dementia-friendly communities

Dementia, which is 'a syndrome of cognitive decline with loss of basic functioning for daily life' (Wu *et al.* 2015: 793), has become more prevalent in Asia. From 2015 to 2050, numbers of people with dementia (PWD) will have increased threefold in Asia, but less than twofold in Europe, and somewhat more than twofold in North America (Prince *et al.* 2015: 1). In response to an increasing prevalence of dementia, governments in Asia have created dementia-friendly communities (DFCs) to support PWD to live more independent lives for as long as possible and to help reduce caregiver burden, stress, and fatigue. In Taiwan, the Dementia Friendly Store project was introduced in 2013 to encourage shop owners to make prior arrangements with families to enable PWD to continuously use their services (Alzheimer's Disease International 2017: 19). For example, advance payment for products for which the PWD may come in is arranged (Alzheimer's Disease International 2017: 19). In Japan, the government introduced the Orange

Plan (2013–2017) and the New Orange Plan (2015–2025), which are national strategies aiming to promote the development of DFCs (Fukawa 2018). The New Orange Plan called for a comprehensive package of measures to tackle dementia, ranging from raising public awareness on dementia, having more specialized medical staff, and regular home visits to offering support for family caregivers (McCurry 2018b). In Singapore, there are eight DFCs where 'the neighbourhood at large are [sic] aware of dementia and understand[s] how to better support PWD and their caregivers' (Alzheimer's Disease Association 2018). These DFCs have touch points to help PWD reunite with their caregivers and use digital devices to keep a lookout for anyone with dementia (TODAYonline 2016).

Adopting new care models

Older adults are not a homogeneous group (Lee and Kim 2016). They come from diverse backgrounds and have different life experiences, lifestyles, interests, and needs. In recent years, governments in Asia have adopted a more holistic and humanistic approach to providing healthcare and long-term care (LTC) for older adults and facilitating ageing in place. In China, the government puts forward the integration of healthcare and nursing services for the elderly. Such integration encourages nursing homes to 'cooperate in various forms with surrounding medical institutions to offer services such as consultation and health management to their residents' (Reynolds 2015). It also encourages nursing homes to set up internal medical departments to provide older residents with more convenient access to healthcare services (Reynolds 2015). Emphasis is put on prevention of diseases and maintaining good physical and mental health of older people. This helps reduce demand for medical care at public hospitals. In Taiwan, senior care centers implement the Time Dollar-Mutual Support program, which is a 'volunteer hours exchange service' program to let volunteers store their service hours (i.e. time dollars) and then use these hours when they need assistance in the future (HONDAO Senior Citizen's Welfare Foundation 2006; Sng 2019). The program aims to promote compassion, dignity in old age, mutual help, and develop mutual trust (HONDAO Senior Citizen's Welfare Foundation 2006; Sng 2019). It can also provide older volunteers a sense of purpose in life and thereby improve their spiritual wellness.

In Hong Kong, the Jockey Club Centre for Positive Ageing was established in 2000 to provide PWD with integrated support services, including daycare service, residential service, discharge support, rehabilitation service, and training courses and health seminars for family caregivers of PWD (The Jockey Club Centre for Positive Ageing n.d.). In Singapore, Kampung Admiralty was established as a one-stop hub integrating housing for older adults with a wide range of healthcare, communal, social, commercial, and retail facilities (Housing & Development Board 2019). It promotes active living among older adults and supports intergenerational bonding (Channel News Asia 2018).

In Japan, the government urged all municipalities to establish the Community-based Integrated Care System (CbICS) by 2025 to help older adults live independently in their communities through the integration of healthcare services, nursing care, preventive care, housing, and livelihood support (Sudo *et al.* 2018: 8). The CbICS contains four elements, including self-help (*Ji-jo*), mutual aid (*Go-jo*), social solidarity care (*Kyo-jo*), and government care (*Ko-jo*) (Sudo *et al.* 2018: 10). In the ROK, the government in November 2018 announced that a comprehensive community care system will be established by 2025 to provide older adults with medical, residential, nursing, and care services in their homes and neighborhoods (Hwang and Park 2018). It will provide older adults with more affordable housing equipped with safety features such as automatic gas cutoffs and located very close to public health care and caregiving centers (The Korea Herald 2018). It will also increase the number of older adults receiving home visits from medical staff from 1.25 million in 2018 to 3.93 million by 2025 (The Korea Herald 2018). It is expected that the comprehensive community care system will provide better housing support, medical care, and LTC services to older adults (The Korea Herald 2018).

Conclusion

'Wellbeing is an integral component of adding life to years in the presence of increasing longevity' (Cosco *et al.* 2017: 581). Fostering healthy ageing through maintaining and improving physical wellness, social wellness, financial wellness, and spiritual wellness of older adults requires leadership and commitment, strong engagement from diverse sectors and different levels of government, the adoption of a positive view of ageing, and a rights-based approach which informs and engages, and consulting older adults in formulating and developing policies that affect them (World Health Organization 2017b: 7–10). Looking forward, healthy ageing will help build more inclusive, cohesive, and resilient societies.

Acknowledgement

This chapter is supported by the Start-Up Grant (SUG) of Nanyang Technological University, Singapore (Grant number: M4082137.SS0.).

Bibliography

Abdullah, W. J. (2016) 'Managing Minorities in Competitive Authoritarian States: Multiracialism and the Hijab Issue in Singapore', *Indonesia & the Malay World*, 44 (129): 211–28.

Abdullah, W. J. (2017) 'Bringing Ideology in: Differing Oppositional Challenges to Hegemony in Singapore and Malaysia', *Government and Opposition*, 52 (3): 483–510.

Abdullah, W. J. (2018) 'Selective History and Hegemony-Making: The Case of Singapore', *International Political Science Review*, 39 (4): 473–86.

Abeysinghe, T., Himani and Lim, J. (2011) 'Equity in Singapore's Healthcare Financing', in P. Wilson (ed.) *Challenges for the Singapore Economy after the Global Financial Crisis*, Hackensack, NJ: World Scientific Pub. Co., pp. 119–38.

Ackrill, R. and Kay, A. (2011) 'Multiple Streams in EU Policy-Making: The Case of the 2005 Sugar Reform', *Journal of European Public Policy*, 18 (1): 72–89.

AgeWell Cincinnati (2018) *Social Wellness Critical to Older Adults' Mental, Physical Health*. Online. Available HTTP: https://agewellcincy.org/social-wellness-critical-to-older-adults-mental-physical-health/ (accessed 4 September 2019).

Ahn, B. Y. (2009) 'Globalization and Welfare Reform in South Korea under the Kim Dae Jung Government', in Y. Chang, H. Seok and D. Baker (eds.) *Korea Confronts Globalization*, London; New York: Routledge, pp. 229–49.

Ahn, C. (2001) *Korean Democracy under Kim Dae Jung: A Stalled Progression?* Online. Available HTTP: http://s-space.snu.ac.kr/bitstream/10371/90006/1/13%20Research%20Article%20Korean%20Democracy%20under%20Kim%20Dae%20Jung%20%20A%20Stalled%20Progression%20%20-%28Chung%20Si%20Ahn%29.pdf (accessed 10 November 2018).

Aitchison, L. R. (1997) *Bureaucratic Reform in a Transitional Economy: The Role of Urban Chinese Health Care*, PhD dissertation, Harvard University, Cambridge, MA.

Alves, E. M. (2014) 'Brazilian Environmental Public Policies Analysis', *International Journal of Environmental and Ecological Engineering*, 8 (4): 997–1001.

Alzheimer's Disease Association (2018) *Building Dementia-Friendly Communities in Singapore*. Online. Available HTTP: https://alz.org.sg/building-dementia-friendly-communities-in-singapore/ (accessed 10 September 2019).

Alzheimer's Disease International (2017) *Dementia Friendly Communities: Global Developments*, 2nd edn. Online. Available HTTP: www.alz.co.uk/adi/pdf/dfc-developments.pdf (accessed 10 September 2019).

American Senior Communities (2016) *The Importance of an Active Social Life*. Online. Available HTTP: www.asccare.com/caregiver-support/importance-active-social-life/ (accessed 4 September 2019).

Anderson, J. E. (2015) *Public Policymaking*, 8th edn, Wadsworth: Cengage Learning.

Arivalagan, Y. (2019) 'Demography', in K. H. Phua, L. G. Goh and M. T. Yap (eds.) *Ageing in Asia: Contemporary Trends and Policy Issues*, Singapore: World Scientific Publishing Co Pte Ltd, pp. 1–57.

Asher, M. G. and Nandy, A. (2006) 'Health Financing in Singapore: A Case for Systemic Reforms', *International Social Security Review*, 59 (1): 75–92.

AsiaOne (2015) 'Japan's Govt Plans More Special Nursing Homes for Elderly', 25 September. Online. Available HTTP: www.asiaone.com/asia/japans-govt-plans-more-special-nursing-homes-elderly (accessed 10 June 2019).

Asia-Pacific Economic Cooperation (2012) *2012 APEC Finance Ministerial Meeting*. Online. Available HTTP: www.apec.org/Meeting-Papers/Sectoral-Ministerial-Meetings/Finance/2012_finance (accessed 9 September 2019).

Auer, M. R. (2007) 'The Policy Sciences in Critical Perspective', in J. Rabin, W. Bartley Hildreth and G. J. Miller (eds.) *Handbook of Public Administration*, 3rd edn, Boca Raton: CRC/Taylor & Francis, pp. 541–62.

Aviva (2015) *The 1 Thing You Need to Have for Your Retirement Planning*. Online. Available HTTP: www.aviva.com.sg/en/money-banter/2015/1-thing-for-retirement-planning/ (accessed 18 May 2019).

Bakir, C. (2009) 'Policy Entrepreneurship and Institutional Change: Multilevel Governance of Central Banking Reform', *Governance: An International Journal of Policy, Administration, and Institutions*, 22 (4): 571–98.

Bakir, C. and Jarvis, D. S. L. (2017) 'Contextualising the Context in Policy Entrepreneurship and Institutional Change', *Policy and Society*, 36 (4): 465–78.

Barany, Z. (2012) *The Soldier and the Changing State: Building Democratic Armies in Africa, Asia, Europe, and the Americas*, Princeton, NJ: Princeton University Press.

Barr, M. (2005) 'Singapore', in R. Gauld (ed.) *Comparative Health Policy in the Asia-Pacific*, Maidenhead: Open University Press, pp. 146–73.

Basu, M. and Rohaidi, N. (n.d.) *Exclusive: How Singapore Health Uses AI to Track Its Elderly Care*. Online. Available HTTP: https://govinsider.asia/innovation/bruce-liang-ihis-population-profiling/ (accessed 3 September 2019).

BBC News (2019) 'Why Some Japanese Pensioners Want to Go to Jail', *BBC News*, 31 January. Online. Available HTTP: www.bbc.com/news/stories-47033704 (accessed 5 September 2019).

Beijing Business Today (2014) 'Some Regions Experience a Deficit in the Medical Insurance Fund', Chinese Version. *Beijing Business Today*, 9 December. Online. Available HTTP: www.cn-healthcare.com/article/20141209/content-465355.html (accessed 6 July 2019).

Béland, D. (2009) 'Ideas, Institutions, and Policy Change', *Journal of European Public Policy*, 16 (5): 701–18.

Béland, D. (2016) 'Kingdon Reconsidered: Ideas, Interests and Institutions in Comparative Policy Analysis', *Journal of Comparative Policy Analysis: Research and Practice*, 18 (3): 228–42.

Béland, D. and Howlett, M. (2016) 'The Role and Impact of the Multiple-Streams Approach in Comparative Policy Analysis', *Journal of Comparative Policy Analysis: Research and Practice*, 18 (3): 221–7.

Béland, D. and Waddan, A. (2012) *The Politics of Policy Change: Welfare, Medicare, and Social Security Reform in the United States*, Washington, DC: Georgetown University Press.

Bell, D. A., Brown, D., Jayasuriya, K. and Jones, D. M. (eds.) (1995) *Towards Illiberal Democracy in Pacific Asia*, New York: St. Martin's Press.

Berenson, R. A., Upadhyay, D. K., Delbanco, S. F. and Murray, R. (2016) *Global Budgets for Hospitals*. Online. Available HTTP: www.urban.org/sites/default/files/05_global_budgets_for_hospitals.pdf (accessed 25 August 2018).

Berman, S. (2001) 'Ideas, Norms, and Culture in Political Analysis', *Comparative Politics*, 33 (2): 231–50.

Blank, R. and Burau, V. (2007) *Comparative Health Policy*, 2nd edn, Basingstoke, England; New York: Palgrave Macmillan.

Boasiako, A. and Asare, B. E. (2015) 'The Multiple Streams Framework and the 1996 and 2007 Educational Reforms in Ghana', *Advances in Research*, 5 (3): 1–15.

Bochorodycz, B. (2010) *The Changing Patterns of Policy Making in Japan: Local Policy Initiative of Okinawa Prefecture in the 1990s*. Online. Available HTTP: https://repozytorium.amu.edu.pl/bitstream/10593/679/4/Bochorodycz_tekst.pdf (accessed 27 March 2019).

Boswel, C. and Rodrigues, E. (2016) 'Policies, Politics and Organisational Problems: Multiple Streams and the Implementation of Targets in UK Government', *Policy & Politics*, 44 (4): 507–24.

Breton, M., Lamothe, L. and Denis, J. (2014) 'How Healthcare Organisations Can Act as Institutional Entrepreneurs in a Context of Change', *Journal of Health Organization and Management*, 28 (1): 77–95.

Brewer, G. D. and deLeon, P. (1983) *The Foundations of Policy Analysis*, Homewood, IL: Dorsey Press.

Bridges, B. (2001) *Korea after the Crash: The Politics of Economic Recovery*, London; New York: Routledge.

Burau, V. D., Theobald, H. and Blank, R. H. (2007) *Governing Home Care: A Cross-National Comparison*, Cheltenham: Edward Elgar Publishing.

Bureau of Labor Insurance (2010) *60 Years of Labour Insurance*, Chinese Version. Online. Available HTTP: www.bli.gov.tw/sub.aspx?a=H20Yxf085Dw%3D (accessed 9 August 2018).

Bureau of Labor Insurance (2013) *Introduction to Farmers Insurance*, Chinese Version. Online. Available HTTP: www.bli.gov.tw/sub.aspx?a=RxE1RBebaZo%3d (accessed 11 August 2018).

Bureau of National Health Insurance (2009) *National Health Insurance in Taiwan 2009*. Online. Available HTTP: www.nhi.gov.tw/Resource/webdata/Attach_15545_1_NHI%20profile.pdf (accessed 16 June 2019).

Bureau of National Health Insurance (2010) *National Health Insurance in Taiwan 2010*. Online. Available HTTP: www.nhi.gov.tw/resource/webdata/attach_15634_1_national%20health%20insurance%20in%20taiwan%202010.pdf (accessed 10 August 2018).

Busse, R., Blümel, M., Knieps, F. and Bärnighausen, T. (2017) 'Statutory Health Insurance in Germany: A Health System Shaped by 135 Years of Solidarity, Self-Governance, and Competition', *The Lancet*, 390: 882–97.

Busse, R., Saltman, R. B. and Dubois, H. F. W. (2004) 'Organization and Financing of Social Health Insurance Systems: Current Status and Recent Policy Developments', in R. B. Saltman, R. Busse and J. Figueras (eds.) *Social Health Insurance Systems in Western Europe*, Maidenhead: Open University Press, pp. 33–80.

Cabinet Office (2001) *Annual Report on Japan's Economy and Public Finance 2000–2001*. Online. Available HTTP: www5.cao.go.jp/zenbun/wp-e/wp-je01/wp-je01-00301.html (accessed 25 February 2019).

Cairney, P. and Jones, M. D. (2016) 'Kingdon's Multiple Streams Approach: What Is the Empirical Impact of This Universal Theory?', *The Policy Studies Journal*, 44 (1): 37–58.

Campbell, J. C. (1992) *How Policies Change: The Japanese Government and the Aging Society*, Princeton, NJ: Princeton University Press.

Campbell, J. C. (1997) 'Initiating Public Long-Term-Care Insurance in Japan', *The Journal of the International Institute*, 5 (1). Online. Available HTTP: https://quod.lib.umich.edu/j/jii/4750978.0005.104?view=text;rgn=main (accessed 7 April 2019).

Campbell, J. C. (2011) *Japan's Universal Long-Term Care Insurance: Generous, Affordable, Workable*. Online. Available HTTP: http://asia-center.utah.edu/_documents/humis/docs/organization-669-1328047588.pdf (accessed 8 June 2019).

Campbell, J. C. (2014) 'Japan's Long-Term Care Insurance System', in J. C. Campbell, U. Edvardsen, P. Midford and Y. Saito (eds.) *Eldercare Policies in Japan and Scandinavia: Aging Societies East and West*, New York: Palgrave Macmillan, pp. 9–30.

Campbell, J. C. and Ikegami, N. (1998) *The Art of Balance in Health Policy: Maintaining Japan's Low-Cost, Egalitarian System*, Cambridge: Cambridge University Press.

Campbell, J. C., Ikegami, N. and Kwon, S. (2009) 'Policy Learning and Cross-National Diffusion in Social Long-Term Care Insurance: Germany, Japan, and the Republic of Korea', *International Social Security Review*, 62 (4): 63–80.

Campbell, J. L. (1998) 'Institutional Analysis and the Role of Ideas in Political Economy', *Theory and Society*, 27 (3): 377–409.

Campbell, J. L. (2002) 'Ideas, Politics, and Public Policy', *Annual Review of Sociology*, 28: 21–38.

Cao, P. (2006) 'The Rural Cooperative Medical System before Reform and the Opening: Up of China, Chinese Version', *Zhonggong Dangshi Ziliao*, 3: 134–44.

Case, W. (2006) 'Manipulative Skills: How Do Rulers Control the Electoral Arena?', in A. Schedler (ed.) *Electoral Authoritarianism: The Dynamics of Unfree Competition*, Boulder, CO: L. Rienner Publishers, pp. 95–112.

Census and Statistics Department (2000) *Hong Kong Annual Digest of Statistics 2000 Edition*. Online. Available HTTP: www.statistics.gov.hk/pub/hist/1991_2000/B10100032000AN00B0100.pdf (accessed 11 January 2019).

Census and Statistics Department (2012) *Demographic Trends in Hong Kong: 1981–2011*. Online. Available HTTP: www.statistics.gov.hk/pub/B112001703-2012XXXXB0100.pdf (accessed 2 January 2019).

Census and Statistics Department (2017a) *"Demographic Trends in Hong Kong 1986–2016" Published*. Online. Available HTTP: www.censtatd.gov.hk/press_release/pressReleaseDetail.jsp?charsetID=1&pressRID=4352 (accessed 26 June 2019).

Census and Statistics Department (2017b) *Hong Kong Population Projections 2017–2066*. Online. Available HTTP: www.statistics.gov.hk/pub/B1120015072017XXXXB0100.pdf (accessed 26 June 2019).

Census and Statistics Department (2017c) *Thematic Household Survey Report No. 63*. Online. Available HTTP: www.statistics.gov.hk/pub/B11302632017XXXXB0100.pdf (accessed 27 June 2019).

Census and Statistics Department (2019) *Hong Kong Monthly Digest of Statistics June 2019*. Online. Available HTTP: www.statistics.gov.hk/pub/B10100022019 MM06B0100.pdf (accessed 27 June 2019).

Center for Strategic and International Studies (2016) *Does China Have an Aging Problem?* Online. Available HTTP: https://chinapower.csis.org/aging-problem/ (accessed 14 September 2019).

The Central Committee of the Communist Party of China, and the State Council (1997) *The Decision Concerning Health Reform and Development*, Chinese Version. Online. Available HTTP: www.law-lib.com/law/law_view.asp?id=64056 (accessed 7 December 2018).

Central Provident Fund Board (2015) *General Information on MediShield Scheme*. Online. Available HTTP: www.cpf.gov.sg/assets/members/documents/general informationonmedishieldscheme.pdf (accessed 13 May 2019).

Central Provident Fund Board (2019a) *Self-Employed Scheme*. Online. Available HTTP: www.cpf.gov.sg/Members/Schemes/schemes/self-employed-matters/self-employed-scheme (accessed 12 May 2019).

Central Provident Fund Board (2019b) *Medisave*. Online. Available HTTP: www. cpf.gov.sg/Members/Schemes/schemes/healthcare/medisave (accessed 12 May 2019).

Central Provident Fund Board (2019c) *ElderShield*. Online. Available HTTP: www. cpf.gov.sg/Members/Schemes/schemes/healthcare/eldershield (accessed 17 May 2019).

Centre for Health Protection (2019a) *Life Expectancy at Birth (Male and Female), 1971–2018*. Online. Available HTTP: www.chp.gov.hk/en/statistics/data/10/27/ 111.html (accessed 15 September 2019).

Centre for Health Protection (2019b) *Death Rates by Leading Causes of Death, 2001– 2018*. Online. Available HTTP: www.chp.gov.hk/en/statistics/data/10/27/117. html (accessed 27 June 2019).

Chan, A., Raman, P., Ma, S. and Malhotra, R. (2015) 'Loneliness and All-Cause Mortality in Community-Dwelling Elderly Singaporeans', *Demographic Research*, 32 (49): 1361–82.

Channel News Asia (2018) 'Kampung Admiralty Wins Top Global Architecture Award', *Channel News Asia*, 2 December. Online. Available HTTP: www.channel-newsasia.com/news/singapore/kampung-admiralty-wins-top-global-architecture-award-10988872 (accessed 10 September 2019).

Chen, S. (2019) 'Taiwan Seeks to Share Its Advances in Digital Healthcare', *The Diplomat*, 9 May. Online. Available HTTP: https://thediplomat.com/2019/05/ taiwan-seeks-to-share-its-advances-in-digital-healthcare/ (accessed 16 June 2019).

Cheng, K. (2019a) 'Explainer: Why Doctors and Nurses Say Hong Kong's Health System Is Sick', *Hong Kong Free Press*, 9 February. Online. Available HTTP: www.hongkongfp.com/2019/02/09/explainer-doctors-nurses-say-hong-kongs-health-system-sick/ (accessed 26 June 2019).

Cheng, K. (2019b) 'Hospital Authority Temporarily Boosts Overtime Pay Scheme for Medical Professionals amid Winter Flu Surge', *Hong Kong Free Press*, 28 January. Online. Available HTTP: www.hongkongfp.com/2019/01/28/hospital-authority-temporarily-boosts-overtime-pay-scheme-medical-professionals-amid-winter-flu-surge/ (accessed 28 June 2019).

Cheng, T. M. (2003) 'Taiwan's New National Health Insurance Program: Genesis and Experience So Far', *Health Affairs*, 22 (3): 61–76.

Cheng, T. M. (2009) 'Lessons from Taiwan's Universal National Health Insurance: A Conversation with Taiwan's Health Minister Ching-Chuan Yeh', *Health Affairs*, 28 (4): 1035–44.

Cheng, T. M. (2010) 'Taiwan's National Health Insurance System: High Value for the Dollar', in K. G. H. Okma and L. Crivelli (eds.) *Six Countries, Six Reform Models: The Healthcare Reform Experience of Israel, the Netherlands, New Zealand, Singapore, Switzerland and Taiwan*, Singapore; Hackensack, NJ: World Scientific, pp. 171–204.

Cheng, T. M. (2015) 'Reflections on the 20th Anniversary of Taiwan's Single-Payer National Health Insurance System', *Health Affairs*, 34 (3): 502–10.

Cheung, A. B. L. (1997) 'Rebureaucratization of Politics in Hong Kong: Prospects after 1997', *Asian Survey*, 37 (8): 720–37.

Cheung, A. B. L. (2000) *How to Work the Unworkable? The Long-Term and Short-Term Solutions to Hong Kong's Constitutional Anomalies*. Online. Available HTTP: www.legco.gov.hk/yr99-00/english/panels/ca/papers/1076e01.pdf (accessed 27 January 2019).

Cheung, A. B. L. (2004) 'Strong Executive, Weak Policy Capacity: The Changing Environment of Policy-Making in Hong Kong', *Asian Journal of Political Science*, 12 (1): 1–30.

Cheung, A. B. L. (2005) 'Hong Kong's Post-1997 Institutional Crisis: Problems of Governance and Institutional Incompatibility', *Journal of East Asian Studies*, 5 (1): 135–67.

Cheung, A. B. L. (2007) 'Executive-Led Governance or Executive Power "Hol lowed-Out": The Political Quagmire of Hong Kong', *Asian Journal of Political Science*, 15 (1): 17–38.

Cheung, A. and Gu, X. (2002) 'Health Finance', *The Chinese Economy*, 35 (6): 34–67.

Cheung, E. and Tsang, E. (2019) 'Hong Kong's Health Care System Is Teetering on the Brink: What's Wrong with It, What Can Be Done to Fix It and Will the Budget Provide Some Answers?', *South China Morning Post*, 26 February. Online. Available HTTP: www.scmp.com/news/hong-kong/health-environment/article/2187630/hong-kongs-health-care-system-teetering-brink (accessed 27 June 2019).

Cheung, T. (2019) 'Protesting Hong Kong Nurses Demand Action over Staffing Shortages, Saying Public Hospitals Need More Staff Not Money', *South China Morning Post*, 20 January. Online. Available HTTP: www.scmp.com/news/hong-kong/health-environment/article/2182915/protesting-hong-kong-nurses-demand-action-over (accessed 28 June 2019).

Chia, N. and Tsui, A. K. C. (2005) 'Medical Savings Accounts in Singapore: How Much Is Adequate?', *Journal of Health Economics*, 24 (5): 855–75.

Chiang, T. (1997) 'Taiwan's 1995 Health Care Reform', *Health Policy*, 39 (3): 225–39.

Chiang, T. (2008) *No More Impoverished People in Healthcare: A Collection of Essays on National Health Insurance*, Chinese Version, Taipei City: National Taiwan University Press.

China Ageing Finance Forum (2018) *Older People Suffer from Chronic Illnesses and They Have to Pay 50 PerCent of Medical Expenses on Their Own*, Chinese Version. Online. Available HTTP: www.caff50.net/index.php?c=article&id=941 (accessed 6 July 2019).

China Daily (2018) 'China's Basic Medical Insurance Covers 1.35 bln People', *China Daily*, 12 February. Online. Available HTTP: www.chinadaily.com.cn/a/201802/12/WS5a81b398a3106e7dcc13c5cc.html (accessed 6 July 2019).

Chiu, S. W. K., Ho, K. C. and Lui, T. (2012) 'Reforming Health: Contrasting Trajectories of Neoliberal Restructuring in the City-States', in B. Park, R. C. Hill and A. Saito (eds.) *Locating Neoliberalism in East Asia: Neoliberalizing Spaces in Developmental States*, Malden, MA: Wiley-Blackwell, pp. 225–56.

Chiu, T., Yu, H., Goto, R., Lai, W., Li, H., Tsai, E. and Chen, Y. (2019) 'From Fragmentation toward Integration: A Preliminary Study of a New Long-Term Care Policy in a Fast-Aging Country', *BMC Geriatric*, 19: 159.

Choi, J. W., Kim, T. H., Jang, S. I., Jang, S. Y., Kim, W. and Park, E. C. (2016) 'Catastrophic Health Expenditure According to Employment Status in South Korea: A Population-Based Panel Study', *BMJ Open*, 6: e011747.

Choi, Y. and Chung, C. (2002) *Social Impact of the Korean Economic Crisis*. Online. Available HTTP: http://citeseerx.ist.psu.edu/viewdoc/download?doi=10.1.1.54 5.3768&rep=rep1&type=pdf (accessed 18 September 2018).

Chon, Y. (2014) 'The Expansion of the Korean Welfare State and Its Results: Focusing on Long-Term Care Insurance for the Elderly', *Social Policy & Administration*, 48 (6): 704–20.

Chong, Z. L. (2016) 'Budget 2016: PAP Seniors Group Seeks Review of Elder-Shield', *The Straits Times*, 11 March. Online. Available HTTP: www.straitstimes. com/singapore/budget-2016-pap-seniors-group-seeks-review-of-eldershield (accessed 19 May 2019).

Chou, S., Dearden, J., Deily, M. E. and Lien, H. (2014) *Provider Responses to a Global Budget System: The Case of Drug Expenditures in Taiwan Hospitals*. Online. Available HTTP: www3.nccu.edu.tw/~hmlien/health/lecture/Complete%20 Draft%20March%2031.pdf (accessed 25 August 2018).

Chu, M. (2018) *Why Do Doctors Oppose Mooncare?* Online. Available HTTP: www. koreabiomed.com/news/articleView.html?idxno=3360 (accessed 23 June 2019).

Chun, C. B., Kim, S. Y., Lee, J. Y. and Lee, S. Y. (2009) *Republic of Korea: Health System Review*. Online. Available HTTP: www.euro.who.int/__data/assets/pdf_ file/0019/101476/E93762.pdf (accessed 16 September 2018).

Chung, M. (1992) *State Autonomy, State Capacity, and Public Policy: The Development of Social Security Policy in Korea*, PhD thesis, Indiana University.

Colombo, F., Llena-Nozal, A., Mercier, J. and Tjadens, F. (2011) *Help Wanted? Providing and Paying for Long-Term Care*. Online. Available HTTP: https://read. oecd-ilibrary.org/social-issues-migration-health/help-wanted_9789264097759- en#page3 (accessed 25 August 2019).

Community Medical Support Network (n.d.) *The Elderly Health Assessment Pilot Programmes*. Online. Available HTTP: www.cmsn.org.hk/Site/portal/Site.aspx? id=A73-3586&lang=en-US (accessed 3 September 2019).

Conrad, H. (2017) 'Social Policy Responses to the "Gap Society": The Structural Limitations of the Japanese Welfare State and Related Official Discourse since the 1990s', in D. Chiavacci and C. Hommerich (eds.) *Social Inequality in Post-Growth Japan: Transformation during Economic and Demographic Stagnation*, London; New York: Routledge, pp. 121–33.

Consumer Financial Protection Bureau (2015) *Financial Well-Being: The Goal of Financial Education*. Online. Available HTTP: https://files.consumerfinance.gov/ f/201501_cfpb_report_financial-well-being.pdf (accessed 7 September 2019).

Copper, J. F. (1989) 'The Evolution of Political Parties in Taiwan', *Asian Affairs: An American Review*, 16 (1): 3–21.

Corbley, M. (2019) *"All My Pain Disappears": South Korean Seniors Are Finding Healing in New Nightclub for the Elderly*. Online. Available HTTP: www.

goodnewsnetwork.org/south-korean-seniors-heal-in-daytime-discos/ (accessed 5 September 2019).

Cortell, A. P. and Peterson, S. (1999) 'Altered States: Explaining Domestic Institutional Change', *British Journal of Political Science*, 29 (1): 177–203.

Cosco, T. D., Howse, K. and Brayne, C. (2017) 'Healthy Ageing, Resilience and Wellbeing', *Epidemiology and Psychiatric Sciences*, 26: 579–83.

Curry, N., Castle-Clarke, S. and Hemmings, N. (2018) *What Can England Learn from the Long-Term Care System in Japan?* Online. Available HTTP: www.nuffieldtrust.org.uk/files/2018-05/1525785625_learning-from-japan-final.pdf (accessed 24 February 2019).

Curtis, G. L. (1999) *The Logic of Japanese Politics: Leaders, Institutions, and the Limits of Change*, New York: Columbia University Press.

Department of Government Employees Insurance, and Bank of Taiwan (2011) *Statistical Data for Government Employee and School Staff Insurance*, Chinese Version. Online. Available HTTP: www.bot.com.tw (accessed 10 August 2018).

Department of Health (2012) *Primary Care Directory*. Online. Available HTTP: www.pcdirectory.gov.hk/english/welcome/welcome.html (accessed 27 June 2019).

Department of Health (2019) *Towards 2025: Strategy and Action Plan to Prevent and Control NCD in Hong Kong*. Online. Available HTTP: www.change4health.gov.hk/en/saptowards2025/ (accessed 27 June 2019).

Department of Health, Executive Yuan (n.d.) *Why Are There Deficit in the National Health Insurance?*, Chinese Version. Online. Available HTTP: www.nhi.gov.tw/Default.aspx (accessed 16 June 2019).

Diamond, L. (2002) 'Elections without Democracy: Thinking about Hybrid Regimes', *Journal of Democracy*, 13 (2): 21–35.

Dominy, N. and Kempson, E. (2006) *Understanding Older People's Experiences of Poverty and Material Deprivation*. Online. Available HTTP: www.bristol.ac.uk/media-library/sites/geography/migrated/documents/pfrc0606.pdf (accessed 7 September 2019).

Dong, W. (2001) *Health Care Reform in Urban China*. Online. Available HTTP: https://pdfs.semanticscholar.org/765c/3e6f88c5159e4ccea25fd67c944c278 59e24.pdf (accessed 7 December 2018).

Dovlo, D., Nabyonga-Orem, J., Estrelli, Y. and Mwisongo, A. (2016) 'Policy Dialogues: The "Bolts and Joints" of Policy-Making: Experiences from Cabo Verde, Chad and Mali', *BMC Health Services Research*, 16 (4): 216.

Duckett, J. (2011) *The Chinese State's Retreat from Health: Policy and the Politics of Retrenchment*, Abingdon, Oxon; New York: Routledge.

East-West Center (2002) *The Future of Population in Asia*. Online. Available HTTP: www.eastwestcenter.org/publications/future-population-asia (accessed 10 August 2019).

Eberstadt, N. (2018) *China's Demographic Prospects to 2040: Opportunities, Constraints, Potential Policy Responses*. Online. Available HTTP: www.hoover.org/research/chinas-demographic-prospects-2040-opportunities-constraints-potential-policy-responses (accessed 14 September 2019).

Eck, T. (2018) *South Korea's Demographic Deficit*. Online. Available HTTP: www.lowyinstitute.org/the-interpreter/south-korea-s-demographic-deficit (accessed 23 June 2019).

Efron, S. (1996) 'In New Japan Corruption Scandal, Official Quits amid Bribery Charges', *Los Angeles Times*, 20 November. Online. Available HTTP: www.latimes.com/archives/la-xpm-1996-11-20-mn-1009-story.html (accessed 27 April 2019).

ElderShield Review Committee (2018) *ElderShield Review Committee Report.* Online. Available HTTP: www.moh.gov.sg/docs/librariesprovider6/resources/eldershield-review-committee-report.pdf (accessed 17 May 2019).

Estévez-Abe, M. (2002) 'Negotiating Welfare Reforms: Actors and Institutions in the Japanese Welfare State', in B. Rothstein and S. Steinmo (eds.) *Restructuring the Welfare State: Political Institutions and Policy Change,* New York: Palgrave Macmillan, pp. 157–83.

Eto, M. M. (2000) 'The Establishment of Long-Term Care Insurance', in O. Hideo (ed.) *Power Shuffles and Policy Process: Coalition Government in Japan in the 1990s,* Tokyo; New York: Japan Center for International Exchange, pp. 21–50.

Eto, M. M. (2001) 'Public Involvement in Social Policy Reform: Seen from the Perspective of Japan's Elderly-Care Insurance Scheme', *Journal of Social Policy,* 1: 17–36.

EuroHealthNet, Altgeld, T. and Sinclair-Cohen, J. (2012) *Healthy and Active Ageing.* Online. Available HTTP: www.healthyageing.eu/sites/www.healthyageing.eu/files/featured/Healthy%20and%20Active%20Ageing.pdf (accessed 12 September 2019).

Exworthy, M., Lee, B. and Powell, M. (2002) 'How Great Expectations in Westminster May Be Dashed Locally: The Local Implementation of National Policy on Health Inequalities', *Policy and Politics,* 30 (1): 79–96.

Farrell, C. (2016) *Why Pressure Will Grow to Change Long-Term Care Financing.* Online. Available HTTP: www.forbes.com/sites/nextavenue/2016/05/24/why-pressure-will-grow-to-change-long-term-care-financing/#34f6ca9b4cf8 (accessed 12 August 2019).

Fell, D. (2012) *Government and Politics in Taiwan,* Milton Park, Abingdon, Oxon; New York: Routledge.

The Financial Consumer Agency of Canada (2017) *National Strategy for Financial Literacy Phase 1: Strengthening Seniors' Financial Literacy.* Online. Available HTTP: https://cnpea.ca/images/seniorsstrategyfinancialliteracy_en.pdf (accessed 9 September 2019).

Fioretos, O., Falleti, T. G. and Sheingate, A. (2016) 'Historical Institutionalism in Political Science', in O. Fioretos, T. G. Falleti and A. Sheingate (eds.) *The Oxford Handbook of Historical Institutionalism,* Oxford: Oxford University Press, pp. 3–30.

Fong, B. C. H. (2015) *Hong Kong's Governance under Chinese Sovereignty: The Failure of the State-Business Alliance after 1997,* Abingdon, Oxon; New York, NY: Routledge.

Food and Health Bureau (2008) *Your Health Your Life: Healthcare Reform Consultation Document.* Online. Available HTTP: www.fhb.gov.hk/beStrong/files/consultation/Condochealth_full_eng.pdf (accessed 1 January 2019).

Food and Health Bureau (2010) *My Health My Choice: Healthcare Reform Second Stage Public Consultation Consultation Document.* Online. Available HTTP: www.myhealthmychoice.gov.hk/pdf/consultation_full_eng.pdf (accessed 28 June 2019).

Food and Health Bureau (2011) *My Health My Choice: Healthcare Reform Second Stage Public Consultation Consultation Report.* Online. Available HTTP: www.myhealthmychoice.gov.hk/pdf/report/full_report_eng.pdf (accessed 28 June 2019).

Food and Health Bureau (2014) *Consultation Document on Voluntary Health Insurance Scheme.* Online. Available HTTP: www.vhis.gov.hk/doc/en/information_centre/consultation_full_eng.pdf (accessed 28 June 2019).

Food and Health Bureau (2017a) *Voluntary Health Insurance Scheme Consultation Report*. Online. Available HTTP: www.legco.gov.hk/yr16-17/english/panels/hs/papers/hs20170116-rpt201701-e.pdf (accessed 28 June 2019).

Food and Health Bureau (2017b) *Consultation Report on Voluntary Health Insurance Scheme*. Online. Available HTTP: www.legco.gov.hk/yr16-17/english/panels/hs/papers/hs20170116cb2-554-1-e.pdf (accessed 28 June 2019).

Food and Health Bureau (2017c) *Report of the Strategic Review on Healthcare Manpower Planning and Professional Development*. Online. Available HTTP: www.fhb.gov.hk/download/press_and_publications/otherinfo/180500_sr/e_sr_final_report.pdf (accessed 26 June 2019).

Food and Health Bureau (2019a) *Code of Practice for Insurance Companies under the Ambit of the Voluntary Health Insurance Scheme*. Online. Available HTTP: www.vhis.gov.hk/doc/en/information_centre/e_cop.pdf (accessed 28 June 2019).

Food and Health Bureau (2019b) *Legislative Council Panel on Health Services Review on the Elderly Health Care Voucher Scheme*. Online. Available HTTP: www.legco.gov.hk/yr18-19/english/panels/hs/papers/hs20190318cb2-962-1-e.pdf (accessed 25 June 2019).

Food and Health Bureau and Hospital Authority (2019) *Corporate Governance and Manpower Situation of the Hospital Authority*. Online. Available HTTP: www.legco.gov.hk/yr18-19/english/panels/hs/papers/hs20190319cb2-965-1-e.pdf (accessed 27 June 2019).

Forbes (2018) *Why Japan's Aging Population Is an Investment Opportunity*. Online. Available HTTP: www.forbes.com/sites/japan/2018/11/12/why-japans-aging-population-is-an-investment-opportunity/#74b333a4288d (accessed 22 June 2019).

Foyle, D. (1999) *Counting the Public in: Presidents, Public Opinion and Foreign Policy*, New York: Columbia University Press.

Freedom House (2015) *Freedom in the World: Singapore*. Online. Available HTTP: http://freedomhouse.org/report/freedom-world/2015/singapore (accessed 3 June 2019).

Freedom House (2018) *Freedom in the World 2018: Singapore*. Online. Available HTTP: http://freedomhouse.org/report/freedom-world/2018/singapore (accessed 3 June 2019).

Fu, A. (2012) *Integrated Shield Plans: Past, Present & Future*. Online. Available HTTP: www.actuaries.org.sg/files/library/forum_presentation/2012/2012%20HIC/S05.%20Integrated%20Shield-Past,%20Present%20&%20Future%20-%20Alvin%20Fu.pdf (accessed 13 May 2019).

Fu, L. (1995) 'The Political Economy of National Health Insurance Development in Taiwan and the United State', in L. Chang (ed.) *Social Welfare and Policy Systems in the Eastern and Western Societies*, Chinese Version, Taipei: Institute of European and American Studies, Academia Sinica, pp. 31–71.

Fujii, M. and Kawai, M. (2010) *Lessons from Japan's Banking Crisis, 1991–2005*. Online. Available HTTP: www.adb.org/sites/default/files/publication/156077/adbi-wp222.pdf (accessed 25 February 2019).

Fujii, M. and Reich, M. R. (1988) 'Rising Medical Costs and the Reform of Japan's Health Insurance System', *Health Policy*, 9 (1): 9–24.

Fukawa, T. (2002) *Public Health Insurance in Japan*. Online. Available HTTP: http://unpan1.un.org/intradoc/groups/public/documents/APCITY/UNPAN020063.pdf (accessed 16 February 2019).

Fukawa, T. (2018) 'Prevalence of Dementia among the Elderly Population in Japan', *Health and Primary Care*, 2 (4): 1–6.

Fulco, M. (2018) *Taiwan Primes for Old Age Apocalypse with Long-Term Care Plan.* Online. Available HTTP: https://international.thenewslens.com/article/106124 (accessed 25 August 2019).

Fulda, A. M. (2002) 'The Politics of Factionalism in Taiwan's Democratic Progressive Party', *Internationales Asienforum*, 33 (3–4): 323–50.

Gao, J., Tang, S., Tollhurst, R. and Rao, K. (2001) 'Changing Access to Health Services in Urban China: Implications for Equity', *Health Policy and Planning*, 16 (3): 302–12.

Garcia, A. and Wong, P. (2018) *Towards Successful Aging in Asia.* Online. Available HTTP: www.milkeninstitute.org/reports/towards-successful-aging-asia (accessed 10 August 2019).

Garud, R., Hardy, C. and Maguire, S. (2007) 'Institutional Entrepreneurship as Embedded Agency: An Introduction to the Special Issue', *Organization Studies*, 28 (7): 957–69.

Garud, R. and Karnøe, P. (2001) 'Path Creation as a Process of Mindful Deviation', in R. Garud and P. Karnoe (eds.) *Path Dependence and Creation*, Mahwah, NJ: Lawrence Erlbaum Associates, pp. 1–38.

Gauld, R. (1997) 'Health', in P. Wilding, A. S. Huque and J. Tao (eds.) *Social Policy in Hong Kong*, Cheltenham, UK; Lyme, US: E. Elgar, pp. 23–38.

Gauld, R. and Gould, D. (2002) *The Hong Kong Health Sector: Development and Change*, Hong Kong: The Chinese University Press.

The General Office of the State Council (1992) *The Notification of the State Council on the Further Reform of the Healthcare System for Staff and Workers*, Chinese Version. Online. Available HTTP: http://law.lawtime.cn/d609273614367.html (accessed 9 December 2018).

Geva-May, I. (2004) 'Riding the Wave of Opportunity: Termination in Public Policy', *Journal of Public Administration Research and Theory*, 14 (3): 309–33.

Gibson, J. (n.d.) *Korea Unveils Ambitious Plans for "Mooncare".* Online. Available HTTP: http://keia.org/korea-unveils-ambitious-plans-mooncare (accessed 23 June 2019).

Government Administration Council (1951) *The Labour Insurance Regulations of the People's Republic of China*, Chinese Version. Online. Available HTTP: http://m.law-lib.com/law/law_view.asp?id=686&page=1 (accessed 24 November 2018).

Government Administration Council (1952) *The Directive Regarding the Implementation of the Government-Funded Healthcare and Prevention Scheme for Personnel of the People's Governments, Parties, Organizations and Institutions at Various Levels in the Nation*, Chinese Version. Online. Available HTTP: www.china.com.cn/guoqing/2012-09/05/content_26746358.htm (accessed 25 November 2018).

Government Administration Council (1953) *The Labour Insurance Regulations of the People's Republic of China*, 2nd edn. Online. Available HTTP: www.cia.gov/library/readingroom/docs/CIA-RDP83-00418R006200350008-6.pdf (accessed 24 November 2018).

The Government of the Hong Kong Special Administrative Region (2017) *LCQ17: Manpower of Healthcare Professionals.* Online. Available HTTP: www.info.gov.hk/gia/general/201707/12/P2017071200517.htm?fontSize=1 (accessed 27 June 2019).

The Government of the Hong Kong Special Administrative Region (2018) *Government Launches Strategy and Action Plan to Prevent and Control Non-Communicable Diseases*. Online. Available HTTP: www.info.gov.hk/gia/general/201805/04/P2018050400399.htm?fontSize=1 (accessed 27 June 2019).

The Government of the Hong Kong Special Administrative Region (2019) *Voluntary Health Insurance Scheme to be Fully Implemented Next Monday*. Online. Available HTTP: www.info.gov.hk/gia/general/201903/29/P2019032900570.htm?fontSize=1 (accessed 28 June 2019).

The Government Information Centre (2008) *LCQ9: Medical Fee Waivers for the Elderly*. Online. Available HTTP: www.info.gov.hk/gia/general/200803/12/P200803120183.htm (accessed 1 January 2019).

The Government Information Centre (2015) *LCQ10: Private Hospitals*. Online. Available HTTP: www.info.gov.hk/gia/general/201502/25/P201502250586.htm (accessed 1 January 2019).

The Government Information Centre (2019) *SWD Invites Eligible Elderly Persons to Apply for Additional Vouchers under Second Phase of Pilot Scheme on Community Care Service Voucher for the Elderly*. Online. Available HTTP: www.info.gov.hk/gia/general/201908/26/P2019082600308.htm (accessed 27 August 2019).

Government of Singapore (2018) *Understanding ElderShield*. Online. Available HTTP: www.moneysense.gov.sg/articles/2018/10/eldershield (accessed 17 May 2019).

GovHK (2019) *Tax Deduction for Qualifying Premiums Paid under the Voluntary Health Insurance Scheme (VHIS) Policy*. Online. Available HTTP: www.gov.hk/en/residents/taxes/salaries/allowances/deductions/vhis.htm (accessed 28 June 2019).

Graham, T. W. (1994) 'Public Opinion and U.S. Foreign Policy Decision Making', in D. Deese (ed.) *The New Politics of American Foreign Policy*, New York: St. Martin's Press, pp. 190–215.

Graham, W. C. K. and Bilger, M. (2017) 'Financing Long-Term Services and Supports: Ideas from Singapore', *The Milbank Quarterly*, 95 (2): 358–407.

Greenhalgh, S. and Winckler, E. A. (2005) *Governing China's Population: From Leninist to Neoliberal Biopolitics*, Stanford, CA: Stanford University Press.

Groffen, D. A. I., Bosma, H., Van den Akker, M., Kempen, G. I. J. M. and van Eijk, J. Th. M. (2007) 'Material Deprivation and Health-Related Dysfunction in Older Dutch People: Findings from the SMILE Study', *European Journal of Public Health*, 18 (3): 258–63.

Gu, E. (2001a) 'Dismantling the Chinese Mini-Welfare State? Marketization and the Politics of Institutional Transformation, 1979–1999', *Communist and Post-Communist Studies*, 34 (1): 91–111.

Gu, E. (2001b) 'Market Transition and the Transformation of the Health Care System in Urban China', *Policy Studies*, 22 (3/4): 197–215.

Gubhaju, B. B. and Moriki-Durand, Y. (2003) 'Below-Replacement Fertility in East and Southeast Asia: Consequences and Policy Responses', *Journal of Population Research*, 20 (1): 1–18.

Guo, B. (2010) *China's Quest for Political Legitimacy: The New Equity-Enhancing Politics*, Lanham, MD: Lexington Books.

Guo, J. (2016) *How Long Does It Last for 720 Million Retired Employees Not Paying Health Insurance Premium?*, Chinese Version. Online. Available HTTP: www.yicai.com/news/4733894.html (accessed 7 July 2019).

Hacker, J. S. (2002) *The Divided Welfare State: The Battle over Public and Private Social Benefits in the United States*, Cambridge: Cambridge University Press.

Hall, P. A. (1992) 'The Movement from Keynesianism to Monetarism: Institutional Analysis and British Economic Policy in the 1970s', in S. Steinmo, K. Thelen and F. Longstreth (eds.) *Structuring Politics: Historical Institutionalism in Comparative Analysis*, Cambridge: Cambridge University Press, pp. 90–113.

Hall, P. A. and Taylor, R. C. R. (1996) 'Political Science and the Three New Institutionalisms', *Political Studies*, 44 (5): 936–57.

The Hankyoreh (2009) *Citizens' Coalition for Economic Justice Celebrates 20th Anniversary*. Online. Available HTTP: www.hani.co.kr/arti/english_edition/e_national/385353.html (accessed 3 November 2018).

Hanvoravongchai, P. (2002) *Medical Savings Accounts: Lessons Learned from International Experience*. Online. Available HTTP: www.who.int/healthinfo/paper52.pdf (accessed 17 August 2019).

Hartung, R. (2017) 'Plugging the Gaps in Your Financial Knowledge', *TODAYonline*, 8 July. Online. Available HTTP: www.todayonline.com/singapore/new-ways-become-financially-savvy (accessed 9 September 2019).

The Harvard Team (1999) *Improving Hong Kong's Health Care System: Why and for Whom?*, Hong Kong: Printing Department.

Haseltine, W. A. (2013) *Affordable Excellence: The Singapore Healthcare Story: How to Create and Manage Sustainable Healthcare Systems*, Washington, DC: Brookings Institution Press.

Hashimoto, R. and Takahashi, M. (1995) 'Between Family Obligation and Social Care: The Significance of Institutional Care for the Elderly in Japan', *The Journal of Sociology & Social Welfare*, 22 (4): 47–67.

Haynes, L. (2018) *Korea: Prioritising AI in Healthcare Innovation*. Online. Available HTTP: https://pharmaboardroom.com/articles/korea-prioritising-ai-in-healthcare-innovation/ (accessed 3 September 2019).

He, W., Goodkind, D. and Kowal, P. (2016) *International Population Reports, P95/16–1, an Aging World: 2015*, U.S. Government Publishing Office, Washington, DC. Online. Available HTTP: http://cdn.cnsnews.com/attachments/census_bureau-an_aging_world-2015.pdf (accessed 9 August 2019).

He, Z. and Zhou, J. (2017) 'Can Zero-Markup Policy for Drug Sales in Public Hospitals Resolve the Problem of "Seeing a Doctor Is Too Expensive" in China? A Case Study of Four Municipal General Tertiary Hospitals at H City in Z Province', *Journal of Chinese Governance*, 2 (3): 329–42.

Health and Welfare Bureau (2000) *Lifelong Investment in Health: Consultation Document on Health Care Reform*, Hong Kong: Health and Welfare Bureau.

Health Care Voucher Unit (2019) *Key Statistics on the Elderly Health Care Voucher Scheme for 2015–2018*. Online. Available HTTP: www.hcv.gov.hk/files/pdf/Key_Statistics_on_HCVS_(ENG).pdf (accessed 25 June 2019).

HealthHub (2017) *National Steps Challenge™ Season 3: Frequently Asked Questions*. Online. Available HTTP: www.healthhub.sg/sites/assets/Assets/Programs/nsc-2017/National%20Steps%20Challenge%20Season%203_Main%20FAQs.pdf (accessed 3 September 2019).

HealthHub (2019) *ElderShield*. Online. Available HTTP: www.healthhub.sg/a-z/costs-and-financing/8/eldershield (accessed 17 May 2019).

Health Policy Plus (n.d.) *Health Financing: The Basics*. Online. Available HTTP: www.fpfinancingroadmap.org/learning/health-financing-concepts/health-financing-basics (accessed 15 August 2019).

Health Promotion Board (2016) *HPB Dishes Out "Recipe for Healthy Ageing" to Guide Seniors towards Healthy Eating*. Online. Available HTTP: www.hpb.gov.

sg/article/hpb-dishes-out-recipe-for-healthy-ageing-to-guide-seniors-towards-healthy-eating (accessed 3 September 2019).

Health, Welfare and Food Bureau (2004) *Studies on Health Care Financing and Feasibility of a Medical Savings Scheme in Hong Kong*. Online. Available HTTP: www.legco.gov.hk/yr03-04/english/panels/hs/papers/hs0614cb2-2692-3e.pdf (accessed 28 June 2019).

Heikkinen, E. (2003) *What Are the Main Risk Factors for Disability in Old Age and How Can Disability be Prevented?*, Copenhagen, WHO Regional Office for Europe. Online. Available HTTP: www.euro.who.int/__data/assets/pdf_file/0008/74708/E82970.pdf (accessed 19 September 2019).

Hieda, T. (2012) *Political Institutions and Elderly Care Policy: Comparative Politics of Long-Term Care in Advanced Democracies*, London: Palgrave Macmillan.

Hill, M. and Hwang, Y. (2005) 'Taiwan: What Kind of Social Policy Regime?', in A. Walker and C. Wong (eds.) *East Asian Welfare Regime in Transition: From Confucianism to Globalization*, Bristol, UK: The Policy Press, pp. 145–64.

Hirano, Y. (2017) *Foreign Care Workers in Japan: A Policy without a Vision*. Online. Available HTTP: www.nippon.com/en/currents/d00288/foreign-care-workers-in-japan-a-policy-without-a-vision.html (accessed 10 June 2019).

Ho, A. H. Y. (2019) *Project ARTISAN: Aspiration and Resilience through Intergenerational Storytelling and Art-Based Narratives*. Proceedings for the 2019 Arts & Culture Research Symposium. Online. Available HTTP: www.nac.gov.sg/dam/jcr:855fa58e-cbf1-4ecc-bdff-3b32de5d3b9b (accessed 5 September 2019).

Ho, K. L. (2010) 'Political Consolidation in Singapore: Connecting the Party, the Government and the Expanding State', in T. Chong (ed.) *Management of Success: Singapore Revisited*, Singapore: Institute of Southeast Asian Studies, pp. 67–79.

Ho, T. (2017) *Seniors' Guide to Healthcare Schemes, Grants and Subsidies in Singapore*. Online. Available HTTP: https://dollarsandsense.sg/complete-guide-government-healthcare-schemes-singapore-seniors/ (accessed 15 May 2019).

Hogwood, B. W. and Gunn, L. A. (1984) *Policy Analysis for the Real World*, Oxford: Oxford University Press.

Hollingsworth, J. (2017) 'Hongkongers Top Life Expectancy Rankings Worldwide for Second Year in a Row', *South China Morning Post*, 29 July. Online. Available HTTP: www.scmp.com/news/hong-kong/health-environment/article/2104584/hongkongers-top-life-expectancy-rankings-worldwide (accessed 15 September 2019).

HONDAO Senior Citizen's Welfare Foundation (2006) *Current Services*. Online. Available HTTP: www.hondao.org.tw/en/index.html (accessed 10 September 2019).

Hong Kong Government (1964) *Development of Medical Services in Hong Kong*, Hong Kong: Government Printer.

Hong Kong Government (1974) *The Further Development of Medical and Health Services in Hong Kong*, Hong Kong: Government Printer.

Hong Kong Government (1993) *Towards Better Health: A Consultation Document*, Hong Kong: The Government Printer.

The Hong Kong Medical Association (1999) *Improving the Health Care System of Hong Kong: Change to Improve Not for the Sake of Changing*, Hong Kong: The Hong Kong Medical Association.

Hong Kong Special Administrative Region Government (1997) *The 1997 Policy Address*, Hong Kong: Printing Department.

Hong Kong Special Administrative Region Government (2018) *Elderly Health Care Voucher Scheme*. Online. Available HTTP: www.hcv.gov.hk/files/pdf/hk%20leaflet_out%20put_outline.pdf (accessed 25 June 2019).

Hong Kong Special Administrative Region Government (2019) *Relief and Enhancement Measures under Elderly Health Care Voucher Scheme*. Online. Available HTTP: www.info.gov.hk/gia/general/201906/05/P2019060500533.htm (accessed 25 June 2019).

The Hong Kong Special Administrative Region of the People's Republic of China (2018) *Towards 2025: Strategy and Action Plan to Prevent and Control Non-Communicable Diseases in Hong Kong*. Online. Available HTTP: www.chp.gov.hk/files/pdf/saptowards2025_fullreport_en.pdf (accessed 27 June 2019).

Hong Kong Standard (1998) 'Health Finance Panel "Lacks Grassroot Input"', *Hong Kong Standard*, 30 December. Online. Available HTTP: http://libwisenews.wisers.net (accessed 12 January 2019).

Hong Kong Standard (1999a) 'Chamber Attacks Proposed Insurance Schemes', *Hong Kong Standard*, 13 April. Online. Available HTTP: http://libwisenews.wisers.net (accessed 12 January 2019).

Hong Kong Standard (1999b) 'Public Input Needed for Reform Decision', *Hong Kong Standard*, 18 April. Online. Available HTTP: http://libwisenews.wisers.net (accessed 12 January 2019).

Hong Kong Standard (1999c) 'Tax Rise "No Cure" for Health Funding', *Hong Kong Standard*, 18 April. Online. Available HTTP: http://libwisenews.wisers.net (accessed 12 January 2019).

Hong Kong Standard (1999d) 'Authority Worried about Spiralling Costs', *Hong Kong Standard*, 19 April. Online. Available HTTP: http://libwisenews.wisers.net (accessed 12 January 2019).

Hong Kong Standard (1999e) 'Mandatory Insurance Plan Slammed in Health-Care Poll', *Hong Kong Standard*, 24 April. Online. Available HTTP: http://libwisenews.wisers.net (accessed 12 January 2019).

Hong Kong Standard (1999f) 'Warning Sounds on Health Payments', *Hong Kong Standard*, 26 April. Online. Available HTTP: http://libwisenews.wisers.net (accessed 12 January 2019).

Hong Kong Standard (1999g) 'At the End of the Day the Decision Is Ours, Not the Harvard Team's', *Hong Kong Standard*, 29 April. Online. Available HTTP: http://libwisenews.wisers.net (accessed 12 January 2019).

Hoshino, S. (1996) 'Paying for the Health and Social Care of the Elderly', in S. Bass, R. Morris and M. Oka (eds.) *Public Policy and the Old Age Revolution in Japan*, New York: The Haworth Press, pp. 37–56.

Hospital Authority (1997) *Hospital Authority Annual Report 1996–1997*, Hong Kong: Hospital Authority.

Hospital Authority (2010) *Hospital Authority Statistical Report 2008–2009*. Online. Available HTTP: www3.ha.org.hk/data/HAStatistics/DownloadReport/10 (accessed 26 June 2019).

Hospital Authority (2018) *Hospital Authority Statistical Report 2017–2018*. Online. Available HTTP: www3.ha.org.hk/data/HAStatistics/StatisticalReport/2017-2018 (accessed 26 June 2019).

Hospital Authority (2019a) *Waiting Time for Stable New Case Booking at Specialist Out-Patient Clinics*. Online. Available HTTP: www.ha.org.hk/haho/ho/sopc/dw_wait_ls_eng.pdf (accessed 26 June 2019).

Hospital Authority (2019b) *Public Hospitals Key Statistics during Service Demand Surge*. Online. Available HTTP: http://gia.info.gov.hk/general/201901/24/P2019012400247_302516_1_1548295577125.pdf (accessed 26 June 2019).

Housing & Development Board (2019) *Kampung Admiralty*. Online. Available HTTP: www.hdb.gov.sg/cs/infoweb/residential/where2shop/explore/woodlands/kampung-admiralty (accessed 10 September 2019).

Howlett, M. and Giest, S. (2015) 'The Policy-Making Process', in E. Araral, S. Fritzen, M. Howlett, M. Ramesh and X. Wu (eds.) *Routledge Handbook of Public Policy*, 2nd edn, London; New York: Routledge, pp. 17–28.

Howlett, M. and Ramesh, M. (1995) *Studying Public Policy: Policy Cycles and Policy Subsystems*, Toronto: Oxford University Press.

Hsiao, W. C. (1995) 'Medical Savings Accounts: Lessons from Singapore', *Health Affairs*, 14 (2): 260–6.

Hsü, I. C. Y. (2000) *The Rise of Modern China*, 6th edn, New York: Oxford University Press.

Hsu, J. C. Y. (2010) *Medical Savings Accounts: What Is at Risk?* Online. Available HTTP: www.who.int/healthsystems/topics/financing/healthreport/MSAsNo17FINAL.pdf (accessed 17 August 2019).

Hu, T., Ong, M., Lin, Z. and Li, E. (1999) 'The Effects of Economic Reform on Health Insurance and the Financial Burden for Urban Workers in China', *Health Economics*, 8 (4): 309–21.

Hu, W., Yeh, C., Shiao, A. and Tu, T. (2015) 'Effects of Diagnosis-Related Group Payment on Health-Care Provider Behaviors: A Consecutive Three-Period Study', *Journal of the Chinese Medical Association*, 78: 678–85.

Huang, C. (2016) 'MOH Appoints 14-Member Panel to Review ElderShield', *The Business Times*, 7 October. Online. Available HTTP: www.businesstimes.com.sg/government-economy/moh-appoints-14-member-panel-to-review-eldershield (accessed 19 May 2019).

Huang, H., Sheng, M. and Liu, H. (2012) *National Health Insurance*, Chinese Version, Taiwan: Wu-Nan Book Inc.

Huber, M. (1999) 'Health Expenditure Trends in OECD Countries, 1970–1997', *Health Care Financing Review*, 21 (2): 99–117.

Huenchuan, S. (2013) *Ageing, Solidarity and Social Protection in Latin America and the Caribbean: Time for Progress towards Equality*. Online. Available HTTP: https://repositorio.cepal.org/bitstream/handle/11362/2620/1/S2012882_en.pdf (accessed 10 August 2019).

Hugh, S. M. Mc, Perry, I. J., Bradley, C. and Brugha, R. (2014) 'Developing Recommendations to Improve the Quality of Diabetes Care in Ireland: A Policy Analysis', *Health Research Policy and Systems*, 12: 53.

Hundt, D. (2009) *Korea's Developmental Alliance: State, Capital and the Politics of Rapid Development*, London: New York: Routledge.

Hurd, M. D. (1990) 'Research on the Elderly: Economic Status, Retirement, and Consumption and Saving', *Journal of Economic Literature*, 28 (2): 565–637.

Hurley, J. E. and Guindon, G. E. (2008) 'Medical Savings Accounts: Promises and Pitfalls', in M. Lu and E. Jonsson (eds.) *Financing Health Care: New Ideas for a Changing Society*, Weinheim: Wiley, pp. 125–47.

Hurst, D. (2018) 'Japan Lays Groundwork for Boom in Robot Carers', *The Guardian*, 6 February. Online. Available HTTP: www.theguardian.com/world/2018/feb/06/japan-robots-will-care-for-80-of-elderly-by-2020 (accessed 10 June 2019).

Hwang, G. (2006) *Pathways to State Welfare in Korea: Interests, Ideas and Institutions*, Aldershot, England; Burlington, VT: Ashgate.

Hwang, G. (2008) 'Going Separate Ways? The Reform of Health Insurance Funds in Germany, Japan and South Korea', *Policy Studies*, 29 (4): 421–35.

Hwang, Y. and Park, H. (2018) 'Comprehensive Community Care System to Allow Elderly Koreans to Live in Their Homes by 2025', *The Hankyoreh*, 21 November. Online. Available HTTP: http://english.hani.co.kr/arti/english_edition/e_national/871188.html (accessed 10 September 2019).

Ikegami, N. (2005) 'Japan', in R. Gauld (ed.) *Comparative Health Policy in the Asia-Pacific*, Maidenhead: Open University Press, pp. 122–45.

Ikegami, N. (2007) 'Rationale, Design and Sustainability of Long-Term Care Insurance in Japan: In Retrospect', *Social Policy & Society*, 6 (3): 423–34.

Ikegami, N., Yoo, B., Hashimoto, H., Matsumoto, M., Ogata, H., Babazono, A., Watanabe, R., Shibuya, K., Yang, B., Reich, M. R. and Kobayashi, Y. (2011) 'Japanese Universal Health Coverage: Evolution, Achievements, and Challenges', *The Lancet*, 378: 1106–15.

Independent Age (2016) *If You're Feeling Lonely: How to Stay Connected in Older Age*. Online. Available HTTP: https://independent-age-assets.s3.eu-west-1.amazonaws.com/s3fs-public/2016-11/Advice-Guide-If-youre-feeling-lonely.pdf (accessed 5 September 2019).

Information Services Department (2002) *A Report on the First Five Years of the Hong Kong Special Administrative Region of the People's Republic of China*. Online. Available HTTP: www.info.gov.hk/info/sar5/content_e.htm (accessed 10 January 2019).

Inoguchi, T. (1997) 'A Step toward One-Party Predominance: Japan's General Election of 20 October 1996', *Government and Opposition*, 32 (1): 48–64.

The Institute for Health Metrics and Evaluation (2018) *Findings from the Global Burden of Disease Study 2017*. Online. Available HTTP: www.healthdata.org/sites/default/files/files/policy_report/2019/GBD_2017_Booklet.pdf (accessed 12 September 2019).

International Committee for Human Rights in Taiwan (1993) *New Political Map of Taiwan*. Online. Available HTTP: www.taiwandc.org/twcom/tc58-int.pdf (accessed 4 September 2018).

International Labour Organization (2015) *Pros and Cons of Key Financing Mechanisms for Social Health Protection*. Online. Available HTTP: www.social-protection.org/gimi/gess/ShowTheme.action?id=3108 (accessed 17 August 2019).

International Monetary Fund (2001) 'Hong Kong SAR and Crisis Recovery', *IMF Survey*, 30 (12). Online. Available HTTP: www.imf.org/external/pubs/ft/survey/survey01.htm (accessed 10 January 2019).

The Investor and Financial Education Council (2019) *Financial Literacy Strategy 2019*. Online. Available HTTP: www.ifec.org.hk/common/pdf/fls/financial-literacy-strategy-2019.pdf (accessed 9 September 2019).

Iwagami, M. and Tamiya, N. (2019) 'The Long-Term Care Insurance System in Japan: Past, Present, and Future', *JMA Journal*, 2 (1): 67–9.

Izuhara, M. (2003) 'Social Inequality under a New Social Contract: Long-Term Care in Japan', *Social Policy & Administration*, 37 (4): 395–410.

Japan Health Policy NOW (n.d.) *Long-Term Care Insurance*. Online. Available HTTP: http://japanhpn.org/en/longtermcare/ (accessed 9 June 2019).

The Japan Institute for Labour Policy and Training (2016) *Labor Situation in Japan and Its Analysis: General Overview 2015/2016*. Online. Available HTTP: www.jil.go.jp/english/lsj/general/2015-2016/2015-2016.pdf

The Japan Times (1998) 'Health Officials Face Prison over Nursery Home Subsidies', *The Japan Times*, 22 April. Online. Available HTTP: www.japantimes.co.jp/news/1998/04/22/national/health-officials-face-prison-over-nursery-home-subsidies/#.XMOuE-gzaUk (access 27 April 2019).

The Japan Times (2018a) 'Fill the Gap in Nursing Care Workers', *The Japan Times*, 26 June. Online. Available HTTP: www.japantimes.co.jp/opinion/2018/06/26/editorials/fill-gap-nursing-care-workers/#.XP3W2IgzY2w (accessed 10 June 2019).

The Japan Times (2018b) 'Centenarians in Japan Hit Record 69,785, Nearly 90% of Them Women', *The Japan Times*, 14 September. Online. Available HTTP: www.japantimes.co.jp/?post_type=news&p=1487590#.XP5IdYgzY2z (accessed 10 June 2019).

Jenike, B. R. (2003) 'Parent Care and Shifting Family Obligations in Urban Japan', in J. W. Traphagan and J. Knight (eds.) *Demographic Change and the Family in Japan's Aging Society*, Albany: State University of New York Press, pp. 177–202.

Jeon, B. and Kwon, S. (2017) 'Health and Long-Term Care Systems for Older People in the Republic of Korea: Policy Challenges and Lessons', *Health Systems & Reform*, 3 (3): 214–23.

Jeong, H. (2011) 'Korea's National Health Insurance: Lessons from the Past Three Decades', *Health Affairs*, 30 (1): 136–44.

Jing, Y., Cui, Y. and Li, D. (2015) 'The Politics of Performance Measurement in China', *Policy and Society*, 34 (1): 49–61.

Jo, Y. (2013) *Korea's Universal Health Coverage*. Online. Available HTTP: www.kdevelopedia.org/Resources/social-development/koreas-universal-health-coverage-04201311190129113.do?fldIds=TP_SOC%7CTP_SOC_HE%7CTP_GOV%7CTP_GOV_PA#.W53DVOgzaUk (accessed 16 September 2018).

The Jockey Club Centre for Positive Ageing (n.d.) *Service*. Online. Available HTTP: https://jccpa.org.hk/en/home/index.html (accessed 10 September 2019).

Johnson, C. (1982) *MITI and the Japanese Miracle: The Growth of Industrial Policy, 1925–1975*, Stanford, CA: Stanford University Press.

Jones, G. W. (2007) 'Delayed Marriage and Very Low Fertility in Pacific Asia', *Population and Development Review*, 33 (3): 453–78.

Joshua, L. (2017) *Aging and Long Term Care Systems: A Review of Finance and Governance Arrangements in Europe, North America and Asia-Pacific*. Online. Available HTTP: http://documents.worldbank.org/curated/en/761221511952743424/Aging-and-long-term-care-systems-a-review-of-finance-and-governance-arrangements-in-Europe-North-America-and-Asia-Pacific (accessed 15 August 2019).

Kamei, T., Itoi, W., Kajii, F., Kawakami, C., Hasegawa, M. and Sugimoto, T. (2011) 'Six Month Outcomes of an Innovative Weekly Intergenerational Day Program with Older Adults and School-Aged Children in a Japanese Urban Community', *Japan Journal of Nursing Science*, 8: 95–107.

Kang, M. S., Jang, H. S., Lee, M. and Park, E. (2012) 'Sustainability of Korean National Health Insurance', *Journal of Korean Medical Science*, 27: S21–S24.

Kao, E. and Tsang, E. (2019) 'Non-Urgent Patients Wait Up to 8 Hours at Hong Kong's Public Hospitals amid Flu Surge: And Things Unlikely to Get Better before Lunar New Year', *South China Morning Post*, 6 January. Online. Available HTTP: www.scmp.com/news/hong-kong/health-environment/article/2180897/non-urgent-patients-wait-8-hours-hong-kongs-public (accessed 26 June 2019).

Kasza, G. J. (2002) 'War and Welfare Policy in Japan', *The Journal of Asian Studies*, 61 (2): 417–35.

Keegan, M. (2018) 'Hong Kong's "Cardboard Grannies": The Elderly Box Collectors Living in Poverty', *South China Morning Post*, 24 April. Online. Available HTTP: www.theguardian.com/cities/2018/apr/24/hong-kong-cardboard-grannies-elderly-box-collectors-recycling-poverty (accessed 7 September 2019).

Keeler, J. T. S. (1993) 'Opening the Window for Reform: Mandates, Crises and Extraordinary Policy-Making', *Comparative Political Studies*, 25 (4): 433–86.

Khalik, S. (2017) '$5 Health Screening for 1.8 Million Singaporeans: Letters Out from August', *The Straits Times*, 16 April. Online. Available HTTP: www.straitstimes.com/singapore/health/5-health-screening-for-18-million-singaporeans-letters-out-from-august (accessed 3 September 2019).

Khew, C. (2016) 'New Toolkit by Health Promotion Board to Help Senior Citizens Eat Healthily', *The Straits Times*, 15 May. Online. Available HTTP: www.straitstimes.com/singapore/health/new-toolkit-by-health-promotion-board-to-help-senior-citizens-eat-healthily (accessed 3 September 2019).

Kim, H. and Cheng, S. (2018) 'Assessing Quality of Primary Diabetes Care in South Korea and Taiwan Using Avoidable Hospitalizations', *Health Policy*, 122: 1222–31.

Kim, S. (2005) 'Economic Crisis, Domestic Politics and Welfare State Changes', *The Pacific Review*, 18 (3): 375–91.

Kim, S. (2017) *Solidarity, Labour, and Institution: The Politics of Health Insurance Reform in Japan and South Korea*, PhD thesis, University of Sheffield. Online. Available HTTP: http://etheses.whiterose.ac.uk/17866/1/Thesis_May28_Seongjo Kim.pdf (accessed 10 September 2018).

Kim, S. (2019) 'S. Korea Faces Heated Debate over Retirement Age Extension amid Rapid Aging', *Yonhap News Agency*, 26 June. Online. Available HTTP: https://en.yna.co.kr/view/AEN20190625006500315 (accessed 10 September 2019).

Kim, S. and Jang, H. (2017) 'Korea Officially Becomes Aged Society', *The Chosunilbo*, 4 September. Online. Available HTTP: http://english.chosun.com/site/data/html_dir/2017/09/04/2017090401307.html (accessed 21 September 2019).

Kim, Y., Lee, J., Moon, Y., Kim, K. J., Lee, K., Choi, J. and Han, S. (2018) 'Unmet Healthcare Needs of Elderly People in Korea', *BMC Geriatrics*, 18: 98.

Kimura, R. (2002) 'Bioethical Public Policy and the Making of the 1997 Japanese Long-Term Care Insurance Law', in H. Conrad (ed.) *Aging and Social Policy: A German-Japanese Comparison*, Munich: Iudicium, pp. 335–50.

King, D. S. (1992) 'The Establishment of Work-Welfare Programs in the United States and Britain: Politics, Ideas, and Institutions', in S. Steinmo, K. Thelen and F. Longstreth (eds.) *Structuring Politics: Historical Institutionalism in Comparative Analysis*, Cambridge: Cambridge University Press, pp. 217–50.

Kingdon, J. W. (1984) *Agendas, Alternatives, and Public Policies*, New York: HarperCollins Publishers.

Kingdon, J. W. (2011) *Agendas, Alternatives, and Public Policies*, updated 2nd edn, White Plains: Pearson Longman.

Kitazawa, K. (2015) 'The Fukushima Nuclear Accident: Lost Opportunities and the "Safety Myth"', in Y. Funabashi and B. Kushner (eds.) *Examining Japan's Lost Decades*, Abingdon, Oxon; New York, NY: Routledge, pp. 118–34.

Kobayashi, Y. (2009) 'Five Decades of Universal Health Insurance Coverage in Japan: Lessons and Future Challenges', *JMAJ*, 52 (4): 259–62.

Korea Centers for Disease Control and Prevention (2017) *Chronic Disease Management Research & Development*. Online. Available HTTP: www.cdc.go.kr/CDC/

eng/contents/CdcEngContentView.jsp?cid=74297&menuIds=HOME002-MNU0576-MNU0582 (accessed 23 June 2019).

Korea Herald (2017) 'National Health Insurance Rate to Go Up 2.04% in 2018', *Korea Herald*, 29 August. Online. Available HTTP: www.koreaherald.com/view.php?ud=20170829000720 (accessed 22 June 2019).

The Korea Herald (2018) 'Korea to Expand Caregiving to Seniors in Their Homes', *The Korea Herald*, 20 November. Online. Available HTTP: www.koreaherald.com/view.php?ud=20181120000723 (accessed 10 September 2019).

Krauss, E. S. and Pekkanen, R. J. (2010) 'The Rise and Fall of Japan's Liberal Democratic Party', *The Journal of Asian Studies*, 69 (1): 5–15.

Ku, Y. (1997) *Welfare Capitalism in Taiwan: State, Economy and Social Policy*, Houndmills, Basingstoke, Hampshire: Macmillan Press; New York: St. Martin's Press.

Ku, Y. (1998) 'Can We Afford It? The Development of National Health Insurance in Taiwan', in R. Goodman, G. White and H. Kwon (eds.) *The East Asian Welfare Model: Welfare Orientalism and the State*, London; New York: Routledge, pp. 119–38.

Kulaç, O. and Özgür, H. (2017) 'An Overview of the Stages (Heuristics) Model as a Public Policy Analysis Framework', *European Scientific Journal*. Online. Available HTTP: https://eujournal.org/index.php/esj/article/viewFile/9250/8789 (accessed 11 July 2018).

Kwon, H. (2001) 'Globalization, Unemployment and Policy Responses in Korea: Repositioning the State?', *Global Social Policy*, 1 (2): 213–34.

Kwon, H. (2007) 'Advocacy Coalitions and Health Politics in Korea', *Social Policy & Administration*, 41 (2): 148–61.

Kwon, S. (2003) 'Health Care Financing Reform and the New Single Payer System in the Republic of Korea: Social Solidarity or Efficiency?', *International Social Security Review*, 56 (1): 75–94.

Kwon, S. (2007) 'The Fiscal Crisis of National Health Insurance in the Republic of Korea: In Search of a New Paradigm', *Social Policy & Administration*, 41 (2): 162–78.

Kwon, S. (2009) 'Thirty Years of National Health Insurance in South Korea: Lessons for Achieving Universal Health Care Coverage', *Health Policy and Planning*, 24 (1): 63–71.

Kwon, S. (2011) 'Health Care Financing in Asia: Key Issues and Challenges', *Asia-Pacific Journal of Public Health*, 23 (5): 651–61.

Kwon, S. (2015) *Republic of Korea: Merger of Statutory Health Insurance Funds*. Online. Available HTTP: https://core.ac.uk/download/pdf/51181417.pdf (accessed 16 September 2018).

Kwon, S., Lee, T. and Kim, C. (2015) *Republic of Korea Health System Review*, Manila: World Health Organization, Regional Office for the Western Pacific. Online. Available HTTP: www.searo.who.int/entity/asia_pacific_observatory/publications/hits/hit_korea/en/ (accessed 18 June 2019).

Kwon, S. and Reich, M. R. (2005) 'The Changing Process and Politics of Health Policy in Korea', *Journal of Health Politics, Policy and Law*, 30 (6): 1003–25.

Lai, O. (2002) 'Long-Term Care Policy Reform in Japan', *Journal of Aging & Social Policy*, 13 (2–3): 5–20.

Lam, J. T. M. (2003) 'Party Politics in Hong Kong during the Political Transition', in M. Sing (ed.) *Hong Kong Government and Politics*, Hong Kong: Oxford University Press, pp. 218–38.

Lam, S. (2017) 'Poor and on Their Own, South Korea's Elderly Who Will 'Work until They Die', *Channel News Asia*, 19 March. Online. Available HTTP: www. channelnewsasia.com/news/asia/poor-and-on-their-own-south-korea-s-elderly-who-will--work-until-8577758 (accessed 7 September 2019).

Lau, S. (2002a) 'Tung Chee-hwa's Governing Strategy: The Shortfall in Politics', in S. Lau (ed.) *The First Tung Chee-hwa Administration: The First Five Years of the Hong Kong Special Administrative Region*, Hong Kong: Chinese University Press, pp. 1–39.

Lau, S. (2002b) 'Preface', in S. Lau (ed.) *The First Tung Chee-hwa Administration: The First Five Years of the Hong Kong Special Administrative Region*, Hong Kong: Chinese University Press, pp. vii–x.

Lauer, R. H. (1976) 'Defining Social Problems: Public and Professional Perspectives', *Social Problems*, 24 (1): 122–30.

Law, D. S. (2017) 'Alternatives to Liberal Constitutional Democracy', *Maryland Law Review*, 77 (1): 223–43.

Lee, B. H. (1978) 'Singapore: Reconciling the Survival Ideology with the Achievement Concept', *Southeast Asian Affairs*: 229–44.

Lee, C. (2016) *When Solidarity Works: Labor-Civic Networks and Welfare States in the Market Reform Era*, New York, NY: Cambridge University Press.

Lee, C. (2018) 'Doctors Protest against "Moon Jae-in Care"', *The Korea Herald*, 20 May. Online. Available HTTP: www.koreaherald.com/view.php?ud=2018 0520000208 (accessed 23 June 2019).

Lee, E. W. Y. (1999) 'Governing Post-Colonial Hong Kong: Institutional Incongruity, Governance Crisis, and Authoritarianism', *Asian Survey*, 39 (6): 940–59.

Lee, G., Wang, D. and Li, S. (2004) 'Labor', in L. Wong, L. White and S. Gui (eds.) *Social Policy Reform in Hong Kong and Shanghai: A Tale of Two Cities*, Armonk, NY: M.E. Sharpe, pp. 127–58.

Lee, H. (2018a) 'Ministry Approves Korea's First AI-Based Medical Device', *Korea Biomedical Review*, 16 May. Online. Available HTTP: http://m.koreabiomed. com/news/articleView.html?idxno=3294 (accessed 3 September 2019).

Lee, H. (2018b) 'Seoul Approves 2 New AI-Based Medical Devices', *Korea Biomedical Review*, 20 August. Online. Available HTTP: http://m.koreabiomed.com/ news/articleView.html?idxno=3992 (accessed 3 September 2019).

Lee, I. (2019) 'Taipei Urges People Aged 40 and Older Get Free Checkup', *Taipei Times*, 23 January. Online. Available HTTP: www.taipeitimes.com/News/taiwan/ archives/2019/01/23/2003708479 (accessed 3 September 2019).

Lee, J. (2003) 'Health Care Reform in South Korea: Success or Failure?', *American Journal of Public Health*, 93 (1): 48–51.

Lee, K. (2018) '"Moon Jae-in Care" Could Hurt State-Run Healthcare', *The Korea Times*, 6 April. Online. Available HTTP: www.koreatimes.co.kr/www/ nation/2018/04/356_246774.html (accessed 23 June 2019).

Lee, M. (2000) *Chinese Occupational Welfare in Market Transition*, Basingstoke: Palgrave.

Lee, S. H. and Kim, Y. B. (2016) 'Which Type of Social Activities May Reduce Cognitive Decline in the Elderly?: A Longitudinal Population-Based Study', *BMC Geriatric*, 16: 165.

Lee, S. Y., Kim, C. W., Seo, N. K. and Lee, S. E. (2017) 'Analyzing the Historical Development and Transition of the Korean Health Care System', *Osong Public Health and Research Perspectives*, 8 (4): 247–54.

Lee, Y., Lim, S., Kim, S. Y. and Kim, G. (2019) 'Ethical Consideration of National Health Insurance Reform for Universal Health Coverage in the Republic of Korea', *Asian Bioethics Review*, 11: 41–56.

Lee, Y. M. (2013) *Shocks of Ageing Population to Medical Expenses and Ways to Response It*, Chinese Version. Online. Available HTTP: www.nhi.gov.tw/epaper/ItemDetail.aspx?DataID=3431&IsWebData=0&ItemTypeID=5&PapersID=299&PicID= (accessed 16 June 2019).

The Legislative Council (1999) *Official Record of Proceedings Wednesday, 5 May 1999*. Online. Available HTTP: www.legco.gov.hk/yr98-99/english/counmtg/hansard/990505fe.htm (accessed 12 January 2019).

The Legislative Council Commission (2019) *Panel on Health Services*. Online. Available HTTP: www.legco.gov.hk/yr99-00/english/panels/hs/general/ehs.htm (accessed 27 January 2019).

Legislative Council Secretariat (1999a) *LegCo Panel on Health Services (Minutes) 12 April 1999*. Online. Available HTTP: www.legco.gov.hk/yr98-99/english/panels/hs/minutes/hs120499.htm (accessed 25 January 2019).

Legislative Council Secretariat (1999b) *LegCo Panel on Health Services (Minutes) 12 July 1999*. Online. Available HTTP: www.legco.gov.hk/yr98-99/english/panels/hs/minutes/hs120799.htm (accessed 27 January 2019).

Legislative Council Secretariat (1999c) *LegCo Panel on Health Services (Minutes) 21 July 1999*. Online. Available HTTP: www.legco.gov.hk/yr98-99/english/panels/hs/minutes/hs210799.htm (accessed 27 January 2019).

Legislative Council Secretariat (2000) *LegCo Panel on Health Services Minutes of Meeting Held on Thursday, 14 October 1999 at 9:00 am in the Chamber of the Legislative Council Building*. Online. Available HTTP: www.legco.gov.hk/yr99-00/english/panels/hs/minutes/hs141099.pdf (accessed 25 January 2019).

Legislative Council Secretariat (2005) *Background Paper Prepared by the Legislative Council Secretariat for the Meeting on 19 July 2005: Health Care Reform*. Online. Available HTTP: www.legco.gov.hk/yr04-05/english/panels/hs/papers/hs0719cb2-2252-1e.pdf (accessed 5 January 2019).

Legislative Council Secretariat (2016) *Report of the Subcommittee on Health Protection Scheme*. Online. Available HTTP: www.legco.gov.hk/yr15-16/english/panels/hs/hs_hps/reports/hs_hpscb2-1915-e.pdf (accessed 28 June 2019).

Legislative Council Secretariat (2018) *General Outpatient Clinic Public: Private Partnership Programme*. Online. Available HTTP: www.legco.gov.hk/yr17-18/english/panels/hs/papers/hs20180212cb2-827-6-e.pdf (accessed 27 June 2019).

Legislative Council Secretariat (2019) *Elderly Health Care Voucher Scheme*. Online. Available HTTP: www.legco.gov.hk/yr18-19/english/panels/hs/papers/hs20190318cb2-964-5-e.pdf (accessed 25 June 2019).

Leong, S. H. (2018) *Health Care for All: The Good & Not-So-Great of Taiwan's Universal Coverage*. Online. Available HTTP: https://international.thenewslens.com/article/108032 (accessed 16 June 2019).

Leung, J. C. B. (1998) 'The Transformation of Social Welfare Policy: The Restructuring of the "Iron Rice Bowl"', in J. Y. S. Cheng (ed.) *China in the Post-Deng Era*, Hong Kong: Chinese University Press, pp. 617–43.

Lew, S. C. (2006) *Power Structure and Recent Political Development in Korea*. Online. Available HTTP: http://commons.ln.edu.hk/cgi/viewcontent.cgi?article=1080&context=capswp (accessed 6 November 2018).

Li, Q. (2009) *The Study on Realizing the Path to Universal Health Insurance in China*, Chinese Version, Beijing: People's Publishing House.

Li, T. (2015) *The Expenditure Is Greater Than Revenue in the Medical Insurance Funds*, Chinese Version. Online. Available HTTP: http://finance.sina.com.cn/china/20150605/015522352487.shtml (accessed 6 July 2019).

Li, X., Lu, J., Hu, S., Cheng, K. K., Maesenee, J. D., Meng, Q., Mossialos, E., Xu, D. R., Yip, W., Zhang, H., Krumholz, H. M., Jiang, L. and Hu, S. (2017) 'The Primary Health-Care System in China', *The Lancet*, 390: 2584–94.

Li, Y., Wu, Q., Xu, L., Legge, D., Hao, Y., Gao, L., Ning, N. and Wan, G. (2012) 'Factors Affecting Catastrophic Health Expenditure and Impoverishment from Medical Expenses in China: Policy Implications of Universal Health Insurance', *Bulletin of the World Health Organization*, 90: 664–71.

Lieberthal, K. G. (1992) 'Introduction: The "Fragmented Authoritarianism" Model and Its Limitations', in K. G. Lieberthal and D. M. Lampton (eds.) *Bureaucracy, Politics, and Decision Making in Post-Mao China*, Berkeley: University of California Press, pp. 1–30.

Lieberthal, K. G. (2004) *Governing China: From Revolution through Reform*, 2nd edn, New York: W.W. Norton.

Lieberthal, K. G. and Oksenberg, M. (1988) *Policy Making in China: Leaders, Structures, and Processes*, Princeton, NJ: Princeton University Press.

Lim, J. and Saxena, M. (2015) 'Social Challenges in Singapore's Healthcare System', in D. Chan (ed.) *50 Years of Social Issues in Singapore*, Singapore; NJ: World Scientific, pp. 47–60.

Lim, M. (2010) 'Health Care Reforms in Singapore', in K. G. H. Okma and L. Crivelli (eds.) *Six Countries, Six Reform Models: The Healthcare Reform: Experience of Israel, the Netherlands, New Zealand, Singapore, Switzerland and Taiwan: Healthcare Reforms "Under the Radar Screen"*, Singapore; Hackensack, NJ: World Scientific, pp. 111–36.

Lim, Y. T. (2018) *Stabilize the Finance of the National Health Insurance, Insurance Premium Will Not Increase within the Short Period of Time*, Chinese Version. Online. Available HTTP: www.healthnews.com.tw/ (accessed 16 June 2019).

Lin, C. (2002) 'The Policymaking Process for the Social Security System in Taiwan: The National Health Insurance and National Pension Program', *The Developing Economies*, 40 (3): 327–58.

Lin, W. (2006) *Social Welfare in Taiwan: A Historical and Institutional Analysis*, Chinese Version, Taiwan: Wu-Nan Book Inc.

Lin, W. (2012) *Social Welfare in Taiwan: A Historical and Institutional Analysis*, 2nd edn, Chinese Version, Taiwan: Wu-Nan Book Inc.

Liu, D. (2013) *China's New Rural Cooperative Medical Scheme: Evolution, Design and Impacts*, Frankfurt am Main: PL Academic Research.

Liu, E. and Lee, V. (1997) *Long Term Health Care Policy*. Online. Available HTTP: www.legco.gov.hk/yr97-98/english/sec/library/01plc.pdf (accessed 1 January 2019).

Liu, E. and Yue, S. Y. (1998) *Health Care Expenditure and Financing in Hong Kong*. Online. Available HTTP: www.legco.gov.hk/yr97-98/english/sec/library/06plc.pdf (accessed 2 January 2019).

Liu, G. G., Yuen, P., Hu, T., Li, L. and Liu, X. (2004) 'Urban Health Insurance Reform: What Can We Learn from the Pilot Experiment?', in A. Chen, G. G.

Liu and K. H. Zhang (eds.) *Urbanization and Social Welfare in China*, Aldershot, Hants, England; Burlington, VT: Ashgate, pp. 38–62.

Liu, H. Q. (2013) *Government-Funded Health Care Scheme: The Memory That Is Fading Away*, Chinese Version. Online. Available HTTP: http://news.ifeng. com/history/zhongguoxiandaishi/special/maozedongshidaiyiliao/detail_2013_ 11/20/31420417_1.shtml (accessed 24 November 2018).

Liu, L. (1987) 'Social Security Reforms in Japan', *Social Security Bulletin*, 50 (8): 29–37.

Liu, X. and Cao, H. (1992) 'China's Cooperative Medical System: Its Historical Transformations and the Trend of Development', *Journal of Public Health Policy*, 13 (4): 501–11.

Liu, X. and Hsiao, W. C. L. (1995) 'The Cost Escalation of Social Health Insurance Plans in China: Its Implication for Public Policy', *Social Science and Medicine*, 41 (8): 1095–1101.

Liu, X. and Mills, A. (2005) 'The Effect of Performance-Related Pay of Hospital Doctors on Hospital Behaviour: A Case Study from Shandong, China', *Human Resources for Health*, 3 (11). Online. Available HTTP: https://human-resources-health. biomedcentral.com/track/pdf/10.1186/1478-4491-3-11 (accessed 25 December 2018).

Lo, S. (2015) *Hong Kong's Indigenous Democracy: Origins, Evolution and Contentions*, Houndmills, Basingstoke, Hampshire; New York, NY: Palgrave Macmillan.

Lou, I. (2018) 'Rise in Emergency Fees at Hong Kong Public Hospitals Fails to Cut Queues and Waiting Times', *South China Morning Post*, 7 December. Online. Available HTTP: www.scmp.com/news/hong-kong/health-environment/article/ 2176994/rise-emergency-fees-hong-kong-public-hospitals (accessed 26 June 2019).

Lu, J. R. and Chiang, T. (2011) 'Evolution of Taiwan's Health Care System', *Health Economics, Policy and Law*, 6 (1): 85–107.

Lu, J. R. and Hsiao, W. C. (2003) 'Does Universal Health Insurance Make Health Care Unaffordable? Lessons from Taiwan', *Health Affairs*, 22 (3): 77–88.

Lu, P. (2017) *Long-Term Care 2.0 in Taiwan: Respond to an Aging Society*. Online. Available HTTP: www.mohw.gov.tw (accessed 25 August 2019).

Luk, S. C. Y. (2014a) *Health Insurance Reforms in Asia*, Abingdon, Oxon; New York, NY: Routledge.

Luk, S. C. Y. (2014b) 'The Politics of Healthcare Financing Reforms in Hong Kong: Lessons of the Tung and Tsang Administration', *Public Administration and Policy*, 17 (1): 15–31.

Luk, S. C. Y. (2015) 'The Politics of Drug Price Control Policy in China: Regulation, Deregulation and Re-Regulation', *The Journal of Contemporary China Studies*, 4 (1): 41–54.

Luk, S. C. Y. (2017) *Financing Healthcare in China: Towards Universal Health Insurance*, Abingdon, Oxon; New York, NY: Routledge.

Luk, S. C. Y. (2018) 'Moving towards Universal Health Coverage: Challenges for the Present and Future in China', in B. Fong, A. Ng and P. Yuen (eds.) *Sustainable Health and Long-Term Care Solutions for an Aging Population*, IGI Global, pp. 19–45.

Luk, S. C. Y. and Preston, P. (2016) *The Logic of Chinese Politics: Cores, Peripheries and Peaceful Rising*, UK: Edward Elgar Publishing Ltd.

Ma, N. (2002) 'Executive-Legislative Relations: Assessing Legislative Influence in an Executive-Dominant System', in S. Lau (ed.) *The First Tung Chee-hwa Administration:*

The First Five Years of the Hong Kong Special Administrative Region, Hong Kong: Chinese University Press, pp. 349–74.

Ma, N. (2007) *Political Development in Hong Kong: State, Political Society, and Civil Society*, Hong Kong: Hong Kong University Press.

MacLeod, S., Musich, S., Hawkins, K. and Armstrong, D. G. (2017) 'The Growing Need for Resources to Help Older Adults Manage Their Financial and Healthcare Choices', *BMC Geriatric*, 17: 84.

Mahesh, M., Abdin, E., Vaingankar, J. A., Picco, L., Jeyagurunathan, A., Binte Shafie, S., Pang, S., Sagayadevan, V., Seow, E., Chong, S. A. and Subramaniam, M. (2016) 'Disability in Singapore's Elderly Population', *Annals of the Academy of Medicine: Singapore*, 45 (7): 284–96.

Mahoney, J. (2000) 'Path Dependence in Historical Sociology', *Theory and Society*, 29 (4): 507–48.

Mahoney, J., Mohamedali, K. and Nguyen, C. (2016) 'Causality and Time in Historical Institutionalism', in O. Fioretos, T. G. Falleti and A. Sheingate (eds.) *The Oxford Handbook of Historical Institutionalism*, Oxford: Oxford University Press, pp. 71–88.

Mandatory Provident Fund Schemes Authority (2010) *MPF Tenth Anniversary*. Online. Available HTTP: www.mpfa.org.hk/eng/anni_publication/files/MPF_Tenth_Anniversary_Publication.pdf (accessed 12 January 2019).

Mandatory Provident Fund Schemes Authority (2019) *MPF System*. Online. Available HTTP: www.mpfa.org.hk/eng/mpf_system/system_features/contributions/index.jsp (accessed 12 January 2019).

March, J. G. and Olsen, J. P. (1998) 'The Institutional Dynamics of International Political Orders', *International Organization*, 52 (4): 943–69.

Masako, I. (1999) 'Japan and Its Planning toward Family Caregiving', in V. M. Lechner and M. B. Neal (eds.) *Work and Caring for the Elderly: International Perspectives*, Philadelphia, PA: Brunner/Mazel, pp. 84–100.

Matsuda, S. (2009) 'How Has the Japanese Health System Implemented the Care Management System?', *Asian Pacific Journal of Disease Management*, 3 (2): 33–8.

Mauzy, D. K. and Milne, R. S. (2002) *Singapore Politics under the People's Action Party*, New York: Routledge.

McCurry, J. (2018a) 'Japanese Centenarian Population Edges towards 70,000', *The Guardian*, 14 September. Online. Available HTTP: www.theguardian.com/world/2018/sep/14/japanese-centenarian-population-edges-towards-70000 (accessed 10 June 2019).

McCurry, J. (2018b) 'Dementia Towns': How Japan Is Evolving for Its Ageing Population', *The Guardian*, 15 January. Online. Available HTTP: www.theguardian.com/world/2018/jan/15/dementia-towns-japan-ageing-population (accessed 10 September 2019).

McGregor, T. (2019) 'Commentary: Why China Is Making a Strong Push for Financial Literacy in School', *Channel News Asia*, 6 April. Online. Available HTTP: www.channelnewsasia.com/news/commentary/financial-literacy-china-schools-teaching-students-how-11384174 (accessed 10 September 2019).

McGuire, J. W. (2010) *Wealth, Health, and Democracy in East Asia and Latin America*, Cambridge: Cambridge University Press.

McKenna, H., Dunn, P., Northern, E. and Buckley, T. (2017) *How Health Care Is Funded*. Online. Available HTTP: www.kingsfund.org.uk/publications/how-health-care-is-funded (accessed 17 August 2019).

McIntyre, D. and Kutzin, J. (2012) 'Revenue Collection and Pooling Arrangements in Financing', in R. D. Smith and K. Hanson (eds.) *Health Systems in Low- and Middle-Income Countries: An Economic and Policy Perspective*, Oxford: Oxford University Press, pp. 77–102.

MediShield Life Review Committee (2014) *MediShield Life Review Committee Report*. Online. Available HTTP: www.moh.gov.sg/docs/librariesprovider5/default-document-library/medishield_life_review_committee_report_final.pdf (accessed 13 May 2019).

Melnyk, B. M. and Neale, S. (2018) 'Social Wellness: Nurture Your Relationships', *American Nurse Today*, 13 (7): 42–4. Online. Available HTTP: www.americannursetoday.com/social-wellness-nurture-relationships/ (accessed 4 September 2019).

Mengin, F. (2015) *Fragments of an Unfinished War: Taiwanese Entrepreneurs and the Partition of China*, Oxford: Oxford University Press.

Menon, J. and Melendez-Nakamura, A. (2009) *Aging in Asia: Trends, Impacts and Responses*. Online. Available HTTP: www.adb.org/publications/aging-asia-trends-impacts-and-responses (accessed 10 August 2019).

Milakovich, M. E. and Gordon, G. J. (2013) *Public Administration in America*, 11th edn, Boston: Wadsworth Cengage Learning.

Ministry of Culture (2011) *Government Employee and School Staff Insurance*. Online. Available HTTP: http://nrch.culture.tw/twpedia.aspx?id=3957 (accessed 10 August 2018).

Ministry of Foreign Affairs of Japan (1996) *Policy Speech by Prime Minister Ryutaro Hashimoto to the 136th Session of the National Diet*. Online. Available HTTP: www.mofa.go.jp/region/n-america/us/security/alliance/ry_136.html (accessed 7 April 2019).

Ministry of Health (1952) *Implementation Methods of the Government-Funded Healthcare and Prevention*, Chinese Version. Online. Available HTTP: http://laws.66law.cn/law-9425.aspx (accessed 24 November 2018).

Ministry of Health (1983) *The National Health Plan*, Singapore: Ministry of Health.

Ministry of Health (2015) *Medisave: Helping You Save for Your Healthcare Needs*. Online. Available HTTP: www.moh.gov.sg/docs/librariesprovider5/schemes-subsidies/medisave/medisave_booklet_b5_complete_fa_rev2_path.pdf (accessed 12 May 2019).

Ministry of Health (2018a) *Medisave*. Online. Available HTTP: www.moh.gov.sg/cost-financing/healthcare-schemes-subsidies/medisave (accessed 12 May 2019).

Ministry of Health (2018b) *MediShield Life*. Online. Available HTTP: www.moh.gov.sg/cost-financing/healthcare-schemes-subsidies/medishield-life (accessed 14 May 2019).

Ministry of Health (2018c) *Medical Endowment Scheme: Annual Report 2017/2018*. Online. Available HTTP: www.moh.gov.sg/docs/librariesprovider5/default-document-library/fy17-annual-reportfa00bd1805e84b2cba90d4b47417c309.pdf (accessed 15 May 2019).

Ministry of Health (2018d) *Medifund*. Online. Available HTTP: www.moh.gov.sg/cost-financing/healthcare-schemes-subsidies/medifund (accessed 15 May 2019).

Ministry of Health (2018e) *Medifund Continues to Assist Needy Singaporeans with Their Healthcare Needs*. Online. Available HTTP: www.moh.gov.sg/news-highlights/details/medifund-continues-to-assist-needy-singaporeans-with-their-healthcare-needs (accessed 15 May 2019).

Ministry of Health (2018f) *ElderShield Premiums*. Online. Available HTTP: www. moh.gov.sg/careshieldlife/about-eldershield/premiums (accessed 17 May 2019).

Ministry of Health (2018g) *ElderShield Supplements*. Online. Available HTTP: www. moh.gov.sg/careshieldlife/about-eldershield/supplements (accessed 17 May 2019).

Ministry of Health (n.d.) *Introduction to the 3Ms*. Online. Available HTTP: www.moh. gov.sg/docs/librariesprovider5/resources-statistics/educational-resources/3m_ updated_engwebver77d4b49ef2a145d7b242894738b8c835.pdf (accessed 15 May 2019).

Ministry of Health and Ministry of Finance (1984) *Notice on Further Strengthening the Management of the Government-Funded Healthcare Scheme*, Chinese Version. Online. Available HTTP: www.chinalawedu.com/falvfagui/fg22598/23676. shtml (accessed 6 December 2018).

Ministry of Information and the Arts (1994) *Ministerial Statement by Bg (Ns) George Yeo on MediShield Plus in Parliament on 17 January 1994*. Online. Available HTTP: www.nas.gov.sg/archivesonline/data/pdfdoc/yybg19940117s.pdf (accessed 13 May 2019).

Ministry of the Interior (2013) *Farmer Health Insurance Act*. Online. Available HTTP: www.moi.gov.tw/english/english_law/law_detail.aspx?sn=207 (accessed 11 August 2018).

Ministry of Labour and the All-China Federation of Trade Union (1966) *The Circular on Several Questions Concerning the Improvement of the Labour Health Insurance System*, Chinese Version. Online. Available HTTP: http://laws.66law.cn/law-17700. aspx (accessed 24 November 2018).

Mohamed Nasir, K. and Turner, B. S. (2013) 'Governing as Gardening: Reflections on Soft Authoritarianism in Singapore', *Citizenship Studies*, 17 (3–4): 339–52.

Monetary Authority of Singapore (2015) *Review of Accident & Health Regulatory Framework*. Online. Available HTTP: www.mas.gov.sg/~/media/resource/publications/consult_papers/2015/Consultation%20Paper%20on%20Review%20 of%20Accident%20and%20Health%20Regulatory%20Framework%202015.pdf (accessed 13 May 2019).

Moon, T. J. (2011) 'The Light and Dark of Healthcare in South Korea', *Japan Medical Association Journal*, 54 (4): 223–8.

Moon, T. J. (2012) 'Light and Shadows of the Korean Healthcare System', *Journal of Korean Medical Science*, 27: S3–S6.

Mucciaroni, G. (1992) 'The Garbage Can Model & the Study of Policy Making: A Critique', *Polity*, 24 (3): 459–82.

Mulgan, A. G. (2000) *The Politics of Agriculture in Japan*, London: Routledge.

Mutalib, H. (2000) 'Illiberal Democracy and the Future of Opposition in Singapore', *Third World Quarterly*, 21 (2): 313–42.

Na, S. and Kwon, S. (2015) *Building Systems for Universal Health Insurance Coverage in South Korea*. Online. Available HTTP: http://documents.worldbank.org/ curated/en/367221468186565282/pdf/98266-WP-Box385353B-PUBLIC-UHC-in-South-Korea.pdf (accessed 16 September 2018).

Nahm, S. (2014) *The Work of Play: Child Psychotherapy in Contemporary Korea*, Lanham, Maryland: Lexington Books.

Nakamura, R. (1987) 'The Textbook Process and Implementation Research', *Policy Studies Review*, 7 (1): 142–54.

Nam, I. (2015) *Democratizing Health Care: Welfare State Building in Korea and Thailand*, Houndmills, Basingstoke, Hampshire; New York, NY: Palgrave Macmillan.

National Health Insurance Administration (2016a) *Premium Subsidies for the Disadvantaged*. Online. Available HTTP: www.nhi.gov.tw/english/Content_List.aspx?n=504FC0157368B239&topn=1D1ECC54F86E9050 (accessed 15 June 2019).

National Health Insurance Administration (2016b) *If You Are Unable to Pay Your Premiums or Co-Payments*. Online. Available HTTP: www.nhi.gov.tw/english/Content_List.aspx?n=1F99E850D7BF8DC4&topn=1D1ECC54F86E9050 (accessed 15 June 2019).

National Health Insurance Administration (2016c) *2016–2017 National Health Insurance Annual Report*. Online. Available HTTP: www.nhi.gov.tw/Resource/webdata/13767_1_National%20Health%20Insurance%20in%20Taiwan%202016-2017(bilingual).pdf (accessed 16 June 2019).

National Health Insurance Administration (2017) *2017–2018 National Health Insurance Annual Report*. Online. Available HTTP: www.nhi.gov.tw/english/Content_List.aspx?n=8FC0974BBFEFA56D&topn=ED4A30E51A609E49 (accessed 15 June 2019).

National Health Insurance Administration (2018a) *2018–2019 Handbook of Taiwan's National Health Insurance*. Online. Available HTTP: https://ws.nhi.gov.tw/001/Upload/293/RelFile/Ebook/English.pdf (accessed 15 June 2019).

National Health Insurance Administration (2018b) *2018–2019 National Health Insurance Annual Report*. Online. Available HTTP: www.nhi.gov.tw/resource/Webdata/2018-19%E5%85%A8%E6%B0%91%E5%81%A5%E5%BA%B7%E4%BF%9D%E9%9A%AA%E5%B9%B4%E5%A0%B1.pdf (accessed 16 June 2019).

National Health Insurance Service (2014) *2014 National Health Insurance System of Korea: Universal Health Coverage for the World*. Online. Available HTTP: www.coopami.org/en/countries/countries/south_korea/social_protection/pdf/social_protection05.pdf (accessed 18 June 2019).

National Health Insurance Service (2015) *National Health Insurance System of Korea*. Online. Available HTTP: www.nhis.or.kr/english (accessed 18 June 2019).

National Library Board Singapore (2019a) *Medisave*. Online. Available HTTP: http://eresources.nlb.gov.sg/infopedia/articles/SIP_2013-08-19_180653.html (accessed 13 May 2019).

National Library Board Singapore (2019b) *"Have Three, or More If You Can Afford It" Is Announced*. Online. Available HTTP: http://eresources.nlb.gov.sg/history/events/1d106f7e-aca1-4c0e-ac7a-d35d0772707d (accessed 18 May 2019).

Naughton, B. (1997) 'Danwei: The Economic Foundations of a Unique Institution', in X. Lü and E. J. Perry (eds.) *Danwei: The Changing Chinese Workplace in Historical and Comparative Perspective*, Armonk, NY: M.E. Sharpe, pp. 169–94.

Neo, C. C. (2017) 'All Eyes on Payouts as ElderShield Review Gets under Way', *TODAY*, 3 January. Online. Available HTTP: www.todayonline.com/singapore/all-eyes-payouts-eldershield-review-gets-under-way (accessed 19 May 2019).

Ng, G. T. (2007) 'Learning from Japanese Experience in Aged Care Policy', *Asian Social Work and Policy Review*, 1 (1): 36–51.

Ng, N. (2018) 'Hong Kong Short of 200 Nurses as Hospitals Grapple with Deadly Flu Season', *South China Morning Post*, 27 January. Online. Available HTTP: www.scmp.com/news/hong-kong/health-environment/article/2130851/hong-kong-short-200-nurses-hospitals-grapple (accessed 27 June 2019).

The NHS Website (2018) *Loneliness in Older People*. Online. Available HTTP: www.nhs.uk/conditions/stress-anxiety-depression/loneliness-in-older-people/ (accessed 5 September 2019).

Nokubi, F. (2017) *Examining the Acceptance of Foreign Care and Domestic Workers from the Human Rights Perspective.* Online. Available HTTP: www.psaj.org/2017/05/29/examining-the-acceptance-of-foreign-care-and-domestic-workers-from-the-human-rights-perspectives/ (accessed 10 June 2019).

Nomura, S., Sakamoto, H., Glenn, S., Tsugawa, Y., Abe, S. K., Rahman, M. M., Brown, J. C., Ezoe, S., Fitzmaurice, C., Inokuchi, T., Kassebaum, N. J., Kawakami, N., Kita, Y., Kondo, N., Lim, S. S., Maruyama, S., Miyata, H., Mooney, M. D., Naghavi, M., Onoda, T., Ota, E., Otake, Y., Roth, G. A., Saito, E., Tabuchi, T., Takasaki, Y., Tanimura, T., Uechi, M., Vos, T., Wang, H., Inove, M., Murray, C. J. L. and Shibuya, K. (2017) 'Population Health and Regional Variations of Disease Burden in Japan, 1990–2015: A Systematic Subnational Analysis for the Global Burden of Disease Study 2015', *The Lancet*, 390: 1521–38.

Oberländer, C. (2003) 'Universal Health Insurance in Japan', in K. Marshall and O. Butzbach (eds.) *New Social Policy Agendas for Europe and Asia: Challenges, Experience, and Lessons*, Washington, DC: World Bank, pp. 87–99.

OECD Study on Private Health Insurance (2004) *Proposal for a Taxonomy of Health Insurance.* Online. Available HTTP: www.oecd.org/health/health-systems/31916207.pdf (accessed 17 August 2019).

Ogawa, S., Hasegawa, T., Carrin, G. and Kawabata, K. (2003) 'Scaling Up Community Health Insurance: Japan's Experience with the 19th Century Jyorei Scheme', *Health Policy and Planning*, 18 (3): 270–8.

Olivares-Tirado, P. and Tamiya, N. (2014) *Trends and Factors in Japan's Long-Term Care Insurance System*, Dordrecht: Springer; Netherlands: Imprint-Springer.

Oliver, A. and Mossialos, E. (2005) 'European Health Systems Reforms: Looking Backward to See Forward?', *Journal of Health Politics, Policy and Law*, 30 (1–2): 7–28.

One Foundation Hong Kong (2016) *An Investment for the Celebration of Aging.* Online. Available HTTP: www.ourhkfoundation.org.hk/sites/default/files/media/pdf/OHKF_20161206_Aging_eng.pdf (accessed 27 August 2019).

Organization for Economic Co-operation and Development (1997) *OECD Economic Surveys: Japan 1997*, OECD Publishing.

Organization for Economic Co-operation and Development (2003) *OECD Reviews of Health Care Systems: Korea 2003.* Online. Available HTTP: www.oecd-ilibrary.org/social-issues-migration-health/oecd-reviews-of-health-care-systems-korea-2003_9789264299474-en (accessed 20 June 2019).

Organization for Economic Co-operation and Development (2012) *OECD Health Care Quality Review: Korea.* Online. Available HTTP: www.oecd.org/korea/49818570.pdf (accessed 22 June 2019).

Organization for Economic Co-operation and Development (2015) *How Does Health Spending in Korea Compared?* Online. Available HTTP: www.oecd.org/els/health-systems/Country-Note-KOREA-OECD-Health-Statistics-2015.pdf (accessed 22 June 2019).

Organization for Economic Co-operation and Development (2016) *Health Policy in Korea.* Online. Available HTTP: www.oecd.org/korea/Health-Policy-in-Korea-April-2016.pdf (accessed 26 October 2018).

Organization for Economic Co-operation and Development (2017) *Health at a Glance 2017: OECD Indicators.* Online. Available HTTP: www.oecd-ilibrary.org/social-issues-migration-health/health-at-a-glance-2017/avoidable-hospital-admissions_health_glance-2017-31-en (accessed 23 June 2019).

Organization for Economic Co-operation and Development (2019a) *OECD Economic Surveys: Japan 2019*, Paris: OECD Publishing.

Organization for Economic Co-operation and Development (2019b) *PISA 2018 Assessment and Analytical Framework*, Paris: OECD Publishing.

Ortmann, S. (2011) 'Singapore: Authoritarian But Newly Competitive', *Journal of Democracy*, 22 (4): 153–64.

Osaka, C. (2009) 'Japan's Elderly Playgrounds Show Fun Is for Everyone', *Reuters*, 26 October. Online. Available HTTP: www.reuters.com/article/us-japan-playgrounds-idUSTRE59P0XG20091026 (accessed 3 September 2019).

Osawa, M. (2011) *Social Security in Contemporary Japan*, London: Routledge.

Ozawa, M. N. and Kono, S. (1997) 'Child-Wellbeing in Japan: The High Cost of Economic Success', in G. A. Cornia and S. Danziger (eds.) *Child Poverty and Deprivation in the Industrialized Countries, 1945–1995*, New York: Oxford University Press, pp. 307–36.

Ozawa, M. N. and Nakayama, S. (2005) 'Long-Term Care Insurance in Japan', *Journal of Aging & Social Policy*, 17 (3): 61–84.

Padoveze, M. C. and de Figueiredo, R. M. (2014) 'The Role of Primary Care in the Prevention and Control of Healthcare Associated Infections', *Rev Esc Enferm USP*, 48 (6): 1132–8.

Parliament of Singapore (2018) *CareShield Life*. Online. Available HTTP: https://sprs.parl.gov.sg/search/sprs3topic?reportid=motion-47 (accessed 27 May 2019).

Pei, J. (2002) *The Promulgation and Amendments of the National Health Insurance Act in Taiwan*, Chinese Version. Online. Available HTTP: http://b020.hv.knu.edu.tw/ezfiles/20/1020/img/124/739504135.pdf (accessed 26 August 2018).

Pempel, T. J. (1974) 'The Bureaucratization of Policymaking in Postwar Japan', *American Journal of Political Science*, 18 (4): 647–64.

Pempel, T. J. (1992) 'Bureaucracy in Japan', *PS: Political Science and Politics*, 25 (1): 19–24.

Peng, I. (2002) 'Social Care in Crisis: Gender, Demography, and Welfare State Restructuring in Japan', *Social Politics: International Studies in Gender, State & Society*, 9 (3): 411–43.

Peng, I. (2003) 'Gender, Demographic, and Welfare State Restructuring in Japan', in K. Marshall and O. Butzbach (eds.) *New Social Policy Agendas for Europe and Asia: Challenges, Experience, and Lessons*, Washington, DC: World Bank, pp. 215–42.

Peng, I. (2005) 'The New Politics of the Welfare State in a Developmental Context: Explaining the 1990s Social Care Expansion in Japan', in H. Kwon (ed.) *Transforming the Developmental Welfare State in East Asia*, London, UK: Palgrave Macmillan; Imprint-Palgrave Macmillan, pp. 73–97.

Peng, I. (2008) 'Ageing and the Social Security System', in F. Coulmas, H. Conrad, A. Schad-Seifert and G. Vogt (eds.) *The Demographic Challenge: A Handbook about Japan*, Leiden: Brill, pp. 1033–48.

Peng, S. and Chen, L. (2011a) *Reforming China: Major Events (1978–1991)*, Singapore: Enrich Professional Publishing.

Peng, S. and Chen, L. (2011b) *Reforming China: Major Events (1992–2004)*, Singapore: Enrich Professional Publishing.

The People's Action Party Seniors Group (2016) *Singapore Budge 2016 Recommendations by the PAP.SG*. Online. Available HTTP: https://papwebcdn.azureedge.net/upload/item/Events/2016/PAP%20SG%20Budget%202016%20Recommendations.pdf (accessed 19 May 2019).

Peou, S. (2014) 'The Limits and Potential of Liberal Democratisation in Southeast Asia', *Journal of Current Southeast Asian Affairs*, 33 (3): 19–47.

Pew Research Center (2014) *Attitudes about Ageing: A Global Perspective: In a Rapidly Graying World, Japanese Are Worried, Americans Aren't.* Online. Available HTTP: www.pewresearch.org/global/2014/01/30/attitudes-about-aging-a-global-perspective/ (accessed 12 August 2019).

Phua, K. H. and Yap, M. T. (1998) 'Financing Health Care in Old Age: Policy Issues and Implications in Singapore', *Asian Journal of Political Science*, 6 (1): 120–37.

Pierson, P. (1994) *Dismantling the Welfare State? Reagan, Thatcher, and the Politics of Retrenchment*, Cambridge, England; New York: Cambridge University Press.

Pierson, P. (2000) 'Not Just What, But When: Timing and Sequence in Political Process', *Studies in American Political Development*, 14 (1): 72–92.

Pierson, P. (2004) *Politics in Time: History, Institutions, and Social Analysis*, Princeton, NJ: Princeton University Press.

Pierson, P. and Skocpol, T. (2002) 'Historical Institutionalism in Contemporary Political Science', in I. Katznelson and H. V. Milner (eds.) *Political Science: State of the Discipline*, New York: Norton; Washington, DC: American Political Science Association, pp. 693–721.

Population.sg (2016) *Singapore: A Super-Aged Country?* Online. Available HTTP: www.population.sg/articles/singapore-a-superaged-country (accessed 18 May 2019).

Powell, M. and Anesaki, M. (1990) *Health Care in Japan*, London; New York: Routledge.

Prime Minister's Office Singapore (2011) *Speech by Prime Minister Lee Hsien Loong at the Debate on The President's Address, 20 October 2011 at Parliament.* Online. Available HTTP: www.pmo.gov.sg/Newsroom/speech-prime-minister-lee-hsien-loong-debate-presidents-address-20-october-2011 (accessed 3 June 2019).

Prime Minister's Office Singapore (2016) *National Day Rally 2016 Speech (Chinese).* Online. Available HTTP: www.pmo.gov.sg/Newsroom/national-day-rally-2016-speech-chinese (accessed 19May 2019).

Prince, M., Guerchet, M. and Prina, M. (2015) *The Epidemiology and Impact of Dementia: Current State and Future Trends.* Online. Available HTTP: www.who.int/mental_health/neurology/dementia/dementia_thematicbrief_epidemiology.pdf (accessed 10 September 2019).

Quah, S. R. (1977) 'Accessibility of Modern and Traditional Health Services in Singapore', *Social Science & Medicine*, 11 (5): 333–40.

Rechel, B., Doyle, Y., Grundy, E. and McKee, M. (2009) *How Can Health Systems Respond to Population Ageing?* Online. Available HTTP: www.euro.who.int/__data/assets/pdf_file/0004/64966/E92560.pdf (accessed 3 September 2019).

Reid, T. R. (2009a) *The Healing of America: A Global Quest for Better, Cheaper, and Fairer Health Care*, New York: Penguin Press.

Reid, T. R. (2009b) *Four Basic Models of Health Care.* Online. Available HTTP: https://changeagent.nelrc.org/wp-content/uploads/2018/05/Four-Basic-Models-of-Health-Care.pdf (accessed 17 August 2019).

The Research Office of the Legislative Council Secretariat (2019) *Emergency Care Services in Selected Places.* Online. Available HTTP: www.legco.gov.hk/research-publications/english/1819in05-emergency-care-services-in-selected-places-20190131-e.pdf (accessed 26 June 2019).

Reynolds, J. (2015) *China Pushes Integrated Medical and Nursing Care for Elderly.* Online. Available HTTP: www.fiercepharma.com/pharma-asia/china-pushes-integrated-medical-and-nursing-care-for-elderly (accessed 7 July 2019).

Rhee, J. C., Done, N. and Anderson, G. F. (2015) 'Considering Long-Term Care Insurance for Middle-Income Countries: Comparing South Korea with Japan and Germany', *Health Policy*, 119: 1319–29.

Rickards, J. (2019) *The Looming Challenge for National Healthcare Insurance*. Online. Available HTTP: https://topics.amcham.com.tw/2019/05/the-looming-challenge-for-national-healthcare-insurance/ (accessed 16 June 2019).

Ridde, V. (2009) 'Policy Implementation in an African State: An Extension of Kingdon's Multiple-Streams Approach', *Public Administration*, 87 (4): 938–54.

Rigger, S. (2001) *From Opposition to Power: Taiwan's Democratic Progressive Party*, Boulder: L. Rienner Publishers.

Ripley, R. (1985) *Policy Analysis in Political Science*, Chicago, IL: Nelson Hall Publishers.

Rivers, P. A., McLeary, K. J. and Glover, S. H. (2000) 'Long-Term Care Financing: Are Current Methods Enough?', *Journal of Health and Human Services Administration*, 22 (4): 472–94.

Roberts, N. and King, P. (1991) 'Policy Entrepreneurs: Their Activity Structure and Function in the Policy Process', *Journal of Public Administration Research and Theory*, 1 (2): 147–75.

Rodan, G. (1989) *The Political Economy of Singapore's Industrialization: National State and International Capital*, Basingstoke: Macmillan.

Rodan, G. (1993) 'Preserving the One-Party State in Contemporary Singapore', in K. Hewison, R. Robison and G. Rodan (eds.) *Southeast Asia in the 1990s: Authoritarianism, Democracy and Capitalism*, St. Leonards, NSW, Australia: Allen & Unwin, pp. 77–108.

Roemer, M. I. (1976) *Health Care Systems in World Perspective*, Ann Arbor, MI: Health Administration Press.

Roser, M. (2014) *Fertility Rate*. Online. Available HTTP: https://ourworldindata.org/fertility-rate (accessed 11 August 2019).

Roser, M. (2019) *Life Expectancy*. Online. Available HTTP: https://ourworldindata.org/life-expectancy (accessed 12 September 2019).

Sabatier, P. A. (1991) 'Toward Better Theories of the Policy Process', *PS: Political Science and Politics*, 24 (2): 147–56.

Safiliou-Rothschild, C. (2009) 'Are Old People Responsible for High Healthcare Costs?', *CESifo Forum*, 10 (1): 57–64. Online. Available HTTP: www.ifo.de/DocDL/forum1-09-special3.pdf (accessed 11 August 2019).

Sager, F. and Thomann, E. (2017) 'Multiple Streams in Member State Implementation: Politics, Problem Construction and Policy Paths in Swiss Asylum Policy', *Journal of Public Policy*, 37 (3): 287–314.

Saich, T. (2004) *Governance and Politics of China*, 2nd edn, Basingstoke, Hampshire, UK; New York: Palgrave Macmillan.

Sakamoto, H., Rahman, M., Nomura, S., Okamoto, E., Koike, S., Yasunaga, H. *et al.* (2018) *Japan Health System Review*, New Delhi: World Health Organization, Regional Office for South-East Asia. Online. Available HTTP: www.searo.who.int/entity/asia_pacific_observatory/publications/hits/hit_japan/en/ (accessed 17 February 2019).

Saltman, R. B. (2004) 'Social Health Insurance in Perspective: The Challenge of Sustaining Stability', in R. B. Saltman, R. Busse and J. Figueras (eds.) *Social Health Insurance Systems in Western Europe*, Maidenhead: Open University Press, pp. 3–20.

Savedoff, W. (2004) *Tax-Based Financing for Health Systems: Options and Experiences*. Online. Available HTTP: www.who.int/health_financing/taxed_based_financing_dp_04_4.pdf (accessed 17 August 2019).

Scanlon, W. J. (1988) 'A Perspective on Long-Term Care for the Elderly', *Health Care Financing Review*, Annual Supplement: 7–15.

Schedler, A. (2006) 'The Logic of Electoral Authoritarianism', in A. Schedler (ed.) *Electoral Authoritarianism: The Dynamics of Unfree Competition*, Boulder, CO: L. Rienner Publishers, pp. 1–23.

Scheffler, R. and Yu, W. (1998) 'Medical Savings Accounts: A Worthy Experiment', *European Journal of Public Health*, 8 (4): 274–6.

Schieber, G., Baeza, C., Kress, D. and Maier, M. (2006) 'Financing Health Systems in the 21st Century', in D. T. Jamison, J. G. Breman, A. R. Measham, G. Alleyne, M. Claeson, D. B. Evans, P. Jha, A. Mills and P. Musgrove (eds.) *Disease Control Priorities in Developing Countries*, 2nd edn, Washington, DC: World Bank and Oxford University Press, pp. 225–42.

Schoppa, L. (2006) *Race for the Exits: The Unraveling of Japan's System of Social Protection*, Ithaca, NY: Cornell University Press.

ScienceDaily (2016) *A New Exercise Partner Is the Key to Exercising More*. Online. Available HTTP: www.sciencedaily.com/releases/2016/10/161004081548.htm (accessed 17 September 2019).

Seow, J. (2019a) 'National Day Rally 2019: Retirement Age to Go Up to 65, Older Workers' CPF Rates to Be Raised', *The Straits Times*, 18 August. Online. Available HTTP: www.straitstimes.com/politics/national-day-rally-2019-retirement-age-to-go-up-to-65-older-workers-cpf-rates-to-be-raised (accessed 10 September 2019).

Seow, J. (2019b) 'MOM Mulls over Extending Job Redesign Grant for Older Workers', *The Straits Times*, 15 February. Online. Available HTTP: www.straitstimes.com/business/mom-mulls-over-extending-job-redesign-grant-for-older-workers (accessed 10 September 2019).

Shi, J. X. (2003) *The Pattern and Development of Health Insurance in China*, Chinese Version, Beijing: China Price Press.

Shih, M., Sun, M. T. and Wang, G. (2012) 'The Historical Institutionalism Analysis of Taiwan's Administrative Reform', *International Review of Administrative Sciences*, 78 (2): 305–27.

Shin, D. (2003) *Social and Economic Policies in Korea: Ideas, Networks and Linkages*, London; New York: RoutledgeCurzon.

Siaroff, A. (2009) *Comparing Political Regimes: A Thematic Introduction to Comparative Politics*, 2nd edn, University of Toronto Press, Higher Education Division.

Sim, J. B. Y. and Krishnasamy, M. (2016) 'Building a Democratic Society: Exploring Singapore Students' Understandings of Democracy', *Asian Education and Development Studies*, 5 (1): 37–58.

Sims, C. and Miskel, C. (2003) 'The Punctuated Equilibrium of National Reading Policy', in W. Hoy and C. Miskel (eds.) *Studies in Leading and Organizing Schools*, Greenwich, CT: Information Age Publishing, pp. 1–26.

Singapore Department of Statistics (2018) *Population Trends, 2018*. Online. Available HTTP: www.singstat.gov.sg/-/media/files/publications/population/population2018.pdf (accessed 18 May 2019).

Singapore International School (Hong Kong) (2019) *Building Intergenerational Relationships through Art*. Online. Available HTTP: www.singapore.edu.hk/

2019/02/15/building-intergenerational-relationships-through-art/ (accessed 5 September 2019).

Sng, H. L. (2019) 'Commentary: Opening Earlier and More: Some Senior Care Centres in Taiwan Take Service to New Levels', *Channel News Asia*, 21 July. Online. Available HTTP: www.channelnewsasia.com/news/commentary/old-age-singapore-senior-care-what-we-should-talk-about-11666238 (accessed 10 September 2019).

Son, A. H. K. (2001) 'Taiwan's Path to National Health Insurance (1950–1995)', *International Journal of Social Welfare*, 10 (1): 45–53.

Song, S. O., Jung, C. H., Song, Y. D., Park, C., Kwon, H., Cha, B. S., Park, J., Lee, K. and Lee, B. (2014) 'Background and Data Configuration Process of a Nationwide Population-Based Study Using the Korean National Health Insurance System', *Diabetes & Metabolism Journal*, 38: 395–403.

Song, Y. J. (2009) 'The South Korean Health Care System', *JMAJ*, 52 (3): 206–9.

Sorkin, D., Rook, K. S. and Lu, J. L. (2002) 'Loneliness, Lack of Emotional Support, Lack of Companionship, and the Likelihood of Having a Heart Condition in an Elderly Sample', *Annals of Behavioral Medicine*, 24 (4): 290–8.

Spohr, F. (2016) 'Explaining Path Dependency and Deviation by Combining Multiple Streams Framework and Historical Institutionalism: A Comparative Analysis of German and Swedish Labor Market Policies', *Journal of Comparative Policy Analysis: Research and Practice*, 18 (3): 257–72.

The State Commission for Economic Restructuring, Ministry of Finance, Ministry of Labor and Ministry of Health (1994) *Opinions on Test Sites for Reforming the Healthcare System for Staff and Workers*, Chinese Version. Online. Available HTTP: www.chinalawedu.com/falvfagui/fg22598/29355.shtml (accessed 7 December 2018).

The State Council (1994) *Official Reply of the State Council Regarding the Approval of the Plan on Selecting Zhenjiang in Jiangsu Province and Jiujiang in Jiangxi Province as Test Sites for Implementing the Medical Insurance System for Staff and Workers*, Chinese Version. Online. Available HTTP: www.gx-law.gov.cn/xzfg/2025.jhtml (accessed 7 December 2018).

The State Council (1998) *The Decision of the State Council Concerning the Establishment of the Urban Employee Basic Medical Insurance*, Chinese Version. Online. Available HTTP: www.gov.cn/banshi/2005-08/04/content_20256.htm (accessed 13 December 2018).

The State Council (2016) *Opinions on Integrating the Basic Medical Insurance Systems for Urban and Rural Residents*, Chinese Version. Online. Available HTTP: www.gov.cn/zhengce/content/2016-01/12/content_10582.htm (accessed 6 July 2019).

Statistics Bureau (2010) *Laboor Force Status*. Online. Available HTTP: www.stat.go.jp/english/data/kokusei/2010/poj/pdf/2010ch05.pdf (accessed 24 February 2019).

Statistics Bureau (2018) *Statistical Handbook of Japan 2018*. Online. Available HTTP: www.stat.go.jp/english/data/handbook/pdf/2018all.pdf#page=23 (accessed 22 February 2019).

Steinmo, S. (2008) 'Historical Institutionalism', in D. D. Porta and M. Keating (eds.) *Approaches and Methodologies in the Social Sciences: A Pluralist Perspective*, Cambridge: Cambridge University Press, pp. 118–38.

Strong, M. (2019) 'Taiwan Will Be a Super-Aged Society by 2026', *Taiwan News*, 12 February. Online. Available HTTP: www.taiwannews.com.tw/en/news/3636704 (accessed 20 September 2019).

Sudo, K., Kobayashi, J., Noda, S., Fukuda, Y. and Takahashi, K. (2018) 'Japan's Healthcare Policy for the Elderly through the Concepts of Self-Help (Ji-jo), Mutual Aid (Go-jo), Social Solidarity Care (Kyo-jo), and Governmental Care (Ko-jo)', *Bio-Science Trends*, 12 (1): 7–11.

Sugi, N. (2018) 'Despite Staff Shortage, Foreign Care Workers still Face Barriers to Jobs in Japan', *The Mainichi*, 31 August. Online. Available HTTP: https://mainichi.jp/english/articles/20180831/p2a/00m/0na/002000c (accessed 10 June 2019).

Sugita, Y. (2012) 'The 1922 Japanese Health Insurance Law: Toward a Corporatist Framework', *Harvard Asia Quarterly*, 14 (4): 36–43.

Sun, S. Y. (2009) *The Development of the Traditional Cooperative Medical System and Its Characteristics*, Chinese Version. Online. Available HTTP: www.chinalawedu.com/new/15700_169/2009_8_19_ji4304161336191890027008.shtml (accessed 26 November 2018).

Sydow, J., Schreyögg, G. and Koch, J. (2009) 'Organizational Path Dependence: Opening the Black Box', *Academy of Management Review*, 34 (4): 689–709.

Takahashi, M. (2019) 'Retirement Age to Be Raised to 70 to Help Solve Labor Crisis', *The Asahi Shimbun*, 16 May. Online. Available HTTP: www.asahi.com/ajw/articles/AJ201905160042.html (accessed 10 September 2019).

Talcott, P. (2002) 'The Politics of Japan's Long-Term Care Insurance System', in H. Conrad and R. Lützeler (eds.) *Aging and Social Policy: A German-Japanese Comparison*, Munich: Iudicium, pp. 89–122.

Tamiya, N., Noguchi, H., Nishi, A., Reich, M. R., Ikegami, N., Hashimoto, H., Shibuya, K., Kawachi, I. and Campbell, J. C. (2011) 'Population Ageing and Well-being: Lessons from Japan's Long-Term Care Insurance Policy', *The Lancet*, 378: 1183–92.

Tan, F. (2017) *Singapore: Reaching a Critical Demographic Crossroad in 2018*. Online. Available HTTP: www.uobgroup.com/assets/pdfs/research/MN_171206.pdf (accessed 18 May 2019).

Tan, K. P. (2010) *Singapore: A Depoliticized Civil Society in a Dominant-Party System?* Online. Available HTTP: http://library.fes.de/pdf-files/bueros/china/11396.pdf (accessed 3 June 2019).

Tan, T. and Grofman, B. (2018) 'Electoral Rules and Manufacturing Legislative Supermajority: Evidence from Singapore', *Commonwealth & Comparative Politics*, 56 (3): 273–97.

Tang, W. A. (1997) 'State, Politics, and National Health Insurance in Taiwan', *American Asian Review*, 15 (3): 59–103.

Tang, W. A. and Parish, W. L. (2000) *Chinese Urban Life under Reform: The Changing Social Contract*, Cambridge, UK; New York, NY, USA: Cambridge University Press.

Teo, J. (2017) 'HPB National Steps Challenge: Chalk Up 10,000 Steps Daily to Win Air Tickets', *The Straits Times*, 18 April. Online. Available HTTP: www.straitstimes.com/singapore/chalk-up-10000-steps-daily-to-win-air-tickets (accessed 3 September 2019).

Thelen, K. and Steinmo, S. (1992) 'Historical Institutionalism in Comparative Politics', in S. Steinmo, K. Thelen and F. Longstreth (eds.) *Structuring Politics:*

Historical Institutionalism in Comparative Analysis, Cambridge: Cambridge University Press, pp. 1–32.

Thomas, J. W. and Grindle, M. S. (1990) 'After the Decision: Implementing Policy Reforms in Developing Countries', *World Development*, 18 (8): 1163–81.

Thompson, J., Malhotra, R., Love, S., Ostbye, T., Chan, A. and Matchar, D. (2014) 'Projecting the Number of Older Singaporeans with Activity of Daily Living Limitations Requiring Human Assistance through 2030', *Annals of the Academy of Medicine: Singapore*, 43 (1): 51–6.

Tien, H. (1996) 'Elections and Taiwan's Democratic Development', in H. Tien (ed.) *Taiwan's Electoral Politics and Democratic Transition: Riding the Third Wave*, Armonk, NY: M.E. Sharpe, pp. 3–25.

TODAYonline (2016) 'More Than 8,000 Individuals Trained to Help Those with Dementia', *TODAYonline*, 23 May. Online. Available HTTP: www.todayonline. com/singapore/more-8000-individuals-trained-help-those-dementia (accessed 10 September 2019).

Tsang, E. (2016) 'Hong Kong Urged to Think of Ways to Fund Long-Term Elderly Care', *South China Morning Post*, 13 December. Online. Available HTTP: www. scmp.com/news/hong-kong/health-environment/article/2054276/hong-kong-urged-think-ways-fund-long-term-elderly (accessed 27 August 2019).

Tsang, E. (2017) 'Eight-Hour Waits in Emergency Rooms as Hong Kong Hospitals Feel Flu Season Surge over Christmas Holidays', *South China Morning Post*, 26 December. Online. Available HTTP: www.scmp.com/news/hong-kong/ health-environment/article/2125722/eight-hour-waits-emergency-rooms-hong-kong (accessed 26 June 2019).

Tsang, E. (2018) 'Record-High Doctors' Turnover Rate of 5.7 PerCent in Hong Kong Public Hospitals Worsens Manpower Shortage Issues', *South China Morning Post*, 7 January. Online. Available HTTP: www.scmp.com/news/hong-kong/health-environment/article/2127176/record-high-doctors-turnover-rate-57-cent-hong (accessed 27 June 2019).

Tsutsui, T. and Muramatsu, N. (2007) 'Japan's Universal Long-Term Care System Reform of 2005: Containing Costs and Realizing a Vision', *Journal of the American Geriatrics Society*, 55 (9): 1458–63.

Tsutsumi, S. (2014) *Long-Term Care Insurance in Japan: Understanding the Ideas behind Its Design*. Online. Available HTTP: https://socialprotection-humanrights. org/wp-content/uploads/2015/08/Long-term-Care-Insurance-in-Japan.pdf (accessed 25 March 2019).

Tumpane, T. (2017) *Aging Well: The Importance of Intergenerational Bonding*. Online. Available HTTP: www.thehour.com/news/article/Aging-Well-The-importance-of-intergenerational-11095352.php (accessed 5 September 2019).

Underwood, A. (2009) 'Health Care Abroad: Taiwan', *New York Times*, 3 November. Online. Available HTTP: https://prescriptions.blogs.nytimes.com/2009/11/03/ health-care-abroad-taiwan/ (accessed 17 August 2018).

UNFPA Asia Pacific (2017) *Perspectives on Population Ageing in the Asia Pacific Region*. Online. Available HTTP: https://asiapacific.unfpa.org/en/publica tions/perspectives-population-ageing-asia-pacific-region (accessed 10 August 2019).

United Nations (2015) *World Population Ageing 2015*. Online. Available HTTP: www.un.org/en/development/desa/population/publications/pdf/ageing/ WPA2015_Report.pdf (accessed 9 August 2019).

United Nations (2017a) *World Population Ageing 2017*. Online. Available HTTP: www.un.org/en/development/desa/population/publications/pdf/ageing/ WPA2017_Report.pdf (accessed 9 August 2019).

United Nations (2017b) *World Population Ageing 2017: Highlights*. Online. Available HTTP: www.un.org/en/development/desa/population/publications/pdf/ ageing/WPA2017_Highlights.pdf (accessed 9 August 2019).

United Nations (2019) *World Population Prospects 2019: Highlights*. Online. Available HTTP: https://reliefweb.int/sites/reliefweb.int/files/resources/WPP2019_ Highlights.pdf (accessed 9 August 2019).

United Nations Department of Economic and Social Affairs (n.d.) *Ageing and Disability*. Online. Available HTTP: www.un.org/development/desa/disabilities/ disability-and-ageing.html (accessed 12 August 2019).

United Nations Development Programme (2017) *Ageing, Older Persons and the 2030 Agenda for Sustainable Development*. Online. Available HTTP: www.undp.org/ content/undp/en/home/librarypage/poverty-reduction/ageing--older-persons- and-the-2030-agenda-for-sustainable-develo.html (accessed 11 August 2019).

United Nations Economic and Social Commission for Asia and the Pacific (2015) *Long-Term Care of Older Persons in Japan*. Online. Available HTTP: www.unescap. org/resources/long-term-care-older-persons-japan (accessed 8 June 2019).

United Nations Economic and Social Commission for Asia and the Pacific (2017a) *Addressing the Challenges of Population Ageing in Asia and the Pacific*. Online. Available HTTP: www.unescap.org/publications/addressing-challenges-population- ageing-asia-and-pacific-implementation-madrid (accessed 11 August 2019).

United Nations Economic and Social Commission for Asia and the Pacific (2017b) *Ageing in Asia and the Pacific: Overview*. Online. Available HTTP: www.unescap. org/resources/ageing-asia-and-pacific-overview (accessed 23 February 2019).

United Nations Economic and Social Commission for Asia and the Pacific (2018) *Financing for Long-Term Care in Asia and the Pacific*. Online. Available HTTP: www.unescap.org/sites/default/files/SDPB%202018-01.pdf (accessed 25 August 2019).

United Nations Population Fund (2012) *Ageing in the Twenty-First Century: A Celebration and a Challenge*. Online. Available HTTP: www.unfpa.org/publications/ ageing-twenty-first-century (accessed 9 August 2019).

U.S. Treasury Department Office of Economic Policy (2017) *The Economic Security of American Households*. Online. Available HTTP: www.treasury.gov/resource- center/economic-policy/Documents/The%20Economic%20Security%20of%20 American%20Households-The%20Economic%20Security%20of%20Older%20 Women.pdf (accessed 7 September 2019).

Wang, H. S. (2017) *Familial Foundations of the Welfare State*, Cham, Switzerland: Palgrave Macmillan.

Wang, J. C. F. (2002) *Contemporary Chinese Politics: An Introduction*, 7th edn, Upper Saddle River, NJ: Prentice Hall.

Wang, S. (2009) 'Adapting by Learning: The Evolution of China's Rural Health Care Financing', *Modern China*, 35 (4): 370–404.

Wang, Y. (2017) *Social Security in China: On the Possibility of Equitable Distribution*, Singapore: Springer.

Weir, M. (1992) 'Ideas and the Politics of Bounded Innovation', in S. Steinmo, K. Thelen and F. Longstreth (eds.) *Structuring Politics: Historical Institutionalism in Comparative Analysis*, Cambridge: Cambridge University Press, pp. 188–216.

Wong, C., Lo, V. I. and Tang, K. (2006) *China's Urban Health Care Reform: From State Protection to Individual Responsibility*, Lanham, MD: Lexington Books.

Wong, J. (2003) 'Resisting Reform: The Politics of Health Care in Democratizing Taiwan', *American Asian Review*, 21 (2): 57–90.

Wong, J. (2004) *Healthy Democracies: Welfare Politics in Taiwan and South Korea*, Ithaca: Cornell University Press.

Wong, J. (2005a) 'Democracy, Development and Health in Taiwan', in H. Kwon (ed.) *Transforming the Developmental Welfare State in East Asia*, Houndmills; Basingstoke; Hampshire; New York, NY: Palgrave Macmillan, pp. 50–72.

Wong, J. (2005b) 'Adapting to Democracy: Societal Mobilization and Social Policy in Taiwan and South Korea', *Studies in Comparative International Development*, 40 (3): 88–111.

Wong, M. Y. H. (2018) 'Selectorate Theory in Hybrid Regimes: Comparing Hong Kong and Singapore', *Government and Opposition*, 53 (4): 707–34.

Wong, S. H. (2015) *Electoral Politics in Post-1997 Hong Kong: Protest, Patronage, and the Media*, Singapore: Springer.

Wong, V. C. W. (1996) 'Medical and Health', in M. Nyaw and S. Li (eds.) *The Other Hong Kong Report 1996*, Hong Kong: Chinese University Press, pp. 449–467.

Workforce Singapore (2019) *How Mature Workers Can Stay Relevant in the Workforce*. Online. Available HTTP: https://content.mycareersfuture.sg/mature-workers-can-stay-relevant-workforce/ (accessed 10 September 2019).

World Bank (2010) *Fixing the Public Hospital System in China*. Online. Available HTTP: https://openknowledge.worldbank.org/bitstream/handle/10986/27720/584110NWP0V20P10No21Hospital0Reform.pdf?sequence=1&isAllowed=y (accessed 4 December 2018).

World Health Organization (1981) *Global Strategy for Health for All by the Year 2000*. Online. Available HTTP: http://iris.wpro.who.int/bitstream/handle/10665.1/6967/WPR_RC032_GlobalStrategy_1981_en.pdf (accessed 3 September 2018).

World Health Organization (1998) *The World Health Report 1998*. Online. Available HTTP: www.who.int/whr/1998/en/whr98_en.pdf?ua=1 (accessed 12 September 2019).

World Health Organization (2000) *The World Health Report 2000-Health Systems: Improving Performance*. Online. Available HTTP: www.who.int/whr/2000/en/ (accessed 15 August 2019).

World Health Organization (2003) *Diet, Nutrition and the Prevention of Chronic Diseases*. Online. Available HTTP: https://apps.who.int/iris/bitstream/handle/10665/42665/WHO_TRS_916.pdf;jsessionid=86C25EE23370364DA250AB013D618989?sequence=1 (accessed 3 September 2019).

World Health Organization (2005) *Social Health Insurance: Selected Case Studies from Asia and the Pacific*. Online. Available HTTP: http://origin.wpro.who.int/publications/docs/searpno42.pdf (accessed 13 May 2019).

World Health Organization (2007) *Global Age-Friendly Cities: A Guide*. Online. Available HTTP: https://apps.who.int/iris/bitstream/handle/10665/43755/9789241547307_eng.pdf;jsessionid=5D7EAF254FB9EEEC27F1A72D3CECB381?sequence=1 (accessed 11 August 2019).

World Health Organization (2008) *The World Health Report 2008: Primary Health Care (Now More Than Ever)*. Online. Available HTTP: www.who.int/whr/2008/en/ (accessed 3 September 2019).

World Health Organization (2010a) *Population Ageing*. Online. Available HTTP: www.who.int/features/qa/72/en/ (accessed 9 August 2019).

World Health Organization (2010b) *Monitoring the Building Blocks of Health Systems: A Handbook of Indicators and Their Measurement Strategies*. Online. Available HTTP: www.who.int/healthinfo/systems/WHO_MBHSS_2010_full_web. pdf (accessed 15 August 2019).

World Health Organization (2011) *World Report on Disability*. Online. Available HTTP: www.who.int/disabilities/world_report/2011/report.pdf?ua=1 (accessed 18 May 2019).

World Health Organization (2014) *Basic Documents: Forty-Eighth Edition*. Online. Available HTTP: http://apps.who.int/gb/bd/PDF/bd48/basic-documents-48th-edition-en.pdf#page=1 (accessed 12 September 2019).

World Health Organization (2015) *World Report on Ageing and Health*. Online. Available HTTP: www.who.int/ageing/events/world-report-2015-launch/en/ (accessed 12 September 2019).

World Health Organization (2017a) *10 Priorities towards a Decade of Healthy Ageing*. Online. Available HTTP: www.who.int/ageing/10-priorities/en/ (accessed 12 September 2019).

World Health Organization (2017b) *Global Strategy and Action Plan on Ageing and Health*. Online. Available HTTP: www.who.int/ageing/WHO-GSAP-2017. pdf?ua=1 (accessed 12 September 2019).

World Health Organization (2018) *The Political Economy of Health Financing Reform: Analysis and Strategies to Support Universal Health Coverage*. Online. Available HTTP: www.who.int/health_financing/events/liverpool-flyer-2018.pdf (accessed 12 August 2019).

World Health Organization (2019a) *Universal Health Coverage and Ageing*. Online. Available HTTP: www.who.int/ageing/health-systems/uhc-ageing/en/ (accessed 12 August 2019).

World Health Organization (2019b) *Out-of-Pocket Payments, User Fees and Catastrophic Expenditure*. Online. Available HTTP: www.who.int/health_financing/topics/financial-protection/out-of-pocket-payments/en/ (accessed 17 August 2019).

World Health Organization (2019c) *Life Expectancy*. Online. Available HTTP: www. who.int/gho/mortality_burden_disease/life_tables/situation_trends_text/en/ (accessed 12 September 2019).

Wright, M. (2002) *Japan's Fiscal Crisis: The Ministry of Finance and the Politics of Public Spending, 1975–2000*, Oxford: Oxford University Press.

Wu, C. and Dai, S. (2014) 'From Regime Transition to Liberal Democracy: The Case of Taiwan', in E. S. K. Fung and S. Drakeley (eds.) *Democracy in Eastern Asia: Issues, Problems and Challenges in a Region of Diversity*, London; New York: Routledge, pp. 60–80.

Wu, K. X. (1996) 'A Review of Health Insurance System in Taiwan', in Z. L. Yang (ed.) *Health Insurance*, revised edn, Chinese Version, Taipei City: Chiliu Publisher, pp. 157–97.

Wu, Y., Brayne, C. and Matthews, F. E. (2015) 'Prevalence of Dementia in East Asia: A Synthetic Review of Time Trends', *International Journal of Geriatric Psychiatry*, 30: 793–801. Online. Available HTTP: www.ncbi.nlm.nih.gov/pmc/articles/PMC4510821/pdf/gps0030-0793.pdf (accessed 10 September 2019).

Wudunn, S. (1996) 'Japanese Ex-Aide Is Accused of Taking $530,000 in Bribes', *The New York Times*, 5 December. Online. Available HTTP: www.nytimes.

com/1996/12/05/world/japanese-ex-aide-is-accused-of-taking-530000-in-bribes.html (accessed 27 April 2019).

Xiao, Q. (2007) 'A Decade of Change in the Business Environment', in Y. Yeung (ed.) *The First Decade: The Hong Kong SAR in Retrospective and Introspective Perspectives*, Hong Kong: Chinese University Press, pp. 189–214.

Xie, E. (2019) 'China Plans to Offer Investment Education in Schools across Country', *South China Morning Post*, 17 March. Online. Available HTTP: www.scmp. com/news/china/society/article/3002066/china-plans-offer-investment-education-schools-across-country (accessed 10 September 2019).

Yadav, S. S. (2001) 'Disability and Handicap among Elderly Singaporeans', *Singapore Medical Journal*, 42 (8): 360–7.

Yame, D. (2002) *Student Movements for Multiculturalism: Challenging the Curricular Color Line in Higher Education*, Baltimore: Johns Hopkins University Press.

Yang, B. (1996) 'The Role of Health Insurance in the Growth of the Private Health Sector in Korea', *International Journal of Health Planning and Management*, 11 (3): 231–52.

Yang, B. (2002) 'Health Insurance Reform in Korea: Consolidation of Funds', in T. Hu and C. Hsieh (eds.) *The Economics of Health Care in Asia-Pacific Countries*, Cheltenham, UK; Northampton, MA: Edward Elgar, pp. 63–81.

Yang, C. (2017) *The Political Economy of the Small Welfare State in South Korea*, New York: Cambridge University Press.

Yang, J. (2010) 'Serve the People: Understanding Ideology and Professional Ethics of Medicine in China', *Health Care Analysis*, 18 (3): 294–309.

Yang, J. and Son, H. (2019) 'Many Elderly Koreas Are Lonely', *The Chosunilbo*, 5 January. Online. Available HTTP: http://english.chosun.com/site/data/html_dir/2019/01/05/2019010500348.html (accessed 5 September 2019).

Yashiro, N. (1997) 'Aging of the Population in Japan and Its Implications to the Other Asian Countries', *Journal of Asian Economics*, 8 (2): 245–61.

Yau, O. H. M., Leung, W. F., Cheung, F. S. L. and Chow, C. W. C. (2007) 'SARS Versus the Asian Financial Crisis', in O. H. M. Yau and R. P. M. Chow (eds.) *Harmony Versus Conflict in Asian Business: Managing in a Turbulent Era*, New York: Palgrave Macmillan, pp. 209–30.

Ye, J., Gao, F. and Wu, J. (2015) 'Analysis on the Outcome of the Zero-Markup Drug Policy and Measures to It, Chinese Version', *Jiangsu Healthcare Administration*, 26: 116–17.

Yen, B. S. and Lin, J. (2015) 'The Health Insurance Coverage for Chinese Medicine Services in Taiwan', *Science Journal of Public Health*, 3 (2): 191–8.

Yeo, L. H. (2009) 'Democracy and Governance in Singapore: The Sustainability of Singapore's Political System', in B. Bridges and L. S. Ho (eds.) *Public Governance in Asia and the Limits of Electoral Democracy*, Cheltenham, UK; Northampton, MA: Edward Elgar, pp. 172–91.

Yonhap News Agency (2018) 'S. Korea to up Health Insurance Premium 3.2 pct Annually in 2018–2022', *Yonhap News Agency*, 4 September. Online. Available HTTP: https://en.yna.co.kr/view/AEN20180904006800320 (accessed 22 June 2019).

Yonhap News Agency (2019) 'State Health Insurer Logs Deficit in 2018', *Yonhap News Agency*, 13 March. Online. Available HTTP: https://en.yna.co.kr/view/AEN20190313001600320 (accessed 23 June 2019).

Yoon, S. and Lee, H. (2017) *President Announces New 'Mooncare' Healthcare Plan.* Online. Available HTTP: www.korea.net/NewsFocus/policies/view?articleId=148 430 (accessed 23 June 2019).

Yu, L., Hsu, Y. and Fahn, J. (2016) 'The Political Negotiation in the Legislative Process of Taiwan's National Health Insurance, Chinese Version', *NPUST Humanities and Social Sciences Research*, 10 (1): 75–94.

Yu, W. and Ren, M. (1997) 'The Important Issue of Enterprise Reform: Health Care Insurance System', in G. J. Wen and D. Xu (eds.) *The Reformability of China's State Sector*, Singapore; River Edge, NJ: World Scientific, pp. 433–63.

Yuen, P. P. (1997) 'Medical and Health Issues', in J. Y. S. Cheng (ed.) *The Other Hong Kong Report 1997*, Hong Kong: The Chinese University of Hong Kong, pp. 393–409.

Zahariadis, N. (1992) 'To Sell or Not to Sell? Telecommunications Policy in Britain and France', *Journal of Public Policy*, 12 (4): 355–76.

Zahariadis, N. (2007) 'The Multiple Streams Framework: Structure, Limitations, Prospects', in P. A. Sabatier (ed.) *Theories of the Policy Process*, 2nd edn, Boulder, CO: Westview Press, pp. 65–92.

Zahariadis, N. (2008) 'Ambiguity and Choice in European Public Policy', *Journal of European Public Policy*, 15 (4): 514–30.

Zahariadis, N. and Allen, C. S. (1995) 'Ideas, Networks, and Policy Streams: Privatization in Britain and Germany', *Review of Policy Research*, 14 (1–2): 71–98.

Zakaria, F. (1994) 'A Conversation with Lee Kuan Yew', *Foreign Affairs*, 73 (2): 109–26.

Zhang, K. (2018) 'High Demand for Hong Kong Public Health Care among Biggest Challenges for Hospital Authority, Its Next Chief Says', *South China Morning Post*, 1 November. Online. Available HTTP: www.scmp.com/news/hong-kong/ health-environment/article/2171282/high-demand-hong-kong-public-health-care-among (accessed 26 June 2019).

Zhang, M. (2008) 'From Public to Private: The Newly Enacted Chinese Property Law and the Protection of Property Rights in China', *Berkeley Business Law Journal*, 5 (2): 317–63.

Zheng, G. C. (2009) *The Development of Social Security System with Chinese Characteristics*, Beijing: China Labour & Social Security Publishing House.

Zhou, H. and Zhang, J. (2017) *Towards a Society with Social Protection for All: A Concise History of Social Security Transformation in Modern China*, Singapore: Springer Nature.

Zohlnhöfer, R., Herweg, N. and Huß, C. (2015) 'Theoretically Refining the Multiple Streams Framework: An Introduction', *European Journal of Political Research*, 54 (3): 412–8.

Zohlnhöfer, R., Herweg, N. and Huß, C. (2016) 'Bringing Formal Political Institutions into the Multiple Streams Framework: An Analytical Proposal for Comparative Policy Analysis', *Journal of Comparative Policy Analysis: Research and Practice*, 18 (3): 243–56.

Index

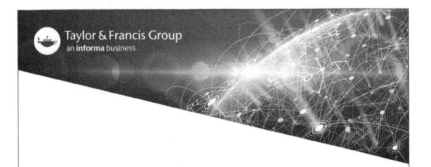